THE *New*

INVITATION TO

Learning

Edited by

MARK VAN DOREN

THE NEW HOME LIBRARY
NEW YORK

THE NEW HOME LIBRARY EDITION PUBLISHED MARCH, 1944
BY ARRANGEMENT WITH RANDOM HOUSE, INC.

THE NEW HOME LIBRARY, 14 West Forty-ninth Street
New York, N. Y.

CL

MANUFACTURED IN THE UNITED STATES OF AMERICA

NB 1983

PREFACE

THE DIALOGUES contained in this second volume of *Invitation to Learning*, like those contained in its predecessor of last year, are printed from transcripts of direct recordings of unrehearsed conversations broadcast weekly by the Columbia Broadcasting System on a coast-to-coast network. The present series of broadcasts ran from November 16, 1941, through May 31, 1942, and so took the program Invitation to Learning a little past the end of its second year. The continuance of the program to this point—and beyond, since it goes steadily on—is something for which the American public first of all is to be thanked. The response has been energetic and intelligent from the start; but, even more heartening, the correspondence from listeners has never given the impression that they took these conversations about great books as substitutes for the reading of the books themselves. Argument has been mixed with praise, and shortcomings have been noted even in the midst of compliment.

But the volume owes other and particular debts which it is a

Preface

pleasure to acknowledge: to CBS and its Adult Education Board for undertaking and continuing an experiment new in radio; to Lyman Bryson, Director of the CBS Department of Education, and to Douglas Coulter, Assistant Director of the CBS Program Division, for encouragement and counsel; to Leon Levine, Assistant Director of the CBS Department of Education, for his untiring attention not only to the principle of the program, but to the many details of its operation; to the Columbia University Press, from whose *Listener's Guide* to the program the passages in italics preceding the dialogues have been reprinted; and to Saxe Commins of Random House for invaluable editorial assistance, expertly and generously given.

M. V. D.

New York, 1942

Contents

[*vii*]

Contents

Contents

INTRODUCTION

THE THIRTY-TWO BOOKS discussed in the following dialogues
are among the relatively few books of the world which can be
so discussed. They are, in other words, great books. Great books,
or classics, are permanently discussable; this is their definition,
as it is the sign of their continuing greatness that they never
cease somehow to be present in men's thoughts. For they are the
source from which thought comes, they are the jewels on which
the talk of men has always turned. And like jewels they are hard;
they wear well. Also, they have many surfaces and reflect much
light.

If they were of softer substance they could be sounded quickly
and let go. They could be satisfactorily summarized, and above
all they could be judged. A great book is not susceptible to syn-
opsis, nor does any critic, however profound, manage to set its
price. It escapes such finalities, being simply and truly alive. It
prefers, and indeed it demands, the kind of attention which only
the dialogue may give. A dialogue is of course not an essay; the

chief mark of its difference being that it does not know how to end. Dialogues stop—because the time is up, because the talkers are tired, because dinner is announced—but they do not end. The end would be only when there was nothing more to say. But on the great subjects, as on the great books, there is always more to say. That is why Invitation to Learning breaks off each discussion with the formal reading of a few sentences from the book at hand. The last speech is thrown to the author.

Not only is it impossible to say the last thing about a great book; it is difficult to say even the first thing well. A great book is never obscure, but it is regularly elusive; it refuses to yield a narrow meaning. To one reader it may mean something quite narrow indeed—as narrow as that reader's mind. Should he undertake, however, to trade his experience with another, he will find to his amazement that he has read a different book. The truth is with both readers, and with as many more readers as may be. A great writer has many minds; which is why he should be discussed by at least three men. It is not that the sum of their judgments will produce an equivalent of his book, but rather that his book will then be free to do what it most likes to do, namely, glance off one mental sphere and strike another, and still another, returning in time to strike the first one with new force. A great book cannot be kept quiet or in place. It was made to move, somewhat as in dialogue truth moves among the speakers, never resting, never giving up.

The foregoing is possibly an answer to those among the audience of Invitation to Learning who write in and suggest that more time be devoted to summaries of the books. All time would not be enough. It is also an answer, perhaps, to those who want readier judgments as to what the books mean today. They mean today what they always did, and it is useless to insist that they justify themselves with maxims for the moment. As good a question is this: What does today mean to them? What maxim of the moment wishes to compete with their more or less timeless wisdom? They are correctives, not manifestoes, and perspective is their charm. They educate by intellectual example. By showing how thought has been, they encourage it to be again.

Not to glorify it too much, something like this is the setting for an Invitation to Learning broadcast. Three persons come together—sometimes it is four—and start the book moving among them. For an hour they do this, neither formally nor solemnly but with a genuine desire in each of them somehow to know the others; and then they are on the air. The only two things they are certain about beforehand are the question to begin with and the passage to be read at the close. The half hour between, except as its agreements and disagreements are colored by memories of the preliminary meeting, is unrehearsed and free. There have been occasions when a disagreement lost something by having been too clearly anticipated; the element of surprise, even of anger, was missing. But on the whole the contrary is true; the argument benefits from previous knowledge of the limits to which it can profitably go.

The art of participating in dialogue is another matter altogether, not to be pursued here because it has its trade secrets. But one observation can be made. Any art has its difficulties, and the difficulty in this case may seem strangely simple. Nevertheless, it is real. It is the difficulty of listening to the other man while preparing to answer him. It is the difficulty of being courteous, mind to mind.

MARK VAN DOREN

POETRY AND DRAMA

THE HOLY BIBLE

The Book of Psalms

THE BIBLE is history, biography, ethics, law, proverbial wisdom, homily, prophecy, and theology. It is also poetry, and the clearest of its lyric strains is to be heard in the Psalms. They were the hymnbook of the Temple, where to the accompaniment of music they uttered the various accents of praise. The proper and indeed the only object of praise is God. Men may compliment one another upon the degrees of excellence they have achieved, but in the nature of things no man is finally excellent. Only God is that, and for Him is reserved the special harmony of praise. For in Him reside all qualities in their highest degree. Praise of God is the praise of qualities, of ideas, of excellences in the abstract; and at its best is praise of Him for His power and His glory, since these are the simplest means whereby we recognize those things. A series of hymns, then, should have one theme throughout, and should aim at the topmost note of joy and worship in the expres-

sion of this theme. To say of such a series that it is monotonous is merely to say that it has done what it should do; for the greatness of God does not change. The Psalms are written in monotone, but the skill with which their one subject is always kept high and exciting is something unique in the world's literature. The ardor of the psalmist—David, according to tradition—never cools, nor does his lyric energy flag; and though he is limited in theme, he seems to recognize no limit among the images and epithets which a burning imagination may command. All are his subjects, as he is the subject of One.

The Psalms have been used as the Jewish hymnal since several centuries B.C. and by Christendom since Apostolic times. The Septuagint canon differs from the Hebrew in the inclusion of Psalm 151 (considered apocryphal by Roman Catholics and Protestants) and in the numbering of some of the others (in this respect the Vulgate and other Roman Catholic versions follow the Septuagint; the Protestant translations, the Hebrew). In the Church of England the version of the Psalter used is that of the Great Bible of 1539-41.

LOUIS UNTERMEYER · IRWIN EDMAN · MARK VAN DOREN

Van Doren: Gentlemen, let us try first, within the limits of human understanding and capacity, to say why it is that the lyric poetry of the Psalms is great lyric poetry. Does it strike you that a reason can be given, Mr. Untermeyer?

Untermeyer: Yes; quite apart from magnificently written poetry, I think you have here, on the part of a great people, a continued expression of faith, a continued communication which is directed to a Force which understands and which acts whether you act or not—an expression which the lyric poetry of today almost completely lacks.

Van Doren: You seem to say that faith is somehow or other an indispensable prerequisite for great lyric poetry. I should say so too. Would you agree, Mr. Edman? Of course you're rather forced to agree, aren't you?

Edman: Not only forced, but persuaded. I agree, because I think when you use the term "faith" you don't mean to commit yourself to a narrow intellectual belief so much as to a profound human conviction concerning the depth and eternity of existence —its divine character. That kind of faith does enter into the Psalms and does explain their extraordinary power, which, as Mr. Untermeyer points out, is precisely what is lacking in so many of the scrupulous self-doubting poems written today.

Van Doren: Or even perhaps the scrupulous self-asserted poems that are written today, because some poems written today express a faith in something or other. I wonder if anything especially distinguishes the faith that we find expressed in the Psalms. I should say, for instance—I wish to offer this—that it

[5]

is not something an individual is represented as having discovered for himself so that he runs to his friends and his neighbors to say: "Look what I believe!" He can count upon their believing it, too. Indeed, the people to whom and for whom he writes and who assist him in singing his psalm, quite clearly are understood as having had, even before he was born, the same faith.

Untermeyer: And more than that. The Hebrews called these poems *Tehillim,* which means literally "praise songs." They were praising God, thanking Him because He existed—they were glad that they could go on their business knowing that there He was, to appeal to, to yield to, even to rail against because for the moment they had been neglected. But, praising God for God's very existence, they did not have to undertake the search which today is so much a matter of desperation. Even when we find Him, we find Him at moments and then He is gone. We are unsure of His existence, whereas the thing they took for granted was this existence, this security—there He was at any moment.

Van Doren: They were not proving that He exists.

Untermeyer: They took it for granted.

Van Doren: That is what gives meaning to your phrase, "thanking Him because He existed."

Edman: I don't think, Mr. Van Doren and Mr. Untermeyer, that they are proving Him; but in a sense they feel that experience has constantly been proving Him. They look around, and even in their personal desperations they find evidence—even in God's terrifying activities—of His existence. They find the world manifesting His glory and His power everywhere, so that they find constant verification, as it were—they don't feel He needs to be proved in view of God's handiwork.

Untermeyer: May I amend that, Mr. Edman, and say they're not proving Him but approving Him?

Edman: Well, that's—

Untermeyer: If you will allow the condescension.

Edman: But approving is rather a mild word for what the Psalms do.

Van Doren: At any rate, there is no doubt in the mind of the psalmist, or, I take it, in the minds of the persons to whom or for whom he is singing, that God exists. God's existence does not seem to depend upon any one's referring to it.

Untermeyer: That is a point I'd like you to emphasize. Can you make it plain why, in such a body of people, there was this acceptance? What was the nature of it? And why did it issue in this kind of a book?

Van Doren: Now you are asking me a question I can't answer. There is no other book like this. There is no book, so far as I know, anywhere in the world which implies so solid and so everlasting a belief, one which makes it possible for us to say that the existence of the thing believed in does not seem to depend upon the belief itself. We are in the habit these days of assuming that we establish God's existence by saying that we believe in Him; but they assumed God's existence first. That is why they were free to write lyric poems like this. There is a great deal of difference.

Edman: I'd like to return for a moment to Mr. Untermeyer's point about the praise and approval of God. The Psalms are so full of it that, it seems to me, this very fulness gives one explanation of their power. It's as if the psalmist simply couldn't find the words to express the inexpressible. Hence these outbursts of daring, which are necessary to say what nothing less than God could deserve, because God was everything, including desolation. God did all kinds of things.

Van Doren: Yes, He was terrible. He was also frequently absent—not non-existent, but absent. There seem to be stretches of time during which the psalmist has thirsted or hungered for His presence. The images of thirst and hunger, which are everywhere in mystical literature, are particularly powerful here. And when God does return, He returns like rain, or like its complement, the sun.

Untermeyer: Well, that was the point I had hoped you might make. Mr. Edman has stressed the metaphorical quality, the passionate outbursts of daring imagery. That is what made the Psalms so surcharged, and so popular. This was an expression

different from that of *Leviticus* and *Numbers,* different from
census-taking, different from the listing of laws. This was the
outburst of man at his most excited pitch, the pitch of poetry.
That is what I would like one of you to speak about. What has
made this not only the expression of confidence in God, but a
particular kind of expression.

Van Doren: What more perfect atmosphere could there be for
a lyric poet to work in? Let us envy a race of men who could
write in this atmosphere—an atmosphere in which exaggeration
was impossible. Any modern poet is bound to worry from time
to time lest he seem to be exaggerating. But the psalmist was
expected—not to exaggerate, perhaps—

Untermeyer: Well, there—in God—you had a subject whose
dimensions you couldn't possibly exaggerate.

Van Doren: That's it.

Untermeyer: Any praise would be understatement, no matter
what it was.

Edman: The psalmist knew that his audience would believe
him because they felt the same way. By the way, when we say
"the psalmist" we are using a conventional short-hand epithet
for what one might call the editor—like Mr. Untermeyer, of a
great anthology. These are the poems of a great people, and the
anthologist apparently made his selection with care. The people
were the anthologists; everything must have dropped out that
wasn't first rate, because all the things that are left in are supreme.

Van Doren: Mr. Untermeyer, are the Psalms an anthology?

Untermeyer: I don't think there is any question about that;
just as *The Song of Songs* is a broken anthology, a rather obscure
anthology of love songs, parts of an ancient marriage ritual.
This is definitely, it seems to me, a winnowing—not only a collection, but a very careful selection of what may have been ten
times as many poems. These Psalms were kept because of their
very vivid imagery, because of the power of their expression, not
merely because they asserted God—although they all did that.
The total original number can never be known.

Van Doren: And again the anthologizing principle was a public one, rather than a private one. You don't conceive, do you, that one man in a study decided for himself which psalms he should select? They had been selected for him.

Untermeyer: No more than the fifty scholars who were also poets at the time of King James were one translator of the Bible.

Van Doren: No, they were persons who miraculously shared a language which was powerful and rich enough for the purpose.

Untermeyer: In both the original document and the translation there was a double refining process—a refiltering, as it were —a distillation. These scholarly men "distilled" a particular language, a language which has now become the model of what great English speech can be. Something must have happened to the language of that time. I think, without being too fantastic, there was some meeting of all the currents of English. And then you had the sheer good luck to have fifty men, almost like Shakespeare, thinking alike. As a matter of fact, there is a persistent rumor that Shakespeare may have been one of the fifty, or the fifty-second, or the fifty-third. He may have had a hand in shaping some parts of Isaiah or the Psalms. A nice idea, don't you think: that he could have been one of the unknown semi-authors?

Van Doren: Decidedly.

Untermeyer: The Psalms are Shakespearean in oratory, pitch, and sonority.

Van Doren: Shakespeare as a playwright was not writing for himself either. He always had an audience that he knew was going to listen to him, that had to understand him, and with which he somehow or other had to agree.

Edman: Mr. Van Doren, there is another point we ought to stress in connection with the public character of the Psalms. I am thinking about their music—the language is so elevated in rhythm, and the English translation catches obviously a good deal of that. We ought to remind ourselves that these poems were sung. They were chorally sung, the first line frequently being recited by a leader. The quality of music in them is more than metaphorical. This gives them a great deal of their power, their character and quality.

Van Doren: And they were songs of praise. I am interested to see that all of us have, of course inevitably, used the word "praise." It is a great advantage for a lyric poem to have something to praise. It is difficult these days, not so much to will the act of praise as to find a thing to praise. That is our greatest difficulty. Praise, again, is something which cannot be exaggerated. A compliment can be exaggerated, but compliments are not paid to God. Compliments are paid to individual persons, and they had better be paid with a smile, because it is clear that no individual deserves more than a modicum of praise. But God is without limits in His deserts, and so, with the greatest solemnity and with all the music and metaphor possible to you, you praise Him freely. He is not an individual; He is everything.

Edman: The psalmist probably was all things to all poets— anything that any poet could possibly think about was justly said about God.

Untermeyer: Speaking of poets, Mr. Edman, couldn't we refer to one of some three centuries ago? May I paraphrase what you say in the words of Sir Philip Sidney? You remember in his beautiful "Defense of Poetry" he spoke of the author of the Psalms, and said he made the reader "see God coming in his majesty, his telling of the beasts' joyfulness and the hills' leaping—a heavenly poetry wherein he showeth himself a passionate lover of that unspeakable and everlasting beauty to be seen by the eyes of the mind, cleared by faith." A magnificent phrase—"a beauty to be seen by the eyes of the mind, cleared by faith."

Edman: That's as good a single summary of the Psalms as you could find.

Untermeyer: I'm afraid it is.

Van Doren: And spoken by a man roughly contemporaneous with the translators of the King James version.

Untermeyer: Something did seem to happen at that particular time.

Van Doren: We have spoken of the metaphors in the Psalms. What do we know about the form of Hebrew verse? Often, as I read translations of Hebrew lyrics, I suspect a method in metaphor. The figures are far from irresponsible or accidental. Can you tell us anything about the way a psalm was written?

Untermeyer: Well, without posing falsely as a Hebrew scholar, which I am not, I think that a great deal of the poetry could be carried over and *was* carried over in translation. That is, the metaphors, the meanings, the balance, the cadence, the repetitions were carried over. But some of the sheer music, the music of vowels and consonants, can never be carried over from one language to the other. The Hebrews notoriously had no rhyme, as we know it, and they didn't have the Latin and Greek accent or "quantity." There was no set rhythm, but they compensated for the lack of it not only with balance, with repetition, with parallelism, but with something that sounds very much to us like assonance and alliteration, even a kind of internal rhyme. May I attempt one line from the 44th Psalm, which begins in the King James version: "We have heard with our ears, O God, our fathers have told us, what work thou didst in their days, in the times of old." Now, allowing for variation and accent, the Hebrew sounds something like this: [Reads in Hebrew]. Perhaps you note the rich alliteration, and an almost insistent semi-rhyme. Of course, all of the Psalms are not like that, but many of them use such devices.

Van Doren: Not rhyme in our sense of the word, I take it, but rhyme in the sense of a repeated sound, a sound repeated with growing emphasis. But you are not aware, are you, that there was anything like a form for the delivery of metaphor? I mean, was there a system by which metaphors were expected to develop? Do you happen to know about that, Mr. Edman?

Edman: I should say there are some obvious things that one can't read more than two or three of the Psalms without becoming aware of—the tendency to use balanced phrases, the tendency to contrast—"There is weeping in the night, but joy cometh in the morning"—and the tendency to slight variations on the same thing that is said: "I shall address the Lord with my lips and speak to him with my mouth." If you haven't said it the first time, say it with more power the second time.

Van Doren: Today we think we must not repeat ourselves; we think it's a crime if we have failed to say a thing once and finally. The opportunity, we assume, has been forever lost. Not so with the authors of the Psalms, the authors of the poetical parts of Job, the authors of much poetry in the Old Testament. They are always perfectly free to go on and on, mounting their metaphors one upon another, without any notion that the pile can be too high.

Edman: Isn't one reason, Mr. Van Doren, that the Psalms were music, and in music you can repeat a theme with variations?

Van Doren: That is true—repetition is necessary in music. I remember that the only ignorance Leonardo Da Vinci ever revealed in himself he revealed in a remark explaining his disinterest in music. He said: I am not interested in music because it seems to me nothing but repetition.

Untermeyer: What you get in the 148th Psalm—"Praise ye the Lord, Praise ye the Lord from the heavens, Praise him in the heights"—and that goes on for eight lines—what you get there is a series of crashing chords. And those chords are not less interesting because they have a slight variation. It's as if they were a basic chord, repeated and redoubled; but within it certain harmonies are changed.

Van Doren: The psalmist is always changing or interweaving his harmonies. I am interested in Mr. Edman's reference to balance, too, because a notion in the reader's ear that a balance is constantly being honored takes away any possible impression of monotony or mere piling up of effect.

Untermeyer: So that we have resonance really matched with reason. It isn't merely a rhetorical resonance.

Van Doren: Let me make one confession. Reading the Psalms this time, I made a discovery. For me, that is to say, it was a discovery. It was the meaning in English of the word "righteous." I'm not at all able to say what idea the word "righteous" translates from Hebrew, but in my own mind, and wrongly, it had somehow or other become tarnished with the notion of self-righteousness. So I looked the word up in a dictionary and discovered, to my great interest, that "righteous" comes from two ancient English words, Anglo-Saxon words, meaning "right" and "wise." The adjective contains the ideas of rightness or straightness and wisdom or prudence—in the deepest sense of the word "prudence."

Edman: That explains, I think, Mr. Van Doren, why the psalmist celebrates the law. The law was not simply legally correct; it was God's wisdom embodied.

Van Doren: Then a law always had something to aim at—it could hope somehow to match the rightness which sitteth in the heavens. If it is a great advantage for a lyric poet to have God to write about, a god whom no one doubts, so it must be an advantage for law-givers.

Untermeyer: Why does the 23rd Psalm, which is so well known that we needn't even refer to it, have that quality, that eternal surety? Although we no longer are agrarian people, we still have the hope, even in these days of unfaith, that the Lord may be our shepherd.

Van Doren: The pastoral language of the Psalms interested me also as I read. As you say, no people are a pastoral people any more, except people who don't get into the newspapers. Albania may still be largely a pastoral region. But here the pastoral language of the Old Testament, and particularly of its lyric poets, is still fastened upon our imagination.

Untermeyer: It has made our imagination. The green pastures have become a symbol to us—they are no longer merely pastures.

Van Doren: Perhaps we all feel an inadequacy in our comments upon the Psalms. Who wouldn't? Let us comfort ourselves with that question. I'm sure the best thing we can do before we finish is to read at least three of them. I should like to begin by reading the 29th Psalm, which has something of the pounding, effective repetition of which Mr. Untermeyer has spoken. Other psalms have different tones and atmospheres, but here is this one.

"Give unto the Lord, O ye mighty, give unto the Lord glory and strength. Give unto the Lord the glory due unto his name;

worship the Lord in the beauty of holiness. The voice of the Lord is upon the waters: the God of glory thundereth; the Lord is upon many waters. The voice of the Lord is powerful; the voice of the Lord is full of majesty. The voice of the Lord breaketh the cedars; yea, the Lord breaketh the cedars of Lebanon. He maketh them also to skip like a calf; Lebanon and Sirion like a young unicorn. The voice of the Lord divideth the flames of fire. The voice of the Lord shaketh the wilderness; the Lord shaketh the wilderness of Kadesh. The voice of the Lord maketh the hinds to calve, and discovereth the forests; and in his temple doth every one speak of his glory. The Lord sitteth upon the flood; yea, the Lord sitteth King for ever. The Lord will give strength unto his people; the Lord will bless his people with peace."

Edman: I should like to read one that illustrates very well what we've been trying, I think, to say—the Psalmist celebrates God because He is God and because He is also all other things in the world, and because He has done all things and can do all things. It is the 8th:

"O Lord our Lord, how excellent is thy name in all the earth! who hast set thy glory above the heavens. Out of the mouth of babes and sucklings hast thou ordained strength because of thine enemies, that thou mightest still the enemy and the avenger. When I consider thy heavens, the work of thy fingers, the moon and the stars, which thou hast ordained; What is man, that thou art mindful of him? and the son of man, that thou visitest him? For thou hast made him a little lower than the angels, and has crowned him with glory and honor. Thou madest him to have dominion over the works of thy hands; thou hast put all things under his feet: All sheep and oxen, yea, and the beasts of the field; The fowl of the air, and the fish of the sea, and whatsoever passeth through the paths of the seas. O Lord our Lord, how excellent is thy name in all the earth!"

Untermeyer: I should like to read the first part of the 137th Psalm, which has to do with the outcry of the Jews in captivity. It is, I think, one of the greatest symbolic poems ever written in any time. Today it has a particular relevance and a more terrific significance than ever. It is the song of the universal refugee, a song in which the words "Jerusalem" and "Zion" are not Jerusalem or Zion alone, but any country—Norway, Poland, Austria, even Germany.

"By the rivers of Babylon, there we sat down, yea, we wept, when we remembered Zion. We hanged our harps upon the willows in the midst thereof. For there they that carried us away captive required of us a song; and they that wasted us required of us mirth, saying, Sing us one of the songs of Zion. How shall we sing the Lord's song in a strange land? If I forget thee, O Jerusalem, let my right hand forget her cunning. If I do not remember thee, let my tongue cleave to the roof of my mouth; if I prefer not Jerusalem above my chief joy."

AESCHYLUS

The Oresteia

THE POWER of Greek tragedy makes itself felt nowhere more perfectly than in the famous trilogy of Aeschylus. The Agamemnon, *the* Choephori, *and the* Eumenides *are three plays but they tell one story to its end: the story of Agamemnon's return from Troy, his murder by his wife Clytemnestra and her lover Aegisthus, their murder in revenge by his daughter Electra and his son Orestes, the pursuit of Orestes by the Furies who would punish him when no mortal is left to do so, and the final resolution of his difficulty by public trial and the intervention of the goddess Athena. Here is the archetype of all poems which deal with the great themes of justice and wrath; or, to put it narrowly, with the theme of feud. Other Greek tragedies told the story of Agamemnon's family; indeed it remains a story that poets cannot leave alone. But no one has told it with the simple grandeur of Aeschylus, or with his genius for overwhelming spectacle. A reader of*

the Oresteia—*or, if he is fortunate, a spectator—never forgets
the moment when Agamemnon steps from his chariot and faces
his queen across the crimson carpet; or when Cassandra, standing outside the palace walls, screams prophecies of the death
within; or when the doors open and reveal the body of the king of
men; or when Electra recognizes her brother at the tomb; or when
the Furies lie in a heap of black at the foot of their altar at the
beginning of the third play. These spectacles are remembered not
only because they are brilliant and terrible. Another and more
important reason is that Aeschylus has made them the focal points
of a profoundly moral narrative. Nothing grander exists in Western literature.*

*Aeschylus was the first of the three great Greek tragedians, the
others being Sophocles and Euripides. Born in Eleusis, he fought
at Marathon and at Salamis, and spent the latter part of his life
at the court of Hiero I of Sicily. Aeschylus probably wrote ninety
plays, of which seven survive in full. Besides the trilogy of the*
Oresteia *these are the* Suppliants; *the* Persians; Seven Against
Thebes; *and* Prometheus Bound. *Aeschylus appears to have introduced costumes, scenic decorations, and the use of supernumer-
aries. With him, the choruses represent ethical commentaries on
the action. As a poet he suffers in translation: this is especially
true of the choral lyrics, which at their best rival the odes of
Pindar.*

WHITNEY J. OATES · JACQUES BARZUN · MARK VAN DOREN

Van Doren: There are one or two external considerations which I think we might begin with today—considerations external to the story Aeschylus is telling in these three plays, though not external to his fame or to the fame of the story. One of them is the existence in our own generation of several very considerable and successful pieces of literature which are based directly upon the *Oresteia.* Eugene O'Neill's masterpiece, perhaps, is *Mourning Becomes Electra,* which is a direct translation of it into modern terms. Another such work is the *Tower Beyond Tragedy* of Robinson Jeffers, the poem by Mr. Jeffers which I think most critics understand to be his best, and again a poem which makes direct use of this material. It is very interesting to me that two outstanding writers of our time have found in Aeschylus the story that each of them can tell best.

Do you think, Mr. Oates, that O'Neill's play is an adequate translation of Aeschylus's story?

Oates: It surely is an excellent version of the essential theme. The thing about O'Neill's trilogy which has most interested me is the fact that in the first two plays you have almost a one-to-one correspondence with the version of Aeschylus.

Van Doren: The Trojan War becomes the American Civil War.

Oates: Right! And in an exceptionally fine way. However, the difference between the two trilogies comes in the third member; there I think one can see, by comparing the two, the essential difference between the ages in which O'Neill and Aeschylus wrote.

[*18*]

Van Doren: What is missing, would you say, in O'Neill's third play that is in Aeschylus? I assume that something is missing.

Oates: I'll have to put it bluntly. It is theology.

Van Doren: Mr. Barzun, would you agree there?

Barzun: I agree with that, but I would put the missing element on the side of Aeschylus. I think something has been added since Aeschylus, and since I have some doubts about the fullness of the Aeschylean trilogy I should like to ask Mr. Oates what he refers to when he says "the essential theme." I'm sure we don't agree as to what it is.

Oates: That's a pretty direct challenge, Mr. Barzun. I'll try to do my best. I think that the essential theme of the *Oresteia* is a theological one. It is Aeschylus's attempt to discover, portray, and express the ultimate power behind the universe. The nature of that power, its relation to man and also, in addition, what man must do when he faces the brute fact of evil in this world.

Barzun: That's not only *an* essential theme, it is perhaps *the* essential theme of literature. What I'm wondering about is the literalness with which Aeschylus does it, his attempt to change two things, as it seems to me—first, his hearer's conception of the gods, making them more just and more humane, and then his hearer's conception of morality: how to behave when a murder is committed in your family. In doing those two things very directly and with, what seems to me, the crudest of motives assigned to people for making the change, he is not in the literary tradition with which we're all familiar, the tradition which emphasizes the complexity of human nature and the impossibility of dealing with such questions in direct terms, except in theological essays.

Oates: You used one word—"crudest"—there; I wish you'd specify, Mr. Barzun, what in the trilogy you regard as very crude.

Barzun: Well, to take the last play first. The Furies come after Orestes and have to be bribed off by the juster gods to desist from their appointed work.

Oates: Just to make things clear, Orestes has killed his mother because she had killed his father.

Van Doren: Because Apollo told him to.

Oates: Yes.

Van Doren: It is very important to remember that he felt it a duty to kill his mother. Indeed, it has been imposed upon him by Apollo.

Oates: Not completely, had it? Completely imposed upon him?

Van Doren: Well, there is the conflict. If there weren't a conflict there wouldn't have been a play.

Barzun: There is very little conflict and there's very little play.

Van Doren: Doesn't Orestes keep saying to us that he has done this deed of slaying his mother because he must?

Oates: It looks like whistling in the graveyard.

Van Doren: But with the full authority of Apollo.

Oates: Yes, indeed, but how far does Apollo's authority stretch at the very beginning?

Barzun: It is one of the crudities of thought in the whole conception that Apollo takes the blame at the trial in the last play. It doesn't seem to exonerate the culprit.

Oates: Of course, it doesn't! That is to say, theologically it is impossible that Apollo's full responsibility should be able to clear Orestes.

Van Doren: I should say the whole point of this play, considered either theologically or morally, considered either divinely or legally, is its resolution of what seems to be an impossible situation. One death shall be avenged by another, which shall be avenged by another, and that by another to the end of time. The solution is arrived at quite arbitrarily.

Barzun: Arbitrarily on which level?

Van Doren: My whole point is this: that in society—let's consider it legally for a minute—the beauty of law is not necessarily that it is just but that it is effective. The very thing that most people complain about in the law, namely, its technicalities, is what makes law important. Law has technicalities which are able, from time to time, to appear in disputes and settle them. The important thing is for disputes to end, not necessarily for them to end in terms of divine justice.

Oates: But they must end equitably. Isn't that the point?

Van Doren: Equitably, yes, but you use a legal term.

Barzun: With a sense, though, of real distinctions—finely drawn, perhaps, but genuine. Now we hear Athena saying that she's going to cast the deciding vote which frees Orestes because she has been born from Zeus direct without a mother and he has only killed his mother. She's on the side of the men, so mothers don't matter. One can hardly say that here is a great mind at work.

Oates: Now just a moment. I think your point would be completely valid, Mr. Barzun, if the play ended precisely at that point. The play does not end at that point. Indeed, a full quarter of the "Eumenides" still remains to be presented, and it strikes me that you get the key to the whole business in that last quarter.

Van Doren: What do you find there, Mr. Oates?

Oates: I find there the justification for my interpretation, to wit, that the play is about theology and not about—

Barzun: —not about law at all.

Oates: No, not about law specifically conceived in human terms. Obviously, the extrication of Orestes immediately in human terms is absurd. Why do you suppose, Mr. Barzun, that the jury voted six to six?

Barzun: Isn't that the natural way of juries?

Oates: No. It takes all twelve in this country.

Van Doren: It seems to me that this is a great play if only because it produces this kind of argument, and because it offers us so sharply a conception of what happens when disputes are settled. A father, for instance, who finds two of his children quarreling begins by asking which of the children is at fault. One tells him that the other is at fault. The other tells him that the first is at fault; and, to be sure, both are. If the father pursues the story back far enough, he doesn't find any end. Both children obviously are at fault and there is no justice to be invoked. The only thing that can happen, the thing that's humanly important to have happen, is that the father should stop the quarrel quite arbitrarily—often on the most trivial of pretexts.

Oates: How far are you carrying this analysis?

Van Doren: I admit it's dangerous. But you know what happens in trials of law. Does anyone pretend that eternal and universal justice is finally achieved?

Oates: I know, but that's not the alternative, Mr. Van Doren. Substantial justice after the ascertainment of fact—surely every trial implies that.

Barzun: Rather than the divine father putting an end to a squabble among his children, which is the attitude, incidentally, of Aeschylus, and the one that he ascribes to Zeus.

Oates: It strikes me, Mr. Barzun, that you have read the play without reading the chorus. That is to say, we are prepared from the very beginning, from the very opening chorus, for the fact that Aeschylus is dealing specifically with a theological problem and that the human story merely provides him with illustrative material on the human level for the large and ultimate problem with which he is primarily concerned.

Barzun: I entirely agree, only I turn the intention of that agreement around and say that precisely because the human side is only illustrative we have a rather literal theology. I find the play not moving and not particularly convincing, and when I come upon such other crudities—since you ask for a list of crudities—as Orestes arguing with his mother about whether he shall kill her or not, I am shocked. I am like Mrs. Bell, a famous wit of Boston toward the end of the last century, who was given this trilogy to read rather late in life and was asked what she thought about it. She said: "Well, the point seems to be—if you don't kill mother, I will."

Van Doren: Yes, but, isn't it clear from the text, and isn't it certain that the actors themselves would make it clear, that Clytemnestra is dishonest? When Orestes first approaches her as a victim to be slaughtered she seems to undermine him. At least, she says things that might undermine anyone else; things, nevertheless, which soon appear to have been disingenuous.

Oates: Oh, she's a complete hypocrite! She keeps offering alibis. She says it was fate that did it.

Barzun: Well, more crudities again! She was, after all, a

human being, and she is being represented here as both a hypocrite and a fool if she thinks the reasons she advances for the murder of her husband and for staving off her own murder at the hand of Orestes are going to carry any weight. I wish you would explain to me, Mr. Oates, why, when Aeschylus, after all, had all of the possible human motives at hand, he invariably chose fantastic ones to have his characters name.

Oates: In answer to that, Mr. Barzun, I'd like to refer again to the even split in the jury, the six-to-six vote. It strikes me that that is full of meaning in that it conveys to the reader the notion that a problem of this sort cannot be solved by any finite mind.

Van Doren: Well, just as the father in the analogy—

Oates: That's why I asked a moment ago how far you were going to press it.

Van Doren: Well, I will press it to the end.

Oates: All right.

Van Doren: Just as a father or a judge, even of a supreme court, is not assumed by any sensible person to have absolute wisdom, to have wisdom which would apply to the particular case before him in the same way that the gods apply their wisdom—

Barzun: It seems to me that we must make a distinction here between divine wisdom, wisdom to which no man lays claim, and human wisdom, which seems to me absent from any of the characters here involved. Why can't a feud be settled by human beings on human lines and with human understanding without all this mechanical apparatus?

Oates: You are setting up a very complete frame of interpretation, Mr. Barzun. You maintain, or I take it that you maintain, that it is possible for human beings, by using reason, understanding, and the like, to settle the differences that may occur among men.

Van Doren: Well, as a matter of fact, don't we find that actually being attempted here? Clytemnestra has reasons for killing Agamemnon—

Oates: Indeed she has!

Barzun: They are very poor.

Oates: Oh, not so poor!

Van Doren: The best in the world from the purely human point of view. He had put to death their daughter ten years before.

Barzun: Do you believe in the great love of Iphigenia which rankles in Clytemnestra for ten years, so that when she sees her husband returning from the wars she kills him?

Van Doren: Of course to that reason is added another one: that she has taken as a lover during his absence Aegisthus, who, by the way, has every reason in the world to want to destroy Agamemnon, too.

Oates: The point, it strikes me, is this: you have a situation that illustrates in the story an inherent fact of life; the fact that crime, wrongdoing, tends to reproduce itself, and that human beings are not able in and of themselves to bring such a sequence to a close.

Van Doren: Don't we have an excellent set of motives here? Clytemnestra has two reasons for killing Agamemnon, Electra and Orestes later have at least one reason—two reasons, if you like—for killing Clytemnestra; not only their desire to avenge their father, but the command of Apollo, because I still remember that, Mr. Oates, is a virtual command.

Oates: It is! But don't you see, up to that time Apollo is merely the vicegerent of Zeus.

Van Doren: He is not the overarching deity.

Oates: Nor, as a matter of fact, all through the play is Zeus himself all that the godhead should be or all that Aeschylus thinks the godhead should be.

Barzun: So this play really is an illustration, according to you, Mr. Oates, of the inconveniences of polytheism—you can't take orders from a single master who will back up his commands.

Van Doren: Well, answering for Mr. Oates, I should say the play—

Oates: Thank you!

Van Doren: I should say the play amply illustrates the value

of polytheism. You have on the lowest level human beings dis-
agreeing with one another and not being able to find justice
among themselves. On a second level above that, and it seems to
me this corresponds very richly to the reality of the world, you
find, as Mr. Oates says, vicegerent deities who disagree with
themselves. And then you have a kind of hierarchy which makes
their disagreement significant at the very top. You find decision
possible only at the top.

Oates: Well, now, wait a minute. Let's go back to Homer for
a second. Zeus is a leading character in the *Iliad,* is he not?

Barzun: Zeus is the leading character who can be swayed by this
one and that, as occasion prompts.

Oates: Not quite so weak-kneed!

Barzun: You think not? If you take hold of his knee and his
chin, as Thetis does, and—

Oates: Well, let's not get off the track. My point is that at any
rate Aeschylus does not present Zeus as a character in his play.
Zeus is not on the stage in *Prometheus Bound.* Zeus does not appear here. Zeus throughout this play is still not an all-compre-
hending, comprehensive deity, because there are all these other
forces, which Zeus absorbs by the time the play is over in that
last sequence, the last two hundred and fifty lines which I was
talking about a moment ago. Zeus assumes that which the Furies
have represented, that is, legal justice. Zeus is the mercy side of
the picture. The Furies are the representatives of legal justice;
and fate and they, in the end, come together in a magnificent
fusion which cannot be understood rationally. Indeed, I agree
with you definitely that the human reasons given are logically
absurd.

Barzun: I entirely agree with you also in your interpretation
of the facts and of the elements involved; but it only confirms
me in the feeling that a play is not the proper place to discuss
ideas. A play may imply and suggest a system of ideas, but it
cannot discuss them because of all the complexities and contradictions which require such exegeses as you have given, or foot-
notes, or things of that sort.

Oates: Why can't a play do it, Mr. Barzun?

Barzun: Because I don't know of any play that does.

Van Doren: This is one of the most famous plays in the world.

Barzun: It is very famous, indeed, but with me its fame doesn't elucidate its endless mysteries, mysteries that are not mysteries if you transport them into the realm of legal discussion or of theological discussion—all sorts of things which are perfectly valid in their own place.

Van Doren: Aren't we giving a very wrong impression on the play by suggesting that discussion goes on in it primarily? Action is going on here, and spectacles of the richest magnificence are being offered. The thing that one remembers, if he has an eye, is two or three spectacles, in my opinion the most beautiful and the most terrible in all literature—the spectacle of Agamemnon's return and his walking over the crimson carpet, but most of all the standing silent of Cassandra until he has entered the palace, and then her beginning to shriek her prophecies. That, I think, has no match anywhere in literature for—if nothing else—purely sensational effect.

Oates: It is sheer dramatic power and impact.

Van Doren: Just as later on, at the beginning of the third play, you have again a spectacle, apparently so terrible in its own time that the audience was if anything too much impressed. The play opens, you remember, with our being told about the Furies at the foot of Apollo's statue behind closed doors. When we have heard about them sufficiently to have them and nothing else in our mind, the doors are suddenly opened. But then we still do not see them in action—they are sleeping with their black clothes piled over them, at the foot of the statue. It is only after that that they suddenly arise and manifest their full terror to us. We have not talked about *that* element in this play, which is present also in the second part, in the recognition scene between Electra and Orestes. We have been assuming, in other words, that the play argues or states things all the way through. It states them; it argues them in the choruses and, indeed, elsewhere in the play, but there is at the core of it a very intense and single activity.

Barzun: Mr. Van Doren, you've cited moments of pageantry rather than of drama, it seems to me; and there are sandwiched in between them long discussions and commentaries upon human life which range all the way from the platitudinous to the deceptive. We have at the beginning of the third play a long history of the religious thought of the Greeks up to the point where the play begins, from the mouth of the Pythoness, and in the long choruses of the first play we have matters that are beautiful in themselves but quite irrelevant to any conflict such as we expect in a play.

Oates: I wouldn't agree with that.

Van Doren: What is the conflict in the first play?

Oates: The conflict in the first play is the conflict that has been engendered by the curse upon the house.

Barzun: You mean the conflict is the simple one, the physical one, that Clytemnestra is planning to hit her husband with an axe.

Van Doren: If you want to put it that way, yes, indeed. That's precisely what she's intending to do.

Barzun: Oughtn't we to have a little more psychological preparation, so that we may feel that we are on both sides of the fence instead of only one?

Oates: Think of the irony in the double meanings in Clytemnestra's opening speeches. You remember how she protests so stoutly her loyalty to her husband, how she has been the watchdog of the home, etc., etc. That certainly gives you a conflict, the kind of conflict that you get in dramatic irony. Going back to Eugene O'Neill's play, there is the scene between General Mannon and his wife as they sit on the front steps of the house; it is one of the most intense and dramatic scenes I have ever witnessed. But I'd like to go on to mention how Clytemnestra comes out and really shrieks her triumph after she has killed him, how she says that his blood is like dew on crops. Do you recall? And then her state of complete emotional exhaustion at the very conclusion of the *Agamemnon,* where she pleads for peace—"Let's call it off!"

Van Doren: Well, Mr. Oates, the disagreement, I take it, between Mr. Barzun and both of us is possibly not a disagreement as to the importance of theology, or as to the importance of religion in drama, because we all assume with the historians that drama begins in religion and always draws its strength from it, but is a disagreement over the question whether this play comes at the right moment in that line of descent from religion to psychology which drama always goes through. I don't suppose there is anything we can really argue about. If to you the play occupies the right position on that line, then it does; and if it doesn't for Mr. Barzun, nothing can be done about it.

Barzun: Especially if we're so far away from a particular religious tradition that we have to learn of it outside the poem.

Oates: We aren't so terribly far away from it, because after all Aeschylus does present us with a deity who has lost his anthropomorphism and is worthy of man's worship. Aeschylus expresses this in a famous chorus at the beginning of the *Agamemnon* which reads as follows:

> *Zeus! Zeus, whate'er He be,*
> *If this name He love to hear*
> *This he shall be called of me.*
>   *Searching earth and sea and air*
> *Refuge, nowhere can I find*
> *Save him only, if my mind*
> *Will cast off before it die*
>   *The burden of this vanity.*
>
> *One there was who reigned of old,*
>   *Big with wrath to brave and blast,*
> *Lo, his name is no more told!*
>   *And who followed met at last*
> *The third-thrower, and is gone.*
>   *Only they whose hearts have known*
> *Zeus, the Conqueror and the Friend,*
>   *They shall win their vision's end;*

Aeschylus: The Oresteia

Zeus, the guide who made man turn
Thoughtward, Zeus, who did ordain
Man by Suffering shall Learn.
So the heart of him, again
Aching with remembered pain,
Bleeds and sleepeth not, until
Wisdom comes against his will.
'Tis the gift of One by strife
Lifted to the throne of life.

(65-8 B.C.)

HORACE

Poems: Odes,
Satires and Epistles

H*ORACE has been for two thousand years one of the best-known poets of the Western world. He exists in innumerable editions, translations, and adaptations; and phrases from his* **Odes** *enjoy a universal circulation, appearing and reappearing even in the speech of those who could not identify their origin. He was possessed of a wonderful felicity with words, so that it has been impossible to improve upon the statements he made. His statements, furthermore, were of familiar things: the things which in all ages have interested men. His last desire was to be original if originality means oddness or uniqueness. For Horace it meant not so much having a new thing to say as knowing better than anyone else how to say the old thing, even the commonplace thing. "What oft was thought but ne'er so well expressed"— Pope has put it precisely; and Pope is one of the many poets who have been content to aim at Horace's mark. Horace took his job*

*to be the job of art, and it was there that he did in fact become
as perfect as human limitations permit. Personally he was sensible, pleasure-loving, skeptical, prudent, and plump. He at no
point, that is, resembles the type of poet which modern times,
temporarily no doubt, have fixed upon as ideal. His temperament
was not specialized, just as his poetry is not eccentric. And his
Satires and Epistles show him to have been a man who could look
with keen, accurate eyes at the behavior of his Roman contemporaries. In short, he was and is in the best sense a worldly poet.
And fashion will never obscure his eminence.*

*Horace was the son of an educated freeman of Venusia. He
studied in Rome and Athens, and joining Brutus and the republicans, fought at Philippi. Introduced by Virgil, Maecenas became
Horace's friend and benefactor and gave him, before 30 B.C., the
Sabine Farm. After Virgil's death, Horace was the chief literary
figure in Rome and the critical arbiter. He represents especially
the spirit of the Augustan Age. His descriptions of Italian scenery
are unique in the classics and his adaptations of Greek meters to
Latin verse are made with consummate skill.*

FRANKLIN P. ADAMS · IRWIN EDMAN · MARK VAN DOREN

Van Doren: Do you suppose, gentlemen, that Horace is really a poet? He was good-natured, easy-going, plump, slightly bald, and he wrote love poems at forty. Nothing that he ever wrote is unintelligible; he said he had girls but it is not certain that he really had them or what it was he really felt about them; he loved the country and yet he always wrote about it from town. He thought nothing was more important than writing a perfect poem, every portion of which was polished and finished. He was not in despair about anything. He felt that life was good, and above all things had a sense of humor. Now, Mr. Adams, do you think I have described a poet in describing Horace?

Adams: Yes, except that he didn't have to work for a living. He had Maecenas, who subsidized him and gave him his farm; there is a poem that ends up: ". . . and what, oh, what is a sabine farm without Maecenas?"

Van Doren: Life was made easy for him. He also seems to have been in favor of his government, does he not?

Adams: Yes, which isn't particularly a liability.

Van Doren: Mr. Edman, do you think we have the right to call Horace a poet in view of the fact that he doesn't seem to fit the prescription of our own time?

Edman: As I understand it, Mr. Van Doren, you are suggesting, I suspect not too seriously, that the reason Horace is not a poet is that he was not constantly in despair, that he was not agonized, that he was sensible, that he enjoyed the minor amusements of life, and that he was careful about his verse, which he was. We have somehow inherited from the nineteenth century the notion that a poet must be long-haired and long-winded—

Van Doren: And short-lived.

Edman: And short-lived, and that he must be full of careless inspiration, and that he must somehow starve. Now Horace did none of these things. By the way, there are some perfectly good poets today who haven't Maecenas; but they have Guggenheim, which doesn't seem to hurt them.

Van Doren: That's true. They don't write poems to Guggenheim, however, as Horace wrote poems to Maecenas and Augustus.

Edman: Well, somehow it is accepted that a man who is amiable or urbane somehow can't be genuinely poetic.

Van Doren: Unfortunately that dogma does exist.

Adams: It's just tradition. It's just nonsense. All the poets I know wear better clothes than I have and do better, and a lot of them pay quite large income taxes.

Van Doren: By the way, Mr. Adams, do they give you the impression, not in their poetry but in their lives, that they know something about the world, that they know how to get around in it?

Adams: If they don't, they're no good.

Van Doren: Horace makes it clear that he knows how to get around in this world, whereas one assumption underlying a great deal of modern poetry is that the author is bewildered, lost in it, can't make anything out of it.

Adams: I know a couple of first-class modern poets who look as though they would be at home in Wall Street. Mr. Mark Van Doren and Mr. Archibald MacLeish for two.

Van Doren: And Mr. Irwin Edman and Mr. Franklin P. Adams for four.

Edman: Well, now that the Horatian amenities have been observed, Mr. Van Doren, I would like to bring up one of the points you mention—the point that somehow Horace couldn't write love poetry because love does not begin at forty.

Adams: Oh, yeah?

Edman: Mr. Van Doren didn't mean that seriously. As a matter of fact, I think Horace felt that you can only write about something, including love, when you have the maturity to understand it and know what you are talking about.

Van Doren: There's another thing about Horace, too, that distinguishes him from almost any modern writer—meaning, by modern writer, a writer of the last 150 years. He is quite content to say things that everyone knows to be true. He isn't breaking his brains to be original in the naked sense of that word. He began by writing satires, you know, and he was perfectly content to make them imitations of Lucilius, a master whom he tried to improve and whom he did improve. Horace took all his subjects for satire from another man, and simply handled them better. One does not find in Horace's poetry unusual, eccentric statements which may or may not be acceptable. I think we all immediately recognize them to be true. As one of his disciples in English poetry, Alexander Pope, put it, he wrote "what oft was thought but ne'er so well expressed."

Edman: Isn't it true that many people call commonplace whatever they recognize when somebody supplies them with sensible feelings about life? They do not know what Horace knows until he puts it into words for them. Such things become commonplace because Horace made them so. Wouldn't you say there was something in that?

Van Doren: Horace helped to make them commonplace, yes. But he also would have insisted that he thought it was the job of the poet to say things which human beings anywhere might recognize as true, but which they would delight in if they were said as well as he could say them.

Adams: I imagine that when people read those obvious things, in those days, although they didn't read them in the papers, they remarked: "Hey, I was saying that only last night." But not quite so well.

Van Doren: Not nearly so well. One of the great tragedies of literature, I think, is that whereas formerly the greatest poets—Shakespeare, Ben Jonson, Herrick, Dryden, Pope, Byron—were proud to rewrite Horace, to translate him, to imitate him, in our day his appearances have been confined to what many people think an unimportant region of poetry, namely, the newspaper column. Now I don't happen to think that it is an unimportant region; indeed, it may be the most important one. But it is significant of our time that persons critically recognized as poets are not supposed to be Horatian. Horace has kept alive in his own place and in his own way, and one reason that I am glad to have both of you here today is that you once assisted in keeping him gloriously alive in the Conning Tower of the New York *World*.

Edman: I should like to say, if it doesn't embarrass Mr. Adams, that for a great many people in this generation, the Horatian philosophy was kept alive only in the Conning Tower, where certain of them learned to express themselves in something like the Horatian mood. And I'd like to make another point about that. A great many people think philosophy is pompous. Now it turns out, when you examine Horace's biography, that he had studied Greek philosophy for years, and what we call his commonplaces are the fruits of a doctrine that numerous philosophers, including Epicurus, arrived at, simply because he managed to state them with cheerfulness and wit and urbanity. We somehow come to think that that is easy to do, or a trivial thing.

Van Doren: In the very first poem of his which we have, the first satire, he says: "I am speaking truth with a smile." That distinguishes him once again from the modern poet whom we have taken as a symbol of our literary time. It wasn't beneath him to speak the truth lightly.

Edman: It occurs to me, Mr. Van Doren, in rereading Horace, that one occasionally comes upon things which seem smiling but are sad. For example, a repeated theme of his is that we have had our day and nobody can take that away from us no matter what happens. That isn't as cheerful as it looks on the surface, is it really?

Van Doren: No, because although he is saying that since life is short we had better enjoy it while we have it, we'd better enjoy the present moment, he does begin with the observation that life is short, and I dare say that is not a necessarily joyous notion. Mr. Adams, would you want to say what it was that Horace believed—that is, what he thought in general?

Adams: He is often trying to say that things might be worse but he doesn't quite see how. Sometimes they might be better. In some of the things he wrote to the gals, whether they existed or not, he says: "Well, I'm through with you, and all that." Roughly, such poems might have been written by Dorothy Parker.

Van Doren: Would you dignify him by saying that he had a philosophy? I don't want to suggest that he should have had one.

Adams: I don't know. I didn't study him, I just translated him.

Edman: I think he did have a philosophy, Mr. Van Doren.

Van Doren: Was it the Epicurean one?

Edman: On the whole it was Epicurean—not with a college education but with a city man's education. He was an Epicurean who lived in town and saw all the things that happened, good, bad and indifferent, and he thought life on the whole pretty precarious. If you didn't ask too much of it, you could make a reasonable go of it, no matter what your particular fate was. And this has been a consolation, a kind of philosophy, to a great many people who aren't fooled about the promise or glory of life but who think you can make pretty good terms with it.

Van Doren: One of his epistles—he wrote not only odes or lyric poems, but longer pieces which are discussions of things—starts off with two very famous words: "Nil admirari," which are to be translated, I take it, "Admire nothing, wonder at nothing." Now there again we see the difference between him and the romantic poet who is supposed to deal in wonder—I suppose it is one of the silliest prescriptions for poetry ever made. Horace said: "No, I have no respect for the man who wonders at everything. I have respect for the man who knows, and so cannot be surprised, cannot be tipped off his balance, can never be completely surprised. He hasn't expected too much; therefore he isn't downcast because too much doesn't happen. Neither has he expected too little."

Edman: I wonder what you think, Mr. Van Doren, saved Horace from being smug. Because he isn't smug, though what you just said would indicate that here was a poet who was terribly careful about not being "taken in." You make him sound frightfully sophisticated, and I don't think Horace gives that impression.

Van Doren: Like every sensible man, Horace runs the risk of being called commonplace and smug; that is always the risk you run if you are sensible.

Adams: And if you are a classic for so many years.

Van Doren: He has been a classic for two thousand years. The fame of this man is one of the most important facts about him; the fame of Horace is almost incredible.

Edman: To use his own phrase, he has become a kind of golden mediocrity—not in our sense of mediocrity but in the sense of a golden level or norm of life.

Van Doren: There are two ways of talking about the golden mean. One way is to suggest that almost anyone can find it—all you have to do is to avoid the extremes. Another way is to suggest that it is very, very difficult to find, the mean being in fact the ideal.

Edman: That is brought out I think by his own practice. We usually come to think a man's philosophy includes his morals; Horace's morals appear not so much in his relation to men and women and life in general as in his relation to his art. He was severely scrupulous. He had a kind of integrity about form that was not casual, and this is probably one of the most important things about him. In that sense too he has become the standard for poets who have an artistic conscience over thousands of years.

Adams: Oh, he was a great old polisher of verses. You can't find false quantities or any of those things, and that is where a great many people who think they study him don't do any such thing. They go after the matter only, and they say: "Oh, well, this is old stuff." As far as the satires are concerned, I've read those in translation only, and I don't think they're half so satirical as the odes and the epistles themselves. How about that, Doc?

Edman: If I may talk back to my first boss who used to correct my quantities in Horace when I tried to submit them to the Conning Tower—

Adams: They were pretty tough, weren't they?

Edman: Well, one does the best one can for Simon Legree. I would like to say that Horace, dealing with the normal commonplaces of life, thought that through him they would become memorable. In fact, one of his most famous odes is one in which he celebrates himself. He thought the way to become memorable was engraving things so perfectly and so plainly that the commonplace would really become immortal. That's a fairly good prescription.

Adams: You don't mean "aere perennius," do you?

Edman: That's exactly what I have reference to.

Van Doren: As a matter of fact, even that sort of statement about a poet's own poetry has become commonplace. One of Shakespeare's most famous sonnets is an attempt to rewrite it, isn't it? "Not marble, or the gilded monuments." Horace, apparently writing a personal poem, wrote one which could be rewritten by other men, who could appear just as personal. He has enormous potency as an artist in that way. Other artists admire him, and are proud and pleased to imitate him.

Edman: The interesting thing is that Horace, trying to find a kind of standard perfection, discovers an accent that is really his own. The more he polishes, the more he becomes himself. I'd like to ask one question, Mr. Van Doren, which occurs to me. Supposing there had been Pulitzer Awards in Rome, mightn't the committee have been a little worried about giving a prize to Horace? Mightn't they have thought: This is a perfect gem of its kind, but a little trivial compared with Virgil, for example?

Adams: They wouldn't have give him honorable mention.

Edman: Do you really think that?

Adams: I really think that. In the first place, his poems are short, they're not ponderous, they have what passed in those days for rhyme, and that is automatically out.

Edman: It is now, but do you think it would have been then?

Van Doren: I can doubt it, because there is every evidence that the thing Horace was trying to do at the time was understood as it would not be understood now. It was believed to be an excellent thing to do if one could do it. For one thing, he made light music, which is a difficult thing to do.

Edman: He was admired for his technical excellence. Even his contemporaries realized that he was expert.

Van Doren: You mentioned Virgil, who of course was one of his best friends. Several of his poems are about Virgil, are they not? He wants Virgil to be safe in the ship which is taking him across the sea. Now Virgil agreed with Horace completely in the matter of polishing. Virgil died before he was able to polish the *Aeneid* to his satisfaction.

Adams: He did all right, though.

Van Doren: Not in his own mind. He left word that the poem should be destroyed because it wasn't perfect.

Adams: By the way, Horace started out as a soldier. I don't think he was so hot, but he was at Philippi, if memory serves.

Edman: Memory serves you very well, Mr. Adams, and I wonder what inference you draw from that. He was a soldier. Did that make him a better poet or a worse one, or did it make no difference?

Adams: I don't know. But he was out quick enough to get into the poetry racket.

Van Doren: You will remember that in his last poem, *The Art of Poetry,* a piece of criticism which has been famous for 2,000 years, he advises you when you write something to put it away for nine years so that you will be sure you have it perfect, because a word once printed can never be recalled. Do you think he is excessive when he says nine years?

Adams: No—especially if you have Maecenas to pay for two or three meals a day and raiment.

Van Doren: Well, who do you think is the better poet, Shakespeare or Ben Jonson?

Adams: I think Shakespeare was a better poet than anybody.

Van Doren: Ben Jonson, however, is on record as saying that Shakespeare would have been still better if he had been able to do what Horace enjoined. Shakespeare never waited at all. He wrote something and there it was.

Adams: He wouldn't have done a bit better the second time.

Van Doren: It seems to me so. I'd just as lieve bet that he wouldn't.

Adams: So would I.

Van Doren: Nine years of waiting is excessive. To be sure, many things would never get published at all if the author waited nine years, and that might be a good thing.

Edman: On the other hand, it would be rather audacious to rely on being Shakespeare, wouldn't it?

Van Doren: Which is a very illuminating statement, Mr. Edman, because after all Horace is ever the artist, isn't he? The thing that he can count on is his art. He doesn't count on being a Shakespeare, he doesn't count on being a Catullus, he doesn't count on being a sudden genius. He counts on the work he knows he can do on his verses.

Edman: I should like to read a poem. I don't know whether it was preserved nine years or not, but I have here a translation of Horace by Mr. Adams which seems very accurately to convey the spirit and temper and quality of Horace itself. It is a translation of the famous "Exegi monumentum":

> *The monument that I have built is durable as brass,*
> *And loftier than the Pyramids which mock the years that pass.*
> *No blizzard can destroy it, nor furious rain corrode—*
> *Remember, I'm the bard that built the first Horatian ode.*
>
> *I shall not altogether die; a part of me's immortal.*
> *A part of me shall never pass the mortuary portal;*
> *And when I die, my fame shall stand the nitric test of time—*
> *The fame of me of lowly birth, who built the lofty rhyme!*

Ay, fame shall be my portion when no trace there is of me,
For I first made Æolian songs the songs of Italy.
Accept, I pray, Melpomene, my modest meed of praise,
And crown my thinning, graying locks with wreaths of Delphic bays!

Van Doren: Mr. Adams, do you remember having written that? Is it true what Mr. Edman says, that you wrote it?

Adams: It's true that I wrote it, but it sounds a good deal better when he reads it than I ever thought it was.

Van Doren: It was written for the Conning Tower, I dare say.

Adams: It was published either in the *World* or in the *Evening Mail,* I don't know which. I have worked so long and for so many papers that I can't remember.

Van Doren: Would you like to read one of your translations yourself, Mr. Adams?

Adams: I should say not. I couldn't read any of my own stuff. I never would have heard of Horace if it hadn't been for Eugene Field.

Van Doren: Did you know Eugene Field?

Adams: No, I didn't. He died in 1895, and I was just out of rompers in those days.

Van Doren: In any collection of translations from Horace that I ever came across, Eugene Field's name was prominent.

Adams: His brother, Roswell M. Field, was an even better translator. Much closer.

Van Doren: I didn't know that. Have you anything from Field that you might read?

Adams: I haven't Field here, but I remember the first thing I read. I'm not sure how it goes exactly, but it began:

> *It is very aggravating*
> *To hear the solemn prating*
> *Of the fossils who are stating*
> *   That old Horace was a prude;*
> *When we know that with the ladies*
> *He was always raising Hades,*
> *And with many an escapade his*
> *   Best productions are imbued.*

There's really not much harm in a
Large number of his carmina,
But these people find alarm in a
  Few records of his acts;
So they'd squelch the muse caloric,
And to students sophomoric
They'd present as metaphoric
  What old Horace means for facts.

We have always thought 'em lazy;
Now we adjudge 'em crazy!
Why, Horace was a daisy
  Who was very much alive!
And the wisest of us know him
As his Lydia verses show him—
Go, read that virile poem—
  It is No. 25.

He was a very owl, sir,
And starting out to prowl, sir,
You bet he made Rome howl, sir,
  Until he filled his date;
With a massic laden ditty
And a classic maiden pretty
He painted up the city,
  And Maecenas paid the freight!

Van Doren: Do you mean to say that that comes out of your memory?

Adams: That comes out of my memory. I think it was the first Field thing from Horace I ever read, and I said: Well, if he can do it, why can't I? And I couldn't.

Van Doren: A magnificent compliment to Field, to Horace, and to you. Mr. Edman, my own memory is that Mr. Adams wrote an alternative version of the "aere perennius" poem. If you have it here, could you read it too?

Adams: I wrote that thing about forty times, I think.

Edman: This is the second version:

Look you, the monument I have erected
High as the Pyramids, royal, sublime,

During as brass—it shall not be affected
  E'en by the elements coupled with time.

Part of me, most of me never shall perish;
  I shall be free from Oblivion's curse;
Mine is a name that the future will cherish—
  I shall be known by my excellent verse.

I shall be famous all over this nation
  Centuries after myself shall have died;
People will point to my versification—
  I, who was born on the Lower East Side!

Come, then, Melpomene, why not admit me?
  I want a wreath that is Delphic and green;
Seven, I think, is the size that will fit me—
  Slip me some laurel to wear on my bean.

Van Doren: That's grand. Very different from the other, and yet the same thing. It justifies me, I think, in calling Mr. Adams a virtuoso in translation. I have still another version of Horace, not a whole poem by any means, but a few lines out of the twenty-ninth ode of the third book, addressed to his patron, Maecenas, about whom Mr. Adams spoke. This is by Dryden, and I think it gets the Epicurean touch perfectly:

Happy the man, and happy he alone,
He who can call today his own;
He who secure within can say
Tomorrow do thy worst, for I have lived today.

Be fair or foul or rain or shine,
The joys I have possessed, in spite of fate, are mine.
Not heaven itself upon the past has power,
But what has been, has been, and I have had my hour.

(1564-1616)

SHAKESPEARE

Hamlet

THE EMINENCE of Hamlet *among tragedies appears most clearly when one considers how many different kinds of play it has been said to be. In modern times it has been taken for granted that Shakespeare's masterpiece has for its hero a man whom an excess of imagination and intellectual subtlety renders unfit to cope with the crude, pressing duties of life. Hamlet, we have said, is too brilliant to act; he can only think, can only be himself. And this interpretation of him and of the play which he dominates has utterly satisfied us. But there have been times when something altogether different was said. Then Hamlet struck no one as paralyzed in will or defective in purpose; it was external obstacles—the King and his guards, a well-populated palace, the meddling of Polonius—that delayed his revenge; or if there were internal obstacles, they were the normal ones of conscience and the desire to be scrupulously right in the selection of a victim. That inter-*

[44]

pretation worked also; and still does. The play will justify any interpretation which takes all of it into account. For among plays it is the one most completely and incessantly alive. Think what we may about Hamlet, we never doubt that we see, hear, and are fascinated by him. We do not know whether he means what he says, but we cannot miss or forget his lines, just as we cannot keep our eyes off his figure as he moves with such swift grace about the stage. An actor himself, he has provided the best-known part for other actors; and has been presented in every conceivable style and dimension. The secret of Hamlet's *eminence is, finally, nothing but the secret of any art when it is wholly successful. It is Shakespeare's signature under his most lifelike portrait.*

William Shakespeare was the son of a Stratford-on-Avon glove-maker. What we know of his life is drawn from official records, contemporary allusions, and oral tradition. He married Anne Hathaway in 1582, probably went to London in 1584, and by 1592 was a recognized playwright. As actor and dramatist for the Lord Chamberlain's (later the King's) company, he wrote a play a year. He extended his financial interest in the London stage, and retired to Stratford in 1610 with a sizable fortune. Of the thirty-eight plays accepted as his work by most scholars, thirty-six comprised the First Folio (1623); eighteen of these were first issued as pamphlets (Quartos) as was the thirty-seventh (Pericles) *; the thirty-eighth* (The Two Noble Kinsmen) *appeared in 1634. Of all thirty-eight, only* Love's Labour's Lost *has no known direct source.*

MARGARET WEBSTER · STRINGFELLOW BARR · MARK VAN DOREN

Van Doren: We have on our hands today the most famous play in the world. I take it to be that, not only because it has had an extended run in London of 340 years since its first production in the year 1600, but because any conversation about drama, and certainly about Shakespeare, sooner or later ends up with *Hamlet*. *Hamlet* somehow gets to the top of any such conversation; it is assumed to be the representative play. Mr. Barr, it occurs to me that the first thing we should ask ourselves today—I don't know whether we can answer the question or not—is: why this eminence? Is it perfectly clear why it is that *Hamlet* has such fame?

Barr: I think it is very far from clear, because, superficially considered, *Hamlet* has less of what most people mean by action than many of Shakespeare's plays, than *Macbeth,* for instance, which Miss Webster is now producing.

Webster: Yet at the same time there are more dead bodies at the end of *Hamlet* than there are at the end of *Macbeth,* and in point of fact Hamlet, who is considered by some a man of weak and indecisive will, incapable of action, actually gets through more murders than anybody else in the cycle of the plays.

Barr: But the murders don't happen very early, do they?

Webster: No, the murders mostly happen toward the end, except, of course, the murder of Polonius. But the play starts right off with the ghost, which might be considered action.

Van Doren: Yes, I was going to say that the most significant murder has taken place before the play begins.

Barr: The ghost of a murdered man.

Webster: The ghost of a murdered man—that promises well for a melodrama, don't you think?

Van Doren: Miss Webster, doesn't it occur to you that Macbeth is also a man of imperfect will? Isn't one of the troubles with Macbeth that he is afraid from the moment the play begins? Afraid of what he's going to do—what he has promised himself and his wife to do?

Webster: There are certain analogies between Hamlet and Macbeth—very interesting ones. And yet to return to your first question, Mr. Van Doren, as to the pre-eminence of *Hamlet,* which has been produced many more times I should imagine than *Macbeth*—Hamlet has come to be considered the crown of any English-speaking actor's career. It is the part which most actors want to play, and, curiously enough, it is an easier part to play than Macbeth.

Van Doren: That is interesting, Miss Webster. Since Hamlet is on the stage almost all of the time and since he is, as legend has it, the play itself so that you can't imagine *Hamlet* without Hamlet, one would suppose that the part was especially difficult.

Webster: It has much more modulation in it than *Macbeth.* Macbeth is a hard, driving part that goes from the beginning of the play to the end with only one brief rest, and calls at the very end for terrific physical exertion. Hamlet is rested by the other characters to a much greater extent than Macbeth is.

Barr: But I hope, Miss Webster, you're not saying that actors are such lazy people that their idea of crowning their careers is to get a part that is less difficult.

Webster: No, I wouldn't put it that way; I wouldn't say that anybody a bit lazy would choose Hamlet.

Barr: Well, why do actors want to play Hamlet? I'd like to know from one who directs Shakespearean plays.

Webster: The opinion of the actor, for all that he is a special kind of animal, coincides with that of the lay audience to a great degree, in the sense that every actor reads himself into Hamlet and Hamlet into himself; in the same way, I think, every reader of *Hamlet* reads him or herself into Hamlet.

Van Doren: I wonder, Miss Webster, if the actor and the layman have the same reason for doing this thing. I grant you that it is done, but the actor, I have always supposed, loves the part because it is the part of an actor, Hamlet himself being always in the process of acting, of playing a part—indeed, of playing many parts. Now, surely, the layman does not think of himself as an actor. Or does he? Perhaps all persons think of themselves as actors. Do you think so, Mr. Barr?

Barr: Maybe so. In any case, Miss Webster's answer throws us back on the original question pretty hard. We could hardly formulate it better now than by asking: Why do people who go to theaters, whose judgment is reflected by the actor's desire to do what they want to see and hear, why do people think that Hamlet is themselves, why is there a tendency to identify oneself peculiarly with Hamlet rather than with Macbeth or with other leading heroes in Shakespeare?

Webster: Is it perhaps the extraordinary variety and range of Hamlet?

Van Doren: I think it must be that, rather than the supposed quality in him—I say "supposed" with emphasis—of indecision, of a paralyzed will, of an inability to act. Surely no one watching the play actually says to himself: "This man cannot act." I am using the word "act," if you like, in two senses. I mean being an actor—

Webster: —and acting in the sense of performing a deed.

Van Doren: Performing a deed as well as performing a part. Surely this man is the most agile and mobile of heroes. He is all over the stage; he is acutely, intensely, intelligently aware of the presence of other persons on the stage—more so, I should say, than any other actor ever has to be. Any scene shows him confronted with persons with whom he must behave in a certain way, or with whom he thinks he must behave in a certain way; he is enormously sensitive to those relations.

Barr: But his own chief impression of himself during the play, if I understand the remarks he makes about himself, is that he cannot act, he cannot perform a deed.

Van Doren: Quite.

Barr: Because unless he performs that deed, all other deeds seem to him rather negligible, rather stupid.

Van Doren: That's quite true. In the fourth act, when he sees Fortinbras marching so briskly and so youthfully to his job in Poland, he considers with himself why it is that he cannot behave this way.

Webster: Because he *can* behave in so many other ways is perhaps one of the answers.

Van Doren: Yes, *Hamlet* is, among other things, the story of a young man who only thinks he wants to do a certain thing to the exclusion of others. Doubtless he does not want to do it. No intellectual young man wants to kill anybody.

Barr: Would it throw any light on the play to ask what in your judgment Hamlet does want to do—just to return to Wittenberg and study and think?

Webster: If there were a definitive answer to that, there would stop being productions of the play, wouldn't there?

Van Doren: Well, he wants to go on being alive in the very rich way in which he has always been alive. He is a man who has charmed everybody who has ever known him. He is a student. He is brilliant. He loves theatricals, amateur and otherwise. He knows the actors, you remember, when they come—knows them all by name, remembers their parts. He is a man to whom the world has always been an intensely interesting and promising place. I suppose he wants to remain in that world. He would like to go on and do the job he has—namely, killing the present king —and remain the sort of man that I have been describing.

Barr: You say he would like to go on living in that world. My chief impression of him, during the play, is that he is paralyzed not so much by fear of taking a human life, because he takes several lives even before the general carnage Miss Webster alludes to, he stabs Polonius and arranges to get rid of Guildenstern and Rosencrantz—

Van Doren: You mean Rosencrantz and Guildenstern.

Barr: My impression is that the thing that horrifies him chiefly is the corruption, the practical life about him.

Van Doren: At the very beginning of the play we see him cast into melancholy for reasons unknown. It isn't at all that he then knows that his father was murdered, if indeed his father was murdered. It is, as you say, that he seems suddenly to have become aware of corruption in the world.

Webster: Do you agree that he should be represented as a very young man?

Barr: Yes, I do, emphatically.

Van Doren: I think so, don't you?

Webster: Yes, I do.

Barr: What is your reason, Miss Webster?

Webster: The thing that you've been speaking of, his sickness at the corruption of the world, is the reaction of a very young man to the initial discovery of a disparity between ideals and the facts of life.

Barr: That is right; and who hates the acceptance by the middle-aged of that corruption.

Van Doren: It is a very complicated young man we have been describing. Although young, he is already complicated.

Webster: But the young are complicated, don't you think?

Van Doren: Well, this young man takes everything hard. That is one way of describing Hamlet. He is a man to whom nothing comes simply. His discovery that the world is corrupt is an overwhelming discovery. But everything else he does he tends to do with that richness and complexity which is part of his nature. When he greets the players, it is, again, with an overwhelming courtesy; when he talks to Ophelia, it is with an overwhelming rudeness. Nothing can be done by him simply; when he conceives the idea of a play to be played before the King which will catch him in his conscience, there again he must set about in the most elaborate and really fascinating way to produce that play.

Barr: It has just occurred to me that one might make this statement as to why the average man or the average woman identifies himself with Hamlet when he watches him on the stage. On the one hand, Hamlet loves life very dearly and feels intensely what its possibilities could be, as all of us feel them. On the other hand, he is horrified by what life is as against what it can be. And that takes in a very wide area of interest for the ordinary man.

Webster: Yes, and comprises within its scope a great variety of different reasons for which almost everybody has felt the same disgust.

Barr: Disappointment.

Webster: Disappointment, and disgust.

Barr: Every disgusted or disappointed person in the world would see a little of himself in Hamlet's frustration.

Webster: And there is practically no person who hasn't at some time or other felt that disappointment.

Van Doren: And yet we should be giving the wrong impression of Hamlet, shouldn't we, if we represented him as a moper? He remains brilliantly articulate, brilliantly alive—he moves about the stage, as I said, always with the agility of a leopard. It isn't as if he were set to talk about himself and became silent the way disgusted and disappointed people often do. His fascination may be that his disgust and his disappointment make him more active than before.

Barr: He is very anxious to act, I take it; he feels a great necessity to act, and not merely because of his father's spirit. Now, if he feels this terrific necessity to act, and yet is tremendously puzzled as to how one would act well in the midst of flattery and general villainy and general treachery and so on, then he is like most of us, because most of us find ourselves either wanting to act or under the necessity to act and unsure how we should do it.

Van Doren: That's right. The simple thing to do cannot be done simply.

Webster: We're doing the very thing that everybody always does in discussions of *Hamlet*—which perhaps is one of the reasons it is so much discussed. We are beginning to discuss Hamlet as a person whom we all know, quite divorced from the particular set of dramatic circumstances and the framework of theater craftsmanship with which he is actually surrounded by Shakespeare.

Van Doren: Which is what always happens, isn't it, to a good play or a good story?

Webster: Of no character does it happen to the same degree as with Hamlet, I think. That is one of the reasons that many fallacious theories of Hamlet as a person have grown up—from people who have ceased to consider Hamlet as a character in the play *Hamlet*.

Van Doren: What is the most fallacious of these theories, would you say, Miss Webster?

Webster: I should say Coleridge's theory of the dreamer and the man incapable of action, the neurotic, pale, moping young man.

Barr: That would put people's teeth on edge if true, wouldn't it?

Webster: I should imagine so.

Barr: Not even neurotics like to look at other neurotics.

Van Doren: Coleridge, perhaps, was making the most elementary mistake that can be made by a critic in not realizing that perhaps the finest hero you can have for a tragedy is a hero who, so to speak, could not do the thing you see him doing. Who are the heroes of great novels in which murder occurs? They are students. Raskolnikov, for instance, or Macbeth again—Macbeth, after all, was a very fine gentleman who shouldn't be killing anybody, and yet he does. A murder story had best have for its hero a man who cannot commit a murder. That is where the interest actually lies.

Barr: Yes, nobody wants to see professional murderers at work.

Webster: No one likes to think that he has a personal sympathy or fellow feeling for habitual murderers.

Van Doren: I quite agree with you, Miss Webster, that we have here not a type but a man. We always lose ourselves if we begin to talk about Hamlet as a type. I suppose we have in Hamlet a man more completely alive than anyone before or since in literature—a man whom you immediately love, a man whose every gesture, every remark, is convincing.

Barr: He isn't one of the types of man, I agree with you, but he is perhaps more typically a man than most heroes in literature.

Van Doren: That is a very important modification to introduce. Yes. All the time that he is a man, he is man.

Barr: Do you remember how frightened he is by the difference between men and animals? He talks of man as the paragon of animals, but he constantly charges the people around him with acting as mere animals—they are gross, they are led by their passions and their appetites. You remember, he praises Horatio because he is free of his animal passions. Maybe what gives him such extraordinary significance for human beings is the struggle between—well, to be banal, the spirit and the flesh.

Van Doren: Not only animals but vegetables. You remember how often the image of gardens, of the unweeded garden, is employed. Man has his place above the animals and the vegetables, also beneath the angels, as he makes clear. I think that is a very important thing to say about the play. It is perhaps a compliment to mankind that it has chosen this play as its favorite, because in it man is represented so perfectly in terms of his potentialities. It is a curious thing—perhaps not curious, either, since we have here the essence of tragedy—that this almost perfect man, this almost perfect gentleman, is in this play never the gentleman or the man that he is, paradoxically enough. We understand that he *was* that man, and toward the end of the play we see him resuming his character, announcing his nobility. I don't mean self-consciously doing so, but simply exposing himself as man. Most of the time, however, he is doing terrible, outrageous things.

Barr: Well, then, is he chiefly significant for pointing out to us the conflict between the animal or vegetable nature in human beings and this peculiar quality they have and animals and vegetables have not? And is the dramatic conflict between those the thing that excites us by pointing out to us that we have special problems that cabbages and lambs haven't got?

Van Doren: I think so, and it is the essence of tragedy that he should be, as we were saying, although always himself, yet at the same time one who can reveal the perils of attempting to be more than oneself. *Hamlet* tells us what a man is. I don't know that any one literary document could be more useful for the definition of man. Yet its hero can show us this only indirectly. He is always threatening to cease to be.

Barr: But I am troubled by your statement that he is aware of the difference not only between himself and an animal, but between himself and the idea of an angel. Shakespeare certainly would have been more familiar with either than our contemporaries are. I'm thinking about Miss Webster's remark that he's rather a young man—because this contradiction between what people actually are around him and what they could be disturbs him in a way that is not characteristic of middle-aged complacency. Maybe he is guilty, a little, Mr. Van Doren, of wanting to go to heaven in a hurry. That is, of wanting to make people around him much better than people actually can be. I'm not asking him to accept the rottenness in the state of Denmark; I'm asking him perhaps to understand it, perhaps to lead a revolution against the King.

Webster: Or just to get a little older, maybe. Well, he should be aging rather rapidly. Don't you think that part of the fascination of the play is the relationship between him and the other characters by whom he is surrounded? Man, in other words, is placed not only against the animals, the vegetables, and the angels, but the various qualities of man are placed in relationship to each other in a way which is extraordinary and dramatic and arresting.

Van Doren: For instance, Miss Webster.

Webster: For instance, the mirrors of man which are placed before you by the other characters—even the small characters—even Guildenstern and Rosencrantz, or Rosencrantz and Guildenstern. Even Fortinbras—very importantly Fortinbras.

Van Doren: And of course Polonius.

Webster: By all means Polonius, whom we all know—and Gertrude, whom we all know.

Van Doren: And Laertes, who is a young man, too.

Webster: He was a young man of a much more common type than Hamlet.

Barr: Even Yorick, who is dead.

Webster: Even Yorick. And certainly the two grave-diggers.

Van Doren: Well, the play is richly populated. And one reason that I remember with such pleasure, Miss Webster, your production of the full version of *Hamlet*—the complete text—is that it populated the palace of the King of Denmark much more than the cut versions do. We saw Polonius's family as a unit, persisting in having its own affairs and hoping that somehow or another the whole life of the palace can somehow weather the existence of Hamlet.

Webster: I was very anxious that people should remember that there were kitchens in the palace, and that it was not just a question of abstract thought delivered in a vacuum, or mostly in the dark on flights of steps.

Van Doren: The paradox of the tragedy, to return to a phrase of mine which may not have much meaning but which now seems to have a little more than it did before, may be that this young man, so representative of the type of man, and able to take us so far in our understanding, must finally die. It is as if he were trying to break the mold, isn't it?

Barr: Yes.

Van Doren: As if he were trying to be more than a man can possibly be.

Barr: Yes, that's what I meant. He is struggling to be more, and it leads him into strange situations. Some of his actions are extraordinarily blind. The first murder he bumps into is the ghost of his murdered father. The first time he commits murder, or makes a ghost, he does it through a curtain, doesn't he? And he doesn't know who it is he has murdered. Life is futile from his point of view. Even when you try to stab somebody, you don't know who it is until later.

Webster: It is indeed just the wrong person.

Van Doren: He acts blindly, as you say, and yet he is one of the most intelligent men we have ever encountered.

Barr: Extremely intelligent in all but action. Is he intelligent in action?

Van Doren: Well, is action ever a matter of intelligence?

Barr: Well, if it's not, then it doesn't matter who is general of an army or who's admiral of a navy.

Webster: That is what Hamlet feels from time to time.

Van Doren: That is what worries him.

Webster: The questions you've just asked are the questions in Hamlet's mind, and one is apt to assume that because it is Shakespeare—because it's that early period—whether you take it as the actual period when the historic Hamlet lived, or the Elizabethan period when Shakespeare lived—one is to judge him a little differently, maybe, from the way in which one would judge a young man today, living on Park Avenue, who suddenly began to suspect that his father whom he adored and who had recently died had perhaps been murdered by his uncle or by the friend of the family, possibly with the connivance of his mother. That might seem a much more poignant situation, fraught with much greater difficulty now than it does when one thinks of it roughly in terms of period. One wouldn't expect a young man living on Park Avenue, automatically without thinking about it, to kill off the best friend of the family because of the suspicion that his father had been murdered.

Van Doren: You'd expect him to do that, perhaps, only if a lot of other elements were there too, wouldn't you?

Webster: Yes.

Van Doren: If he were a certain kind of young man who took everything as hard as Hamlet does.

Barr: Miss Webster speaks of killing on suspicion. I agree with her that Hamlet fusses a good deal because he is uncertain whether his father was murdered. That is true, isn't it?

Webster: That is true until after the play scene, I think, and even after that.

Barr: Even after that. Well, is it possible that the thing that bothers him is precisely the problem of getting ideas into the realm of action? Ideas for him always have a ghostly quality. You're not sure that you ought to perform a certain act—you can't be sure!

Van Doren: If one could just stop thinking and begin to act! On the other hand, we find him always acting too. He is extremely active in the preparation of the play, isn't he?

Webster: And he finds relief in that. Because it is a concrete action. He is rid for a moment of the feeling of indecision.

Van Doren: That's right—his acting is irrelevant, maybe, to his main task. It is a sideline that he takes. Of course, we haven't asked whether the reason for the eminence of *Hamlet* is merely its excellence among plays considered as plays. Maybe it is the play that has the most good scenes in it.

Webster: That may be true. It certainly has the most good acting parts in it, and undoubtedly the best advice on acting that was ever written by any author. Hamlet's speech to the players should be learned by heart by every student of acting today, I think.

Van Doren: It is almost excessive in the play, isn't it? That is, the ham actors whom he is going to have do the job don't need that much advice, nor can you believe that they could take it.

Webster: Let me read it to you, and you judge.

"Speak the speech, I pray you, as I pronounced it to you, trippingly on the tongue; but if you mouth it, as many of your players do, I had as lief the town-crier spoke my lines. Nor do not saw the air too much with your hands, thus, but use all gently; for in the very torrent, tempest, and, as I may say, the whirlwind of your passion, you must acquire and beget a temperance that may give it smoothness. . . . Be not too tame neither, but let your own discretion be your tutor. Suit the action to the word, the word to the action; with this special observance, that you o'erstep not the modesty of nature. For anything so overdone is from the purpose of playing, whose end, both at the first and now, was and is, to hold as 't were the mirror up to nature; to show virtue her own feature, scorn her own image, and the very age and body of the time his form and pressure. Now this overdone or come tardy off, though it makes the unskilful laugh, cannot but make the judicious grieve; the censure of the which one must in your allowance o'erweigh a whole theater of others. . . . And let those that play your clowns speak no more than is set down for them; for there be of them that will themselves laugh to set on some quantity of barren spectators to laugh too, though in the meantime some necessary question of the play be then to be considered. That's villainous, and shows a most pitiful ambition in the Fool that uses it. Go, make you ready.

(1749-1832)

JOHANN
WOLFGANG VON GOETHE

Faust

T HE DRAMATIC *poem which Germany's greatest writer
spent his entire life in composing is more than a story and more
than an idea. It is a world, furnished with all the insights of
Goethe's long-lived and fertile mind. The story of Faust, Wagner,
Mephistopheles, and Margaret is known not only through this
poem but through the opera by Gounod; and hundreds of lines
or passages are the common possession of poets and scholars
who quote them for their concentrated wisdom. The distinction
of* Faust, *however, is greater than such success implies. It is the
distinction proper to the chief work of a master spirit, and to a
work which summed up as well the thought of a whole civilization in its richest and least provincial phase. Germany before*
Faust *and since has tended to look inward at itself.* Faust *looks
out upon the whole world of man as its author and its times conceived this world. Such limits as the conception has are the ines-*

capable limits of a romantic literature which exalts desire and pursuit above the stationary, the formal truth. But no poem is without its limits which define it and in fact announce the secret of its strength. The strength of Faust *continues to be felt by all who come in contact with its text. The beginning is simpler than the end; story is overlaid with symbol as the plan unfolds, and the second part, with its Helena, taxes the ingenuity of commentators. Faust is not, like the* Iliad *or the* Divine Comedy *or* Hamlet, *both profound and transparent. And this is its most serious limitation. Nevertheless it holds its place as the most celebrated of modern poems.*

Johann Wolfgang von Goethe, poet, dramatist, novelist, philosopher, and student of science, was born of wealthy parents in Frankfurt-am-Main. Of deep influence on German letters and thought, he was himself strongly influenced by his loves and by his friends (pre-eminently Herder and Schiller). His drama Götz von Berlichingen *(1773) opened the Sturm and Drang movement, while* The Sorrows of Young Werther *(1774) gave rise to a whole imitative sentimental literature. Other important works include the plays* Iphigenie auf Tauris *(1787) and* Torquato Tasso *(1790); the first modern German novel,* Wilhelm Meister's Apprenticeship *(1795-96); the idyll* Hermann und Dorothea *(1798); and the autobiographical* Dichtung und Wahrheit. *From 1775 Goethe lived in Weimar, serving as principal minister of state to the duke, Charles Augustus, building the state theatre into the greatest in Europe, and continuing his studies.*

ALLEN TATE · JACQUES BARZUN · MARK VAN DOREN

Van Doren: More and more one hears in discussions of the philosopher Nietzsche that he was a source of Fascism or Nazism. The same sort of thing is known to have been said about Goethe. Mr. Barzun, don't you agree in respect to Goethe, as well as to Nietzsche, that we are justified in concluding that he is no such source?

Barzun: I have no doubt in my mind about that. There is simply no justification for the notion that Goethe is an inspirer of Fascism or any such doctrine. The current idea to that effect rests on a misunderstanding of what Goethe says.

Van Doren: What is that?

Barzun: He says that the irrational element in man is a thing that has to be coped with and understood and cannot be explained away. In his view it has to be mastered by reason and knowledge and science. Because a person points to irrationality doesn't mean that he believes in it as a mode of life; the whole course of this poem, the purport of its thought, is away from the thralldom of irrationalism to something else.

Van Doren: Would you agree, Mr. Tate?

Tate: I would agree with everything that Mr. Barzun has said. I would like to add something else. Isn't it possible to go through any literature and pick out writers who seem to exalt instinct and emotion over intellect? For example, if we look at Shakespeare I'm sure we could find many plays and many characters in Shakespeare who would seem to justify violence and force; but I hardly think it would be fair to say that Shakespeare is a Fascist.

Van Doren: It is a fairly popular game these days.

Tate: Take Thomas Carlyle—his hero worship and all that sort of thing. Carlyle would be a very good Fascist, I'm sure.

Van Doren: And Plato is regularly so classified—not because of his praise of passion but because of his praise of reason.

Tate: We have discussed Machiavelli on this program. I'm inclined to think that Machiavelli couldn't be brought into the background for Fascism either. It's very dangerous, in other words, to go back into history and to simplify a great thinker's doctrine into contemporary terms.

Barzun: Particularly the doctrine of those who aren't theorists of the state or government but are writing poems about life, like Goethe.

Van Doren: Mr. Barzun, there is something very harsh said about reason in *Faust*.

> "Man calls it reason—
> Thence his power's increased
> To be far beastlier than any beast."

But that is said by whom? Do you remember?

Barzun: By Mephisto.

Van Doren: Yes, by the devil. It would only be fair to point that out. Reason is obviously a term which can be used with many meanings.

Tate: It's most flexible. Goethe seems to take a great deal of pains to ridicule certain kinds of reasoning, that is, sterile theological speculations and sterile metaphysics and logic. But that is not a very dignified conception of reason, and certainly Goethe wouldn't rest his case for reason on that kind of thing.

Van Doren: Perhaps that question then is answered. I am very happy that it has been so answered, and I am happy at the suggestion from Mr. Tate that perhaps it never needs to be raised here again. We have *Faust* before us. We know and everyone knows its vast reputation and the habit critics have of ranking it among the greatest poems of the world, of ranking its author indeed with the three great poets of the world. I take those to be Homer, Dante, and Shakespeare. George Santayana, you may remember, in a volume dealing with a number of poets, ended with Goethe.

Tate: You refer to his volume *Three Philosophical Poets.*

Barzun: Of course, that is taking a rather occidental view of world literature. I don't think we could get the greater half of humanity to agree to that. They probably wouldn't even know the names of the three world poets.

Van Doren: At any rate, among us Goethe and *Faust* are given very high rank, and that means that *Faust* comes in for comparison with the *Divine Comedy,* with *Paradise Lost,* and with the Book of Job, which also you know starts with a wager between God and the Devil.

Barzun: Obviously this wager in *Faust* is borrowed from Job, isn't it?

Van Doren: I suppose it is. The question we have before us now is whether that rating is justified. Mr. Tate, do you have a distinct, an immediate opinion there?

Tate: I should like to pass the question to Mr. Barzun, and ask him to state the case for Goethe. I believe he is more willing to do that than I am.

Barzun: Well, it's hardly fair to put the burden of proof on me, since after all the poem has a reputation and it's those who want to destroy it who should fire the first gun.

Van Doren: You're not being asked to prove its reputation, because that is known. We take that for granted.

Barzun: No, not its reputation, but its deserving to have it. Well, it seems to me that this poem contains a very definite statement of life as it looks to modern man, I mean man since the Renaissance—a world of strife, a world of self-development, a secular world in which religion is in question and has to be placed and justified, a world in which the proper end of man has to be sought both by reason and by experience. Now, in the course of treating all these things which are symbolic of our modern era, Goethe manages to embody in absolutely perfect form any number of experiences, ideas, traditions, possibilities, hopes, and aspirations which find an answering echo in our breasts.

Van Doren: You are justifying the reputation of the poem by saying that it does something in its time and for its time, that it perfectly represents a current point of view. Let us say you are making it depend for our admiration of it on its doing a job in history.

Barzun: But I don't know of any poem doing anything else at any time.

Tate: Mr. Barzun, let us consider the *Divine Comedy* for a moment. There is a very close resemblance between the purposes of the two poems; that is, in the *Divine Comedy* we have the character of Dante who goes through hell first, then through heaven. He encompasses all experience. And in the case of *Faust,* we have through Faust's wager with Mephistopheles the possibility of encompassing all of experience at the end of the eighteenth century. After that point, where the resemblance is very close, don't we get into differences very quickly? I would strongly question your statement that the *Divine Comedy* does no more than a historical job. Perhaps, Mr. Van Doren—I don't know whether you agree with me or not—we could accuse Mr. Barzun of an occupational disease here. He is a historian and he tends perhaps to read poetry from a historical point of view, that is, in terms of what history it contains.

Barzun: I think, Mr. Tate, you're doing me a kind of injustice through an ambiguity.

Tate: I'm sure I am.

Barzun: History can be considered in two ways: it can be merely the record of things that we've learned from various sources, and if you suppose that I'm merely looking in *Faust* or in the *Divine Comedy* for things that I've read about and learned elsewhere, you're making a mistake.

Tate: The mistake was intentional—just to bring you out.

Barzun: I'm very glad to know that it was. But history is in another sense the sum total of human experiences, and since we don't find those experiences repeating themselves exactly, it is the differences seen through a poetic medium which form the substance of all great poems.

Van Doren: I wonder, Mr. Barzun, if we do not see those experiences being repeated. I think we do. I'm convinced that the same experiences happen to men all the time.

Barzun: But not in the same form.

Van Doren: It is only when you begin to have a philosophy or a theory of experience and begin to use the term itself that a change seems to come over thought with respect to the thing. I think it is very important that Dante nowhere uses the word "experience." I agree with Mr. Tate that all experience is in the *Divine Comedy,* but Dante is not saying so. In this poem we have the word "experience" used with a capital letter.

Barzun: Yes, but you're proving my point. There are times when human beings—presumably similar from the day of creation to the present day—use a given word and there are other times when they do not use it or use another. That difference itself is what gives the shape and form to masterpieces of literature.

Tate: I agree with you, Mr. Barzun, because in no two ages do men apprehend their experience in the same terms. Nevertheless, I think that unless we're going to succumb merely to historical relativity and say that because all these poems have historical value we'll therefore consider them equal, we have to consider something like an absolute standard, although nobody quite knows what kind of standard that is. Now let me ask you this direct question: Which do you think is the greater poem, the *Divine Comedy* or *Faust*? Now let's see if we can get at something through that question.

Barzun: Well, it's a question which, rejecting as I do your hypothetical absolute standard, I can't answer, because in order to measure two things you have to have a yardstick.

Tate: I believe we have a yardstick here.

Van Doren: I think we have, too.

Barzun: I don't see it.

Van Doren: I think we have a yardstick right at that point where we find Goethe making an abstraction out of experience. As soon as that is done, it seems to me, the experience of man dwindles, both in the reason and in the imagination. We find in Homer a vast amount of experience. I've come to think that we find all the experience possible to man somehow there. But Homer does not think he's writing about experience. Homer thinks he has a war to write about. We find in the *Divine Comedy*, to be sure in another dimension and another set of terms, all the experience possible to man. But Dante is not writing about experience. He is writing about God.

Barzun: Yes, but what you two gentlemen are saying is that you prefer the kind of man that Homer and Dante respectively were, and that you prefer the subjects that they treated. You're not really saying that Goethe and his subject are in a testable way inferior or less encompassing.

Tate: I would say that, yes.

Van Doren: You would say what, exactly?

Tate: That Goethe is dealing with an inferior man.

Van Doren: All I ask of a great poem is that it have everything in it, that it have the world in it. I would say that *Faust* singularly lacks the world. We have instead a world of "experience" which Faust makes much of and which even Goethe's God sells himself out to. But this world of experience is curiously meager and abstract.

Barzun: You mean you couldn't make a list of the human experiences delineated in *Faust*?

Van Doren: Precisely. In some of Shakespeare's plays, in the *Divine Comedy*, in Homer I could make you a list of experiences which would be almost endless. Every sentence is an experience.

Barzun: And not here?

Van Doren: Not here.

Tate: Mr. Barzun, I think there is something to be said for your argument just at this point.

Barzun: I should like to think so.

Van Doren: We're being very hard on Mr. Barzun.

Tate: I think he'll rout us in just a minute. Now there is a sense in which I think Mr. Van Doren is wrong about the "experiences" in *Faust*. Goethe manages to cram into this poem all of the paraphernalia from the past,—the historical paraphernalia: mythologies, religions, from all parts of the world; and in that sense there's more in this poem than there is in the *Divine Comedy*.

Barzun: I'm glad you grant that.

Tate: But it seems to me that it has quantitatively more— only that. There is more actually presented to us in terms of dramatic form, in terms of real experience (not Goethe's abstract experience), than there is in Homer and Dante.

Van Doren: Of course, Mr. Tate, that is what I meant was lacking. I didn't mean that Goethe does not say a lot of things and do a lot of things and handle a lot of things in the poem. But many of the things he handles have no dramatic place here. For instance, I think God is out of place here. God has no function here, if He is to remain God.

Tate: Well, he is not the god of Dante, the transcendent god who is not embodied in nature, as here in *Faust*, or in man's divine self.

Van Doren: I agree—if He is to remain anything other than a man, which I suppose God has to be in order to be God. Here He becomes the chairman of the waterworks.

Barzun: Just as the gods of Homer are politicians who take part in a petty quarrel.

Van Doren: That is a mortal wound, as matter of fact, to me; I can't defend the gods of Homer.

Tate: Let me ask you this, Mr. Van Doren. Do you defend the gods that appear in the Greek drama? For example, is Prometheus credible to you? Do you believe in him? Now he is in some sense a god.

Van Doren: There is also Zeus, you remember. Or were you thinking simply of Prometheus?

Barzun: Yes, as the greatest man of that era. But both those characters have meaning only in terms of human experience.

There is no god brought into literature whom we can apprehend as God.

Van Doren: What about the God of the Book of Job?

Tate: He is a character in the book. He is as much a dramatic character in the Book of Job as Job himself. This is all I mean by the irrelevance of Goethe's god. He ceases to be for me what God should be, or rather what God is.

Barzun: That's because you start with a preconceived notion.

Van Doren: Of course I do. My preconceived notion about God is that He is not the world, that He is something in addition to the world, that He is more than the world, and that He is better than the world, that He does not make compromises with the world and is not willing to accept it. He is the thing against which, indeed, we measure the world. Now in this poem, He ceases to be anything by which we can measure the world because He loses himself in it. At the end, why does He forgive Faust? He forgives Faust for having sold his soul to the devil merely because Faust has sunk himself in experience, has thrown himself into the stream of experience and disappeared into it.

Barzun: He has come out of it. But with what? The one true way of saving his soul.

Van Doren: As a man. God is not interested in a man's saving his soul for himself. The place where you save your soul is in heaven.

Barzun: I think that's a very unorthodox doctrine, Mr. Van Doren, isn't it?

Van Doren: I hope not. I hope I haven't committed a heresy. Does one save one's soul by works?

Tate: That is the way Faust saves his soul. I don't think God is particularly interested in that. That is purely for man. It is secularism. I would go even further than Mr. Van Doren. I would say that the God in this poem has no business being here, that Goethe merely includes him out of historical habit; that He's not necessary at all.

Barzun: He is certainly necessary to the first part, which after all takes place in a medieval setting where God exists as a social force and destroys Margaret.

Tate: But just as a social force.

Barzun: Well, that's one of his manifestations surely.

Tate: That's the historical manifestation.

Barzun: Why must we always jump out of our skins and be outside history?

Tate: Because that's where the individual lives; he lives outside history.

Van Doren: And so does God. God lives outside of time.

Barzun: In the same sense that God lives outside of time. He is not knowable outside of time, that is, He is not knowable by people who did not live in a particular place in a particular time. What you're wanting, it seems to me, is a god who shall be just like Dante's god. But if you start with another preconception, say, that of the Greeks, Dante's god is ridiculous, impossible, hopeless. Now you object to Goethe's making experience an abstraction. Dante makes morality an abstraction.

Van Doren: Does he? I wouldn't think so.

Barzun: He pours in all sorts of irrelevant historical matter, drawn from the petty politics of Italian towns and the Papacy, in order to swell out a poem only a few parts of which have genuine meaning for us today.

Tate: I'm delighted that you said that, Mr. Barzun, because that will permit us to get back to the form of this particular poem, *Faust*. I would say of course that there are a lot of things in the *Divine Comedy* which we could imagine not being there. But since they're there, I think they function, have a place. What about this excessively loose form in *Faust?*

Barzun: You mean the absence of system. You don't mean form, because the form of each particular part is as nearly perfect as we can expect it to be from a human work.

Tate: That isn't my point of view. I would take as an example Faust's visit to Gretchen in prison. Dramatically it's very imperfect. The speeches are not in correct proportion; we feel that both characters have ceased to be dramatic characters—

they've become symbols of something, and the scene gradually fades out. I would bring that up as typical of a great many scenes in the poem. I think some things are too long, some too short.

Barzun: And why is that? It is because Faust is a dynamic figure who moves through this cosmos; he is not at a fixed point.

Tate: Is it the cosmos of the poem or the cosmos in general?

Barzun: Well, they're identical for purposes of literary perception, aren't they?

Tate: They should be. That's my point. They should be, but they aren't to me. The only cosmos we're entitled to know in this poem is the cosmos of the poem.

Van Doren: Exactly. Mr. Tate, you use the word proportion. I have never been able to get over the feeling that there is an almost ludicrous lack of proportion between what each part of the poem starts out to produce and what it does produce. The first part produces a seduction.

Barzun: And it's the only seduction story, incidentally, which bears reading. I can't imagine any of the subsequent nineteenth-century novels continuing to be as readable.

Tate: What about *Madame Bovary*?

Barzun: That's in a very different category. And it's hardly a seduction. The comparison strikes me as meaningless.

Van Doren: At any rate, to me the poem regularly tapers down to something small. I grant that a seduction could be a great subject. I don't find this seduction great. So in the second part, it seems to me, the poem dwindles; it tends to reach the small end of a funnel. What we end with—the grand end which brings about Faust's disappearance from the earth and which leads to a colloquy in heaven concerning his eternal destiny—is a decision of his to drain a swamp. Now, I don't like to be vulgar about it, but I can't help feeling that in both cases a mountain has produced a mouse.

Barzun: Mr. Van Doren, vulgarity, I think, is the right note. It is shown in this poem for the first time, it seems to me, that certain very small things like love-affairs, like draining marshes, are in a sense central to man's life and that the constant effort to get away from that and to pretend to be a demigod or a god is a far greater vulgarity than facing the reality.

Tate: I think we're getting into a paradox. Mr. Van Doren, may I shift this question slightly? I don't want to leave it entirely.

Van Doren: Please don't forget what you were going to say. May I interrupt for one moment to suggest that Mr. Barzun misunderstood me. I would say the opposite thing was happening in *Faust*. Faust is represented there as becoming a kind of god through human activity.

Barzun: Through understanding it, willing it, and being satisfied with it.

Van Doren: I quite grant that a very important thing for man to do might be to drain a swamp. I should like to leave it at that.

Tate: Yes, but if by draining a swamp he thinks he's becoming a god, then perhaps the charge of Nazism against Faust is somewhat true, because when you have this secular activity posing as something divine you have trouble in the world.

Barzun: But it was never stated to be divine. It is stated to be right and proper and the true way for man to behave. It becomes possible because pretense to the divine is eliminated.

Van Doren: "The one true way" not on earth but in the universe. That is the background against which these four words are supposed to have meaning.

Barzun: Well, there is no implication that it is proper for man to drain marshes because God drains them also. It is the difference between God and man that is realized, understood through an understanding of nature. And remember that the poem starts with all the abstractions, all the highfalutin philosophy and theology. Faust wins himself or his soul away from these fantastic things that mankind will always run after.

Van Doren: You mean he wins his soul away from God.

Barzun: Not from God; from the imitation doctrines about God.

Van Doren: Well, Mr. Tate, if you do remember now, please go on.

Tate: I think that we've got away from this poem as a work of literature in discussing doctrines. I would like to ask Mr. Barzun about this question of form again. It is a difficult word to use. Mr. Barzun says that Faust is a dynamic character moving through a cosmos, touching things here and there—really touching everything possible to modern man, I suppose you would say. I confess that he does in a certain sense, but I don't find much connection among the scenes as they progress. We are suddenly shifted here and there, and I should say that the only justification for this form would be that in a world in which things are miscellaneous and confused then you must have a literary form that is miscellaneous and confused. . . .

Barzun: No, because it seems to me that what the form of the poem states is a little more subtle than that, a little more complicated. It says that the form we find in the world we help to create, and that we create it by grouping and bunching, that the world is a pluralistic world. Not a world contained within one complete system like the rather naive world of Dante.

Tate: Should the world merely be reflected in art or should art try to do something more with the world than that? That's the main question, it seems to me, that this poem brings out.

Barzun: That is a perfectly good question, but one which can be answered only subjectively. Do you like this sort of world or do you prefer a unitary world? It seems to me that the charge of Fascism then can be retorted on you, because you want a unitary world.

Tate: But in the arts only.

Barzun: Well, practice frequently follows culture.

Van Doren: I am unhappy at your use of the word "naive" in connection with Dante, but then we'll let that pass. We have said a good deal about this swamp and the draining of it. Mr. Barzun, would you like to read the final speech of Faust, in which he realizes that this is his destiny?

Barzun: Yes. He has been talking about the necessity for getting at the swamp-draining, which is of course here only symbolic, and earlier in the poem he has said that he would give his soul to Mephisto when he found a single moment so attractive that he wanted it to linger. And this is what he says, bringing about the catastrophe:

"Yes! to this thought I hold with firm persistence;
The last result of wisdom stamps it true.
He only earns his freedom and existence,
Who daily conquers them anew.
Thus here, by dangers girt, shall glide away
Childhood, manhood, age, the vigorous day.
And such a throng I fain would see,—
Stand on free soil, among a people free!
Then dared I hail the moment fleeing.
'Ah, still delay, thou art so fair!'
The traces cannot, of my earthly being,
In æons perish—they are there!
In proud forefeeling of such lofty bliss,
I now enjoy the highest moment—this!"

(1826-1906)

HENRIK IBSEN

The Wild Duck

*THE WILD DUCK is one of Ibsen's best plays, and by far the
most painful. Written after the storm of controversy which had
followed upon the production of* A Doll's House, Ghosts, *and*
An Enemy of the People, *it goes farther than any previous play
of Ibsen's in its attack on human folly. For it attacks, among other
persons, the author himself, who would seem to be saying now
that the very uncompromising love of truth which his earlier
dramas had defended, and which as an attitude had naturally been
associated with himself, was also evil in its potentialities. Blind
and stubborn idealism is capable of doing deep damage in human
affairs; the reformer can be a destructive agent. Gregers Werle,
the hero of the play if it can be said to have one, is a man warped
by idealism into sinister and fantastic shapes. He brings nothing
but misery into the world where he has his friends, and where he
indulges to the full his instinct for purifying others. Truth as he*

handles it is an ugly thing; and in saying so Ibsen confesses the shortness of his own sight to date. The act of writing such a play from such a motive has few parallels in literature; and The Wild Duck *itself has not been surpassed in modern times for bitterness and power. It is one of Ibsen's best written plays; which is to say that it is one of the best-written plays in the world, swift, terrible, and natural. It is also perhaps the completest revelation we have of his trenchant, tormented mind; and the most potent exercise in symbols which even he ever contrived.*

Henrik Ibsen, Norwegian poet and dramatist, turned from early essays in journalism to an association with the national theatre, first in Bergen and later in Copenhagen. He had written poetry, criticism, and a few plays before producing Love's Comedy (1862), a satirical play in verse which, like its more famous successors, roused a storm of criticism. It was followed by The Pretenders *and by the great dramatic poems* Brand *and* Peer Gynt. In Germany, where he lived from 1874 to 1891, Ibsen wrote, at intervals of about two years, the series of realistic social dramas on which his fame rests: The Pillars of Society (1877); A Doll's House (1879); Ghosts (1881); An Enemy of the People (1882); The Wild Duck (1884); Rosmersholm (1886); The Lady from the Sea (1888); Hedda Gabler (1890); The Master Builder (1892); Little Eyolf (1894); John Gabriel Borkman (1896); When We Dead Awaken (1899).

MARGARET WEBSTER · JOHN MASON BROWN
MARK VAN DOREN

Van Doren: When I read *The Wild Duck* this time I reflected upon its limitations as a tragedy. The chief limitation it seemed to have was in the size of the hero's—or, if you like, the villain's—character. Perhaps I said something then when I hesitated over whether to call Gregers Werle the hero or the villain.

Brown: May I interrupt just for one moment?

Van Doren: I wish you would.

Brown: It is my humble conviction that the play really is not supposed to be a tragedy, at least in the accepted sense. I think it is honestly a sardonic comedy, one of the bitterest things that Ibsen ever wrote, and I think the proof of the fact that it isn't tragic in its conception is that even when the little girl, Hedvig, has shot herself, has committed suicide, the lines that follow are as mercilessly written, as cruel, as devastating and unexalted, as all the lines which have preceded that particular and terrific scene.

Van Doren: Miss Webster, has Mr. Brown broken something down here?

Webster: I quite agree with what Mr. Brown has said. One of the difficulties about the play is that Ibsen denies it the uplifting quality of tragedy; he also denies it, in a sense, the cleansing quality of pure comedy. It has, as Mr. Brown says, a sardonic quality about it, a sour quality almost, and the difficulty of placing either Gregers or Hjalmar as either villain or hero seems to me to make it in some sense an unsatisfactory play.

Van Doren: I suppose that it is what I had in mind when I said I

felt a limitation in it if it were tragedy. In the first place, a tragedy
must have a hero; he must be not only the worst man in the play,
but the best man too. This play reveals its difference at once from
a great tragedy like *Hamlet*. Hamlet can be called the worst man
there—he suspects everybody, he thinks the worst, he brings
about many deaths—and yet his loss is, of course, incalculable.

Brown: But, Mr. Van Doren, if this is not a tragedy, if it is a
satiric comedy, particularly if it is a satire on idealism—and that's
the way I truly see it—then just exactly as a tragedy needs a hero,
doesn't a satire need a fool? It needs a person to be laughed at,
and Hjalmar, the weakling husband, the selfish man, the father
in this play—it seems to me that he is the perfect fool, or rather
the perfectly foolish man.

Van Doren: Yes, but I still want to see whether there is any
point in comparing *The Wild Duck* with, say, *Hamlet*. Now, the
hero of *Hamlet* is clearly wrong. He clearly has delusions; he
clearly is incorrect in assuming that he has to set the world to
right. He doesn't like it, yet he is willing to accept the function.
Nevertheless, he remains admirable and probable to us everywhere, even when he is most terrible, when he is committing the
most destruction; whereas—I quite agree with you—Gregers is
something of a fool from the beginning.

Brown: They both are—both Gregers and Hjalmar, the two
central male characters.

Webster: And yet Hjalmar is very fully realized and Gregers,
it seems to me, is very inadequately realized. Gregers in a curious
way seems to take a back seat in the play. He is the machinery
that sets everything in motion and yet one has so little patience
with him as a person—so little understanding of him, or sympathy with him—that he fades into insignificance beside the
much more fully realized character Hjalmar.

Van Doren: I must stop talking about Hamlet, but the defect,
after all, of either hero is the excess of a virtue, is it not? That
is to say, Hamlet's sensitiveness to disorder and to wrongdoing
is itself a good thing. But somehow there seems to be too much
of it, or it seems to be wild and uncontrolled in him, as in the

case of Oedipus. The destruction which Oedipus brings into the world springs again from the excess of a virtue; his virtue is a desire for the truth, an insistence that it be spoken, a great will, even a great stubbornness. In both cases you can understand where the tragedy comes from. Whereas in Gregers' case we scarcely know. He is merely a man who has lived remote from civilization for years, and who now comes to us with a quaint, curious, twisted idealism which has nothing either personal or philosophical to recommend it.

Brown: Gregers is a man we do hate. I agree with you and Miss Webster that he is poorly realized; he is one of the more unattractive and certainly one of the most glacial characters in Ibsen. But the excuse for Gregers is what Ibsen hoped to do with the character. This was not to correct himself on the eternal warfare in his plays between the sickly and the healthy conscience, but to correct his disciples, the people who had been carried away with the idea of throwing open the window and ventilating the room. He at last wanted to say that perfection has to be reached from within, that the outsider cannot merely by opening a window do anything more, as Somerset Maugham has said, than give everyone on the stage pneumonia so that they all die unhappily.

Webster: Well, if this play is to be saved for a sardonic comedy, then I suppose it must swing around Hjalmar; yet I find Hjalmar absolutely insufferable, so insufferable that at moments he almost ceases to be funny. For instance, the moment where he lets Hedvig do the retouching for him, in spite of the fact that he knows she is in danger of losing her sight. It is funny, it is part of Hjalmar, and yet it is so dreadful that one ceases to have any patience with the man.

Brown: But it is a magnificent comment. The father, knowing that the daughter is going blind, having discussed her blindness, allows her out of his eternal selfishness to touch up the photographs so that he can go into the attic. It seems to me one of the most adroit of Ibsen's miracles. I think Mr. Van Doren and I both feel a little bit embarrassed about discussing Hjalmar, because we both blushed as we read the script; both of us found so much of ourselves—and hope all men are like us—in his selfishness.

Webster: I'm sure you do yourself a grave injustice!

Van Doren: No, I don't think so, Miss Webster. All men are not only selfish, but actors—all men are trying to play a part, and they have wonderful capacities for self-pity.

Brown: But they're just bad actors; women are good actresses and get away with it.

Van Doren: That's right. Of course Miss Webster was acting now when she pretended she didn't know what we were talking about.

Brown: It was one of the politest compliments, but one of the most insincere, ever given.

Webster: No, that's not so. I, to start with, think that Hjalmar is very much of his period. I think he's very definitely 1884.

Brown: Thank you, Miss Webster, that separates us.

Webster: Surely there's a gulf between you! I do think that there are basic things, of course, in Hjalmar's nature which are in a great many men that I know—I won't say present company. But the idiom of Hjalmar seems to me to date the play, just as to me the idiom of Torvald dates *The Doll's House*—that kind of bonhommie, I think, is very much of its period.

Van Doren: Bonhommie? After all, he's a pretty damp, soggy character, isn't he? Is he the life of the party?

Webster: Well, he considers himself the life of the party surely —except when he gets to Tokay, which he doesn't understand.

Van Doren: Yes, he has little jests and quips and cracks, to be sure, but on the whole he's a pretty sad fellow, don't you think, Mr. Brown?

Brown: Yes. His bonhommie is a household commodity.

Van Doren: That's right. He has always acted a series of parts, one of which is the part of the father who knows how to cheer everybody up and who knows how in a very jaunty way to say: Now we shall make the worst of it. I found it really dreadful also to see him compromising his nobility all the time. Incidentally, let me say that he is like all men in that he cannot bear not to seem noble, and of course one of the best ways to seem noble is to seem superior to nobility, as men these days are always saying they don't want to appear noble; yet that is noble too. But do you remember how he compromises his nobility about the butter? Having entered in a great, tragic mood and been offered food by his wife, Gina, he refuses to take it because he is above food; yet he cannot take his eyes and his mind off the beer and the bread and butter.

Brown: Mr. Van Doren, that scene affected me so that I haven't asked for butter in my own home since I reread the play.

Van Doren: And of course you remember the time when he comes home from the dinner at the elder Werle's and is asked by Hedvig whether he has brought something for her—some dainty to eat—because, after all, these people don't have enough to eat. All he has is a crumpled menu in his pocket.

Webster: I'm horrified and shocked by the deep sympathy you both display with Hjalmar. Perhaps that is what makes this play less satisfactory from a woman's point of view than from a man's; because I believe most women would identify themselves with Gina. I certainly would, although I can't claim to cook so well. But the only other person with whom I find myself in any degree of sympathy is Relling, every word of whose dialogue, I think, makes the most admirable sense. Perhaps Gina and Relling, who are not, after all, principal characters in the play, stand up to a modern woman's ideas better than the two men who *are* the principal characters. Perhaps that is what makes it to me, as I've said before, an unsatisfactory play.

Van Doren: Relling is a sort of sensible chorus, isn't he? Any playwright seems to need a chorus of some sort, even if that chorus is only one man. From time to time Relling says what the audience can just not bear not hearing said. He is even more than sensible; he's very cutting. At the end, you remember, he pronounces the word "rubbish" with something like finality. I found Relling interesting because he seemed to represent the true vision of the author, but perhaps we do Ibsen an injustice if we suggest that because Hjalmar and Gregers are both highly disagreeable men *The Wild Duck* as a play is not powerful. You wouldn't say that, would you, Miss Webster?

Webster: I wouldn't say it isn't powerful. I think it has great power, and there are scenes in it—for instance, of course, the scene just before Hedvig goes into the garret to shoot herself—that are infinitely touching, as well as scenes that are brilliantly comic like the very first dinner-party scene. But I'm not quite sure of the addition sum that it makes at the end—I don't find myself knowing quite what you come away with, other than that extraordinarily depressing last line of Gregers'; when he says his destiny is to be the thirteenth at table.

Brown: Well, Miss Webster, Ibsen does end by saying that the idealist will always be thirteenth at table, but aren't you surprised by a new point of view in Ibsen, a point of view his past social dramas haven't included? For the first time, that is, he has recognized the importance in human living of the ideal, of the illusion. He says that without this your life is destroyed. Until now he has been so uncompromising—his dialogue has been so cold—that I've always felt his people were fencing, using icicles as rapiers. The speech has had a glacial quality in spite of its brilliance. But this time there is a sudden—even in this hideously sardonic satire there is a sudden—compassion, a sudden understanding of the importance of the illusion by which we all have to live.

Webster: I think that as regards the question of Ibsen's development the play does occupy a very important place, standing as it does immediately before his last period of playwriting when he got himself into a different dimension. Those to me are the Ibsen plays which don't date, because they deal so much more with universal things.

Brown: You mean when he was working as a symbolist?

Webster: To an extent, yes.

Brown: May I suggest one thing? Don't you think that in the last plays, right down to the very final play, *When We Dead Awaken,* what Ibsen was doing was coming back to the poet in him that had first appeared in the great plays, from *Catiline,* a very bad play, right straight through to *Emperor and Galilean* and the rest of them? You remember, he said once he was going to try photography—comedy by photography? I think it was Edmund Gosse who said—or maybe it was Archer; no, as a matter of fact, it was George Brandes; one of them at any rate said it—that even in his most prosy prose-play he felt that at one stage in Ibsen's career a Pegasus had been shot out from under him.

Webster: Yes.

Van Doren: That is the feeling I had in reading this play. Certainly the first Ibsen was a poet and the last Ibsen was a poet; but then *Peer Gynt* is rather obviously poetry—its symbolism is something of which the hero, the author, is conscious as poetry. And so at the end. But I'm not at all sure that the great poet in Ibsen isn't in these middle plays. From one mountain top he swings down a valley to another mountain top, but I think the swing is what makes him a great playwright. Here, for instance, poetry is, to be sure, frozen—inhibited, thwarted all the time—and yet, perhaps just for that reason, I feel its force. I feel it not only in the coldest and most sardonic of the speeches and in the most dreadful exposures that he makes of human folly—because, after all, one business of a poet is to recognize human folly and expose it—but in the symbolism which actually appears.

Brown: I agree. The attic is the fullest proof that the poet, though for the moment submerged, still exists.

Van Doren: I think Ibsen is a greater poet in *Hedda Gabler* than he is in either *Peer Gynt* or *John Gabriel Borkman* or *The Master Builder.*

Brown: I have to disagree there to a certain extent, much as I love *Hedda Gabler. Peer Gynt* I find one of the most exciting plays in the world, for the simple reason that it has an almost Shakespearean quality of freedom, of ubiquity. It is the play in which the whole expressionistic modern theatre really found its source.

Van Doren: But, Mr. Brown, don't you find these middle plays exciting?

Brown: I find them exciting in a different way.

Van Doren: I should say they are exciting in the way poetry ought to be exciting. Whenever you can read poetry and say you are finding symbols in it, you are not reading the first-rate article. Symbols should be utterly buried in poetry.

Brown: The difference being that what was free in *Peer Gynt* has here the fascination of a jig-saw puzzle. It is superior building. Ibsen is truly a master builder. It is the wonderful inlay. It is the cloisonné work in dialogue, in planning, in sudden revelation—the spiritual strip-tease . . .

Voice: Mmm-huh—

Brown: . . . that is so fine.

Van Doren: I myself prefer poetry when it is not free—when it is struggling with the stuff that it ought to struggle with, namely, life. Expressionistic drama, it seems to me, was bound to be second-rate drama just because it took a short cut. You see, it went from the author's mind to the spectator's mind, not through life at all but through words and symbols—through poetic properties that were somewhat standard.

Brown: I'm sorry I brought up that ugly term "expressionism." It recalls a fortunately forgotten period in the drama. I didn't mean to hold this against *Peer Gynt*. *Peer Gynt* certainly deals with man in the same sense as this, but it struggles against and doesn't conquer the theatre as a medium. It's too big for the theatre, as Hardy's *The Dynasts* is too big. And yet, as something to read, it is one of the glorious free expressions of Ibsen's mind.

Webster: It is a great piece of theatre mastery, *The Wild Duck,* an extraordinary piece of theatre craftsmanship.

Van Doren: I am not denying, of course, that *Peer Gynt* is a great poem. I only want to suggest that *The Wild Duck* might be one too, and that we might understand it as such, especially in view of the very difficulty we have found in deciding whether it is tragedy or comedy. Perhaps you don't agree that we're having the difficulty, because it seems to you so clearly comedy. I can't see it as pure comedy—I am stopped, for instance, by the thought of what Shaw, who is a pure comic genius, would have done with old Werle. He would have let Werle dominate the play as Ibsen never does. Ibsen's Werle remains somewhat sub-dued, submerged. He's a sort of twilight between tragedy and comedy, and perhaps indeed the whole play somehow exists in that twilight—always potentially a tragedy, and yet always, I quite agree with you, in some sense actually a comedy.

Brown: To me the approach in this play seems almost too brutal. It certainly is too brutal for tears, and it's too common-place for exaltation.

Van Doren: I quite agree with that statement.

Webster: I accept that definition entirely.

Van Doren: There's no exaltation here. I only find the desire for it somehow or other, I find the possibility.

Webster: There is less music in this play—poetry and spirit—than in most of the others. I agree, of course, that it's there, in the garret and in old Ekdal, who is, I think, a very touching figure; and of course in Hedvig. But it is very difficult for us to judge that quality in Ibsen correctly. We can apprehend his poetic vision, his poetic conception, but just how far it really comes out in his writings is something which it is hard for us to tell because most of the existing translations have done him such irreparable harm.

Brown: Mr. William Archer—God rest his Scotch soul—was never more thrifty than in his use of poetry. And William Archer, with those antimacassar phrases of his, has done more than any-one else to put Mr. Ibsen definitely in a period.

Webster: I entirely agree.

Van Doren: What about the stage history of *The Wild Duck?* I've seen only one performance of it, in which I remember chiefly Tom Powers as Gregers Werle. Did you see that, Mr. Brown?

Brown: I think you are speaking, Mr. Van Doren, of the Actors Theatre Production of about fifteen years ago.

Van Doren: Yes.

Brown: That production I remember as one of the really fine productions in the theatre of our time. I remember almost everyone in the cast, as if I had just seen it yesterday. I remember particularly how admirably Miss Blanche Yurka played Gina—it seemed to me one of her best performances. Miss Helen Chandler's Hedvig was charming, and so was Mr. John Cromwell's performance of Hjalmar.

Van Doren: Hjalmar would, I should think, be a very difficult part, because the man is such an ass.

Webster: It is what is known as a very "fat" part. Particularly in the German theatre, Hjalmar is one of the most sought-after parts in the whole Ibsen repertoire. Actors love to get their teeth into Hjalmar.

Van Doren: Is he played like the ass that he so obviously is?

Webster: Oh, yes.

Brown: Isn't he almost from the actor's point of view what Hedda Gabler is to the actress? Without the excitement, but with the same—a character equally contemptible, equally unsympathetic, and equally interesting to play for that very reason?

Webster: Well, Hedda has much more range and width and margin to her than Hjalmar. I don't understand myself why people want to play Hjalmar so much, but apparently they do. Hjalmar is less of a problem for the actor than for the director —how to keep Hjalmar in balance with the rest of the play is quite a problem. How to play Hjalmar isn't so difficult.

Brown: He's more of a problem for Gina.

Webster: An intolerable problem for Gina.

Van Doren: His problem, considered intellectually, considered from the point of view of the strategy of the author, is very interesting. He must be, of course, an ass; he must be a man rotten with self-pity and a love of acting. But the point about him seems to be this: he is not the kind of material Gregers is looking for. Gregers Werle, who wants to reform the world by bringing frankness into it, by tearing away all the darkness and self-deceit and so forth, should, if his program is sound at all, look around and be able to recognize a man worthy of the experiment.

Dramatically that is one of the most interesting things here. Gregers is utterly unable to see how small and weak a person Hjalmar is.

Brown: That is one of the greatest human and technical defects in the play. He has missed his man through false hero-worship. Even Gregers would have known more about human nature than that.

Webster: It would have been far better to light on one of the counselors at the first dinner party scene.

Brown: He would have done best of all to light on himself

Webster: That would have been a hopeless problem, I should think.

Van Doren: This is why I do eventually have to agree with both of you that the play is primarily comic. If Ibsen had been bound to write tragedy, he would have had at least as much respect for Hjalmar and for Gregers as he has for Hedda—because I am sure he has a kind of respect for Hedda Gabler.

Brown: And so have we all.

Webster: Certainly, she has great stature—she's a person who matters.

Brown: She has great fascination, great intelligence, but she is spiritually arid.

Webster: Well, don't let's start discussing Hedda, or we'll never get back to *The Wild Duck.*

Van Doren: I should be quite content to range among Ibsen's plays.

Webster: It is quite a range.

Van Doren: Yes, but let us assume that we are free to talk about Ibsen as well as *The Wild Duck.* Those last plays, Miss Webster, which you spoke of—*The Master Builder, John Gabriel Borkman, Little Eyolf,* and *When We Dead Awaken.* Was that the group you had in mind?

Webster: Those are the four—yes. I was also thinking of the plays which immediately preceded them, like *Hedda Gabler* and *Rosmersholm.*

Brown: And *The Lady from the Sea?*

Van Doren: You find them all to be free in various degrees, I dare say, from the chill which is here, from the failure to be tragic.

Webster: Well, it isn't a chill exactly; it is rather a preoccupation with social problems. He is also preoccupied with them in *Rosmersholm,* but they occupy a less dominant place in the later plays.

Van Doren: Yes, I should say that the chief limitation of this play might very well lie in the fact that the author has to be so explicit in his use of the words "ideal," "idealism," "illusion," and so forth. It's as if he had to say: You don't know what this play is about, so I'll tell you. Mr. Brown, would you mind taking parts with me in a dialogue between Dr. Relling, the realist, and Gregers near the end?

Brown: Will Miss Webster direct us?

Webster: Certainly, from the side lines.

Brown: From now on I become Maurice Evans.

Van Doren: It is the scene in which the point about illusion is made.

Brown: I am Relling?

Van Doren: Yes.

Brown: "Well, you see, I'm supposed to be a sort of doctor. I can't help giving a hand to the poor sick folk who live under the same roof with me."

Van Doren: "Oh, indeed. Hjalmar—is he sick, too?"

Brown: "Most people are sick, worse luck!"

Van Doren: "And what remedy are you applying in Hjalmar's case?"

Brown: "My usual one. I'm cultivating the life illusion in him."

Van Doren: "Illusion? I didn't catch what you said."

Brown: "Yes, I said illusion, for illusion, you know, is the stimulating principle."

Van Doren: "May I ask with what illusion Hjalmar is inoculated?"

Brown: "No, thank you. I don't betray professional secrets to quacksalvers. You would probably go and muddle in his case still more than you have already. But my method is infallible. I have applied it to Molvik as well. I have made him daemonic. That is the blister I have put on his neck."

Van Doren: "Is he not really daemonic then?"

Brown: "What the devil do you mean by daemonic? It's only a piece of gibberish I've invented to keep up the spark of life in him. But for that, the poor harmless creature would have succumbed to self-contempt and despair many a long year ago. And then the old Lieutenant—but he's hit upon his own cure, you see."

Van Doren: "Lieutenant Ekdal—what of him?"

Brown: "Just think of the old bear-hunter shutting himself up in that dark garret to shoot rabbits. I tell you there's not a happier sportsman in the world than that old man pottering about in there among all that rubbish. The four or five withered Christmas trees he's saved up are the same to him as the whole great fresh fertile forest. The cock and the hens are the big game birds and the fur pelts. And the rabbits that flop about the garret floor are the bears he has to battle with, this mighty hunter from the mountains."

Van Doren: "Poor unfortunate old man."

Brown: "Indeed, he is."

Van Doren: "Yes, he has indeed had to narrow the ideals of his youth."

Brown: "While I think of it, Mr. Werle, Jr., don't use that foreign word 'ideals.' We have the excellent native word 'lies.' "

Van Doren: "Do you think the two things are related?"

Brown: "Yes, just about as closely as typhus and putrid fever."

Van Doren: "Dr. Relling, I shall not give up the struggle until I have rescued Hjalmar from your clutches."

Brown: "So much the worse for him. Rob the average man of his life illusion and you rob him of the happiness of happiness in the same stroke."

Webster: I shan't hire either of you.

PHILOSOPHY

RENE DESCARTES

A Discourse on Method

THE FAMOUS essay by Descartes which had more to do than any book by Lord Bacon with the inauguration of the new learning—or, to give it a more familiar name, of modern science— had for its full title in 1637: A Discourse on the Method of Rightly Conducting the Reason and Seeking Truth in the Sciences. *Reason, then, was for Descartes an instrument wherewith entrance could presumably be made into the mysteries of nature. But his first effort must be to sharpen the instrument, filing from it every speck of ancient rust and discarding any parts which would make successful entrance less likely. He proceeded to do this by asking himself how much he could doubt, and by what sign he could recognize that which is beyond doubt. His doctrine of clear and distinct ideas was the result of such a meditation, as well as his decision to consider henceforth that mind and matter are mutually exclusive, and his determination to assume*

that the answer to every scientific problem is in the last analysis mathematical. Descartes is one of the great, original mathematicians of the world; which is sometimes lost sight of when he is spoken of as the founder of modern scientific method. There is a necessary connection between the two positions he holds, and this connection throws into relief both the fabulous achievements of science since his day and the limitations which prevent it from doing anything different or more. As for the Discourse *itself, criticism has convicted it of many leading errors; yet nothing has displaced it from the position where it still so brilliantly stands, at the head of our scientific host.*

René Descartes, French philosopher and scientist, was educated in the Jesuit school of La Flèche and the University of Poitiers. He joined the army of Maurice of Nassau, traveled in Germany, lived for a time in Paris, and in 1628 settled in Holland, devoting himself to scientific research—dioptrics, meteors, problems of physiology and psychology, mathematics (Cartesian co-ordinates and analytical geometry)—and to philosophic reflection. The development of his philosophy is contained in Meditationes de Prima Philosophia *and* Principia Philosophiae. *His followers were called Cartesian philosophers.*

Descartes: A Discourse on Method

BERTRAND RUSSELL · JACQUES BARZUN · MARK VAN DOREN

Van Doren: The full title of Descartes' essay, you remember, is *Discourse on the Method of Rightly Conducting the Reason and Seeking Truth in the Sciences,* but one notices immediately upon starting to read the essay that it has narrative form; it is cast, as Descartes himself says, in the guise of a tale. Mr. Russell, does it seem to you that this fact is purely accidental in its interest, or has Descartes been assisted in saying what he wants to say by assuming the posture of a narrator?

Russell: I think it assists him very greatly to say what he has to say. It helps the reader to be interested, and it helps the reader to be able to follow the chain of thought. Most philosophers are extraordinarily dry and very dull; Descartes is neither dry nor dull, and that is very largely because he doesn't confine himself to strict logic, but puts in picturesque material of a biographical sort.

Barzun: I should go farther, Mr. Russell, and say that for me the autobiographical element is the only value I find in the essay. It is interesting to note that the present title is a second choice. The essay was first called *History of My Mind,* and it was the preface to three purely scientific essays. I've often thought that if authors kept to their first titles less dangerous consequences would follow. In the present case we are misled into thinking that here is a discourse on method. I, for one, find no method whatsoever propounded in the essay.

Van Doren: Doesn't he at least propound a method which, according to him, came to him while he was lying in bed?

Russell: I disagree radically with what you say. A great deal

[93]

of what he has to say about method is extremely good; I have found it valuable myself.

Barzun: But perhaps it's only the putting into somewhat rigid form of rather ordinary and self-evident rules: how to avoid mistakes. Certainly the account he gives of how he arrived at his method is unconvincing to me. I don't believe that he went through this process at all.

Russell: Oh, I dare say not! A great deal of that is just picturesque talk. But it's talk of a sort that helps you to understand what he means; therefore it's justifiable.

Barzun: It helps us to understand, but it formed a school of Cartesians who really believed that all this had happened.

Van Doren: I take the narrative form to be more than accidental. It seems to harmonize with the method itself. The impression finally given by the essay is that there is a truth about things which can be discovered in time. At first there is nothing and then there is something—the discovery of a principle of philosophy becomes in Descartes by implication almost a creation of the world.

Russell: You're both very unfair to Descartes.

Barzun: Well, you go ahead.

Russell: He says he's going to have nothing except what is clear and distinct. That is not having nothing.

Barzun: Well, he does say that after his education, for which he was properly grateful, he found that he had to undo it all. That is a common enough experience, but then he goes on to say that the first step was the achievement of a *tabula rasa*. Unlike Locke, who started the infant with a *tabula rasa,* Descartes achieved his with great effort, and then came the clear and distinct ideas. Why are those ideas valid, according to Descartes, Mr. Russell?

Russell: Because he was a mathematician. Of course it won't do as a method in empirical matters at all. But it does do in mathematics, and he was primarily a mathematician; all his remarks are those of a mathematician, and in mathematics it is, after all, the clear and distinct that the mathematician trusts to.

Barzun: That's where my objection comes in, because after setting aside the truths of poetry and literature and art and morals he leaves us only with mathematical truth, which, as I hope you'll admit, is truth about something conceived and not something existent. Yet at the end of the essay he invites us to consider physiology and medicine and the practical arts.

Russell: All that historical explanation is also historical justification. In his day mathematics was the chief machine for discovering facts about nature, and it did discover the most important facts, as in the case of Galileo who was a mathematician. He discovered things about the world, and mathematics was his instrument for doing it.

Barzun: But isn't there a kind of misleading uniformity in the attempt to make a very successful science in one realm apply to other realms?

Russell: It certainly is, and we see that now. Now, I think, his method isn't the right one, because on the whole the mathematical part of the job has been to a great extent done. But in his day it hadn't.

Barzun: But it has taken us three hundred years to get over this little essay of sixty pages. That's where my animus originates.

Russell: It goes back further than that. It goes back to Plato. The undue emphasis on mathematics goes back, in fact, further than Plato. It goes back to Pythagoras; Pythagoras is the villain of the piece.

Barzun: You are admitting then that there is a villain in the piece!

Russell: Well, he's become a villain. For two thousand years he was a saint.

Barzun: In other words, Descartes must have the credit of repeating a great error—is that your position?

Russell: Well, the thing has become an error. It was not an error in his day.

Barzun: I'm afraid I must agree with you there, but there is a further objection in my mind, and that is the tone and temper of the man and the *Discourse.* He was a singularly unamiable, vain, malicious, timid person whose ideas could appeal only, it seems to me, to the narrowest and most sectarian of philosophic minds.

Van Doren: You say he was both vain and timid. Would there be any difficulty in reconciling those two terms, or do you mean both?

Barzun: I hadn't thought of it, but I mean both.

Russell: They are quite easy to reconcile. Newton was both, obviously. But I don't agree with you. When one reads most philosophers they're mostly much worse than he is in all these respects. Philosophers are perhaps a narrow-minded sect.

Barzun: Oh, I don't know! I think if you take a man like Berkeley or Locke you find a fuller, richer atmosphere. I suppose we can overdo this point of the atmosphere of a philosopher, but I think it has a great influence historically.

Van Doren: I find Aristotle to be less vain, if vain at all, than Descartes, and for this reason. He seems to begin with the assumption that a world already exists, a world which is very thick and full about him, a world that he did not create and did not conceive himself. Descartes has the air of being the first, or at any rate the only man. Nothing shall be before him; he wants to clear away all former conceptions and all former ways of talking, so that there will be complete barrenness and emptiness and dryness in the world.

Russell: Well, I wish he'd done it more subtly. The trouble was merely that he didn't do it enough. The world was encumbered with rubbish in his day, intellectual rubbish, and the first thing was to be a scavenger, to get it all out of the way.

Van Doren: When the world is full of rubbish, which it always is, of course, thank God—I much prefer a world full of rubbish to an empty one—isn't the wisest thing to do to order that rubbish?

Barzun: Or a corner of it!

Van Doren: If you can.

Russell: Well, it isn't the custom, if you want to build a fine public building, to leave all the ruins of some previous buildings there; you clear them away.

Barzun: Now we fall back into one of Descartes' metaphors—
Russell: We do!
Barzun:—in the introduction, and we come upon one of his major inconsistencies. First he divides the world into thought on the one hand and matter on the other, and that is a cleaning-up process in itself, since his matter is simply extension and his thought is whatever he finds by the test of clarity and distinctness. But then on top of that he brings in the established social order and a curious set of mixed morals—ethics—partly stoical, partly epicurean. At bottom he is profoundly indifferent, it seems to me, to everything except his few leading principles, which can lead in any direction without producing much result.

Van Doren: His morals, incidentally, he explicitly calls provisory. That is to say, they are temporary morals which he will adhere to until the moment when he knows everything. In Part Three of the *Discourse,* you will remember, he says: pro tem, I shall observe the following rules, not because I think they conduce necessarily to right living but because they are the safe ones to follow; they are the rules that will get me into the least trouble. First, I shall obey the laws and customs of my country if only to escape notice and be left free to think. Then I shall be as firm and resolute in my action as possible; that is to say, not knowing yet what is true, nevertheless, when I do see a course of action or a course of thought, I shall take it straight away—here is the metaphor once again—as a man lost in a forest should do. A man lost in the middle of a forest should keep going in one direction, because anything is better than remaining in the middle of the forest. Then, third, I shall be something of a stoic. I shall try to conquer myself rather than fortune, I shall not ask for things which I cannot have. He is nowhere more contemptuous of morals than here where he assumes that they are but ways of being safe.

Russell: But, look, I must stand up to this. When you come to what he really does feel you learn that he has the most passionate desire to be of use to the human race—to be of use through the discovery of knowledge, which was the way in which he could be most useful. I very much doubt whether any other manner of life that he could have adopted would have made him as useful as he was.

Barzun: But wouldn't you admit that he was perhaps a little bit too adroit and diplomatic, not only in his relations to life but in his writings? For example, many of his contemporary critics said that it is very well to divide thought from matter for purposes of science, but that surely they must unite in the human organism: the mind and the body are connected. There is then a third original idea, which is the union of soul and matter and we feel it or sense it through the senses; but we have to go to his letters to a princess who was interested in philosophy in order to learn that, just as we have to go to other letters and other writings to discover that he believed in the value of the emotions and the passions, that he thought they were all perfectly good, provided that they were used in moderation—which contradicts his stoicism. We have to go again to his letters to discover that he was—oh, almost a Christian Scientist. He said that he had been cured of early tuberculosis by looking on the bright side of things, which simply does not go with the image of Descartes as we see him historically.

Russell: I quite agree, of course, but that is so with any man. Any man, if you take him in his letters, where he's discoursing more or less accidentally, doesn't have the same statuesque appearance that he does when he writes his great works; that's just common humanity.

Van Doren: We don't mean to be as savage as we sound. We're expecting you to annihilate us within the next few minutes. Descartes' claim that he is doing good in the world interests me a great deal. He says, to me if you please, that he is doing me good. Well, that reminds me of my failure ever to believe a scientist when he tells me that he is in the world to do me good. I do not find that he is very much interested in me. I am not, you understand, being personal now; I am putting myself in the place of any human being. I find a curious lack of warmth in his voice as he says he wants to do me good. What he really wants me to believe is that if I shall agree with him—

Barzun: He will tolerate you!

Van Doren: He will tolerate me.

Russell: Let's take this up. It's perfectly true that the pure man of science, as such, is not actuated by philanthropy directly, but he knows perfectly well that the outcome of what he does is likely to be beneficial. Let's take, say, a man who is doing medical research. He is not interested in patients because he's not dealing with them; he is engaged in discovering a method by which others can deal with patients.

Van Doren: I wonder how much good a man like Descartes could do medicine in view of the fact that he distinguished body and mind as sharply as he did? It strikes me as possible that all the good one could do in medical experiment might not balance the harm done by that distinction.

Barzun: And I, for one, am certainly not requiring philanthropy in scientists. They should do things for the ordinary, good enough human reason that they're interesting and ultimately valuable, without any particular love for this or that group of human beings. But the reason I feel so strongly against Descartes—I might as well reveal it—is that his insistence on method has had a bad influence on science and more particularly on French education. It has led, it seems to me, to an over-emphasis on the formal side of all thinking, to organization on a mechanical basis, rather than on the organic unity of thought and the capacity for insight. Now, Descartes was not without insight but he trampled it underfoot. His four rules are simply scaffolding, of very little importance in actual use and of very great harm in the sequel.

Van Doren: What are those four rules, by the way? Have you found them useful, Mr. Russell?

Russell: His four rules may as well be set forth. Never accept anything not known to be true or clear and distinct. Divide difficulties into as many parts as possible. Proceed from the simple to the complex. Make complete enumerations to be sure that nothing is omitted. Now, the second and third especially—divide difficulties into as many parts as possible and proceed from simple to complex—I personally have found it always necessary to insist upon with advanced students who were beginning research. Unless they were very able they tended to take vast problems far beyond their powers, and I find Descartes' rules exactly what one has to tell them.

Barzun: Of course, simple and complex are terms relative to almost any single subject matter, and it is possible to lose the view of the whole through looking at detail. I can take an example from Descartes' own life. He wrote his *Meditations,* of which the full title was *Meditations in Which Are Proved the Existence of God and the Immortality of the Soul,* and, as usual, he sent the manuscript to his friend and critic, Father Mersenne, who read it and said: "It's splendid, but there isn't a word in it about the immortality of the soul!" So that Descartes's enumeration there was imperfect. I don't blame him for that. Geniuses have often made those silly errors. But it shows that he didn't use his method.

Russell: He proved the soul was immaterial and forgot to stick in that what was immaterial is immortal.

Van Doren: Possibly, Mr. Russell, the greatest defect of the higher learning today is that students are too much discouraged from considering hard subjects. If I were going to reform graduate schools, for instance, in the United States, I should begin by insisting that students be encouraged to begin in a very large field and then refine it. There is too much suspicion of the capacities of students. This seems to be a direct result of Descartes's own thought, whose scorn of anything except the clear and the distinct, which often became in his mind the small, means that the capacities of students have actually diminished with the failure to occupy them with larger things.

Russell: There is a compromise at that point, which I think is important. When one is engaged upon a smaller matter it should always be in its relation to a large one and because of its relations, not in itself.

Van Doren: That is precisely, it seems to me, where we can see one unfortunate result of Descartes. Take his discussion of God, which might be considered unessential to an explanation of his method, but which I think is very interesting. He pays all sorts of lip service to God, insists that God exists, and indeed spends time proving that He exists; yet what he is really proving is that after one has said all that one can forget God. God started the world, to be sure, and it is now working as He started it going, or as any mathematician might have started it going; Descartes almost says: "I could have done the same thing. I have proved the world to be exactly what it ought to be because it is intelligible to me." That is his test of existence, namely, intelligibility.

Barzun: It is a reduction of experience to something much more abstract and limited.

Van Doren: I don't want to be fantastic, but why wouldn't it be a good thing to expect students to begin with the contemplation of God? We act as if we thought they should begin with a worm.

Russell: Supposing you do begin with the contemplation of God—I should still uphold Descartes, and say that here he sees a large subject that can be divided into heads which can be taken one at a time.

Barzun: I should be perfectly willing to arrive with Descartes at any conclusions that seem to be useful in physics and mathematics, if he would be wholly candid. But, for example, he never tells us except in letters that the main ideas of his philosophy occurred to him when he was twenty-three in a dream, in a series of dreams on one single night in the year 1619. Instead of that, he gives us the wholly false and "public" view that you can arrive at truth by sitting down in a porcelain stove, as he did, and excogitate truth.

Van Doren: That's curious behavior for a scientist, isn't it?

Russell: I don't think it is. He confesses once that you may happen to hit upon the truth in dreams, especially, he says, in matters that are purely intellectual, and I think that's as much as you can expect of him. If he had come before the public and said that something was revealed to him in a dream it wouldn't have had the right effect.

Barzun: No, but he wouldn't have had to say that. He would have had to say that upon the basis of glimmerings acquired in a dream, his ideas were thought out and verified. I'm comforted, however, by the fact that history took its revenge upon him. When he died in Stockholm, since he was an infidel in a Protestant country, he was buried first in the cemetery devoted to children who die before attaining the age of reason.

Van Doren: How did he happen to die, by the way?

Russell: He died of getting up early! He never used to get up till twelve o'clock, in the middle of the day. Then he went to teach Queen Christina of Sweden, and she insisted on his getting up at five in the morning in the Arctic winter. The poor man died of it.

Van Doren: How soon? How many mornings?

Russell: Oh, in a little time. He died the first winter.

Van Doren: Mr. Russell, I wonder if Mr. Barzun and I have not exaggerated the influence of Descartes and rendered too malicious an account of his thought.

Russell: I do not think Mr. Barzun has exaggerated his influence in France. I, too, if I were French, might agree with all he says. But in other countries his influence has been less, and I think one may say of any man, however great and good, that his influence is bad—everybody's influence is bad if it's great.

Barzun: A very philosophical principle!

Van Doren: Will you go on to elaborate that?

Russell: Yes. It produces a set of disciples who repeat what the man has said instead of thinking. And so Descartes, by the mere fact that he had a great influence, undoubtedly became harmful in France. So would anybody else who had a great influence, but, if you contrast him with the scholastics who went before, I think he was better.

Barzun: And he did start Locke on his path. It was a very different path, but Descartes was the necessary stimulus. And the *Discourse*—I don't want to be misunderstood—remains a wonderful piece of autobiographical writing. Wonderful if only in this: that every sentence has at least two or three intentions and must be deciphered before one quite gathers where Descartes stands and what he wants his readers to believe.

Van Doren: What kind of sentence does he write, Mr. Barzun?

Barzun: In France he is considered one of the first modern prose writers. He writes a rather long and tortuous and complex sentence, but one perfect in its fulfillment of hidden meanings. He's a malicious writer.

Van Doren: But also delicate.

Barzun: A very delicate writer.

Van Doren: Do the translations manage to convey all that is there?

Barzun: They tend to break it up into smaller units of prose that spoil his rhythm.

Van Doren: I have not read him in French, although it is clear to me, as I read him in English, that he must have these qualities. However, I suspect them rather than find them.

Barzun: It is interesting that at the end of the autobiography he says that he wants a subsidy. He was thinking ahead to the large foundation, I think, that supports scientists without asking them to produce anything definite.

Russell: I'm not sure that he didn't want them to produce anything. He certainly wanted a subsidy. He wanted it solely for the purpose of experiments.

Van Doren: I think it would be fair, Mr. Russell, to ask you to read something from Descartes.

Russell: I'll read the last paragraph of his *Discourse on Method,* which will give one, perhaps, a better all-around picture of him than what we've been saying. He says:

"In conclusion, I am unwilling here to say anything very specific of the progress which I expect to make for the future in the sciences, or to bind myself to the public by any promise which I am not certain of being able to fulfill; but this of me I will say, that I have resolved to devote what time I may still have to live to no other occupation than that of endeavoring to acquire some knowledge of Nature, which should be of such a type as to enable us therefrom to deduce rules in medicine of greater certainty than those at present in use; and that my inclination is so much opposed to all other pursuits, especially to such as cannot be useful to some without being hurtful to others, that, if, by any circumstances, I had been constrained to engage in such, I do not believe that I should have been able to succeed. Of this I here make a public declaration, though well aware that it cannot serve to procure for me any consideration in the world, which, however, I do not in the least affect; and I shall always hold myself more obliged to those through whose favor I am permitted to enjoy my retirement without interruption than to any who might offer me the highest earthly preferments."

(1632-1677)

BENEDICT DE SPINOZA

Ethics

THE GEOMETRIC STYLE *in which Benedict de Spinoza treated of the subtlest spiritual states can deceive no one concerning the force with which he felt them. Outwardly the coldest of books, the* Ethics *soon confesses to any reader the fever of excitement with which it was written; and this fever communicates itself sooner or later to those who are capable in whatever measure of the author's intoxication. Spinoza was, the saying goes, a God-intoxicated man. His effort is to convince, by any means at his disposal, all those who suffer the bondage of their passions that there is freedom for them in the contemplation of a universe which is all God. But human freedom cannot be earned by anything less than a total acceptance of this universe. So Spinoza proceeds to demonstrate if he can the necessity of acceptance: the necessity, that is, of accepting necessity. There will be no peace until that point has been attained. Opinion differs as to the*

success of his demonstration, and it can be maintained that he so far establishes the notion of necessity as to leave no reader free to suppose himself free to adopt the ethics which the philosopher of Amsterdam is urging upon him. If everything is inescapably what it is, then we shall not escape from ourselves. But if this difficulty is overlooked, and the same difficulty may be found in Lucretius, what one is left with is a singularly intense and absorbing book which somehow achieves its original purpose. The Ethics *contains as well some of the closest and finest analyses ever made of the human emotions. What Spinoza proposed to entomb in the peace of a superhuman universe he first took the pains to understand in its own tragic terms.*

Baruch, or Benedict, de Spinoza was born in Amsterdam of a family of orthodox Spanish or Portuguese Jews. He lived in Amsterdam until about 1663, and thereafter in other Dutch cities, earning his living by grinding lenses. The study of Descartes and others led him away from Jewish tradition, and he was excommunicated in 1656. In 1663 his "Geometric Version" of Descartes' Principia Philosophiae *was published in Amsterdam and in 1670 at The Hague, his* Treatise on Religious and Political Philosophy, *which was immediately condemned as a sacrilegious and atheistic work. His* Opera Posthuma *(1677) included the* Ethics, *Spinoza's letters, and three incompleted treatises.*

BERTRAND RUSSELL • SCOTT BUCHANAN • MARK VAN DOREN

Van Doren: We have in the *Ethics* of Spinoza a book written by a man who, on the evidence both of the book itself and of its author's life, was profoundly religious, or at any rate profoundly moral. And yet the verdict of many persons, in that time and since, has been that he was dangerous. That suggests an interesting question about him; but it suggests even more ironically the question whether for this particular book that he has written he had any license to choose the title *Ethics*. As everyone knows— certainly every young person who reads Spinoza and becomes intoxicated with him, even as he was intoxicated with God— Spinoza begins by establishing a vast and necessitated world in which nothing seems able to be other than it is, and yet he ends by urging upon us a certain way of life, a way of thinking and being. Does it strike you, Mr. Russell, that there is any real difficulty here? Or does he have license to recommend a course of action to us in a world so necessitated?

Russell: Yes, I should say so. I don't think the question, whether the world is governed by necessary laws or not, bears very much upon whether you should have an ethic. Let me take an illustration. We all think electricity is entirely governed by natural laws, and yet we think it is rational to put up lightning conductors. Well, I should say that an ethic is, as it were, a lightning conductor for human passions, to enable them within a deterministic world to work in a way that produces a minimum of disaster.

Van Doren: Well, that's an analogy which I don't know how to reject. Can you, Mr. Buchanan?

Buchanan: I might try. Supposing everything is determined throughout, you can say that this is all according to general and universal law; but the individual comes under that and has, in certain metaphysics at any rate, a certain kind of contingency. Spinoza is concerned to deny any contingency whatsoever.

Van Doren: For instance, Mr. Buchanan, you would say that the person had been determined to put up the lightning rod when he did?

Buchanan: That would be not according to the laws of electricity, but according to some other law. It might be a contingency between the law that governs his behavior and the law that governs the lightning.

Van Doren: There is then a necessity over-arching both electricity and the man who puts up the lightning rod.

Russell: Certainly in Spinoza there is. But at the same time the man whose necessity leads him to put up that lightning conductor is more fortunate than the man whose necessity leads him not to. Now one of the things that will determine your actions, according to Spinoza, is whether or not you have read his *Ethics,* and if you have read his *Ethics,* you will behave like the man who puts up the lightning conductor.

Buchanan: It seems to me that that is one statement of a general principle he is using throughout here, and that is that any change which takes place—supposing it is a change in human behavior because one has read his *Ethics*—would come under his general deterministic rule. In that sense, there isn't anything that escapes it, and therefore anything that is said about it as good or bad comes within it as well.

Van Doren: One had been determined to read his *Ethics,* hadn't one, just as one had been determined to read Lucretius's poem *On the Nature of Things,* and therefore was already in a position, shall we say, to accept Lucretius or to reject Lucretius, whichever decision had been determined?

Buchanan: Also, according to Spinoza, our natures are so made, so constructed, that we will always want to be better, or, as he would say, want to increase the total amount of being we have.

That would be one of his deterministic laws. In other words, there is a law here to change—not one's nature, but one's being in certain respects.

Russell: You could certainly, I think, say what Spinoza would say if he were here with us now; he would say that we are all determined, but that those who realize that we are determined will be happier than those who do not.

Van Doren: That is where I think my question comes in; I ask it as an amateur in philosophy. Is our recognition, then, something that was not determined?

Russell: Oh, no, it is determined whether we shall recognize it or not, but one of the determining factors is Spinoza's writing his book.

Van Doren: Yes, and our having been born at a time when we would be old enough to read that book. I am interested in your use of the word "fortunate." The man who puts up the lightning rod is more fortunate, you say, than the other, just as the man who reads this book and who lives the life of reason, as Spinoza describes it, is fortunate. That is quite relevant, wouldn't you say, Mr. Buchanan, to Spinoza's whole feeling? There was a doctrine of the elect, it seems to me, in him. Certain men are better than others—certain men are bound to be happier than others, because they are bound to live lives that agree more completely with their nature and with the nature of the universe. And it doesn't seem to occur to him that there's anything to do about that.

Russell: Well, Spinoza thought that in man there are temporary elements and eternal elements, and in proportion as the eternal elements in your nature preponderate, in that proportion you become a happier man and a better man, and he did think that philosophy could enlarge the eternal part of you.

Buchanan: It seems to me the real difficulty is right there; that is, in some sense he has in view what is often called the mystery of human nature. He knows that man is partly eternal and partly temporal, and wherever trouble arises it will be a temporal and material matter; the problem always is to get those two together.

Now I take it, understanding in terms of time and in terms of the modes, as he would call them, the particular things of existence will always be confused. There will never be truth in the sense that he is using the term at all—in any of our observations of time and space, for instance. Modern science would be for him very much a matter of opinion.

Van Doren: Not knowledge.

Buchanan: Not knowledge at all. And one would have to jump somehow the ordinary empirical laws of science to get to anything he is talking about. Now how that takes place seems to me the real mystery in what he is talking about—how you get from confused ideas to clear and distinct ideas, in other words.

Russell: Really, his conception is that things are clear and distinct when they are like mathematical ideas, and I think he would say that in mathematical physics, when it is properly set up, the whole of the time process is viewed from an eternal standpoint in the sort of way that the Divine Mind may be supposed to view it. I think that is what he would say.

Buchanan: Yes. An algebraic formula, a differential equation, has these two aspects in it. But it would take some kind of special understanding of the mathematical formula.

Russell: You have to understand it by the third kind of knowledge, you see, and if you are a sufficiently good mathematician, you will.

Buchanan: And that would be the only saving of both science and, if you want to apply it to human affairs, of human affairs in his terms. Something appears to be denied, theologically; he is denying the doctrine of original sin at the beginning and perhaps all the way through. That is, man is essentially rational; his emotions and his imagination are in harmony with his reason. Except when they are not. And that will be because, in so far as the understanding of things is in time, they are out of whack. In other words, time is the principle of original sin.

Russell: Yes, there's a metaphysical doctrine about that—a number of other philosophers have said the same thing.

Van Doren: Well, sin perhaps is never the word for Spinoza;

it is error or confusion or imperfect knowledge—the first type of knowledge rather than either the second or the third, because both the second and the third are preferable to the first. Rather stubbornly I come back to ask my original question in a slightly different form. I can't quite see, granted this necessitated system, how any unit in it, say, myself or one of you gentlemen, at any given time can err, can be wrong, can exist or think in terms of time rather than in terms of eternity. It seems to me that in a system so perfectly articulated, a system in which every thought and every piece of body or matter has had causes before it in a line reaching back into infinity, any unit in that universe would be functioning properly at a given moment. I don't quite see where man is free to be confused. Just as I don't quite see where he is free to be clear—any clearer than he already is.

Russell: Man can't help being more or less confused, so long as his thinking is in time, but he is in a greater or less degree confused in proportion as time dominates his thought. So I should have thought.

Buchanan: And there is nothing improper about his being confused. It may be unfortunate for him; he may be unhappy about it; but he should accept that along with the rest of the universe, I should think.

Van Doren: There is a proposition in which Spinoza says: A decision by the mind is precisely the same thing as a determination of the body. At the same moment that one is making up one's mind to think a certain thing or to do a certain thing, at that very moment the body is determining the result—determining the thought, so far as I can see.

Russell: That of course is psychophysical parallelism. He thinks that every event is both a physical and a mental event. It is really the same event essentially.

Buchanan: Such a parallelism would not make the problem of body and mind very serious; I don't think that is his problem primarily.

Van Doren: Well, the relations between body and mind in Spinoza are very interesting to me as I read. One of the reasons

I was first interested in this book, when I was an undergraduate, was its very startling statements about the identity of mind and body. His remark, for instance, that one whose body is apt in many things is in so far a resident of eternity.

Russell: Yes.

Van Doren: A profoundly interesting statement; and it underlies the theory of modern education, don't you suppose? He goes on to ask what we are doing with an infant as we educate it. We are trying to make its body do things so that its mind will also be able to do things.

Russell: Don't you think that perhaps we're spending a little too much time on his metaphysic, which after all hardly anybody in the present world would accept, whereas in his ethic there is a great deal that is still of permanent value, to my mind. Perhaps we should do well to emphasize the ethical aspects rather more than the metaphysical.

Van Doren: Would you grant, before we begin to do that, that his ethic is good or attractive by some sort of accident—that is to say, it doesn't follow necessarily from his metaphysic?

Russell: I don't think it follows from his metaphysic in the least. I don't think any ethic can ever follow from any metaphysic. And I think his ethic very good, though not perfect, whereas his metaphysic is completely wrong from beginning to end.

Van Doren: I sometimes hear that no ethic can be significant unless it is supported by a metaphysic. What is your position on that, Mr. Buchanan?

Buchanan: Well, I shouldn't like to disconnect them quite as much as Mr. Russell does. What are the bases then of his ethic, if it isn't his metaphysic?

Russell: The bases of his ethic, so far as I accept his ethic, is that one can discover by experience that there is a certain kind of way of living which seems to most of those who have tried it to be a good way and which is the way which Spinoza recommends—a way in which you get rid of indignation and fear and irrational hope and a number of the things that produce anxiety and perturbation in life, and acquire a certain kind of calm. The kind of calm which Spinoza recommends is, I think, attainable without adopting his metaphysic.

Buchanan: You take more or less the position of the psychoanalyst on this, only you prescribe mathematics instead of some of the tricks they play on their patients.

Russell: Not necessarily mathematics—that depends upon who you are. You might get it just as well from history, or you might get it from music, or you might get it from poetry. There are a hundred ways of getting the kind of thing which Spinoza calls the intellectual love of God.

Van Doren: As a matter of fact, didn't Spinoza get it in part from the Stoics? I find something that sounds to me like stoicism here.

Buchanan: It seems to me that if you take Mr. Russell's position you have a rather interesting sort of background for Freud— if, that is, you take merely the empirical side of Spinoza and his ethic. Freud believed in a certain kind of determinism, and the problem of ethic would be largely medical in that case.

Russell: I think medical is too narrow a term altogether.

Buchanan: Psychiatric then.

Russell: Not even that, because it isn't to be assumed that a person is diseased because he doesn't live the life of a perfect saint, nor is it to be presumed that it is a medical man who will get him out of it. He may get out of it, as I say, through listening to music or through a hundred different things—whatever it is that appeals to that particular man.

Buchanan: Or through studying mathematics.

Russell: Yes, through studying mathematics, if he likes mathematics. If he doesn't like it, it won't be of any use to him.

Buchanan: Can mathematics be of moral assistance to anyone, would you say?

Russell: Undoubtedly, yes—a very great moral assistance to those who feel it in the kind of way that Spinoza talks of.

Van Doren: Could you say more about that, Mr. Russell?

Russell: Well, I think mathematics has the advantage of teaching you the habit of thinking without passion. That seems to me the great merit of mathematics. You learn to use your mind primarily upon material where passion doesn't come in, and having trained it in that way you can then use it passionlessly upon matters about which you feel passionately. Then you're much more likely to come to true conclusions.

Van Doren: And of course if you're not a person capable of feeling passionately about anything, it doesn't make much difference what you think, does it?

Buchanan: You're not saying that mathematics is free of emotion, are you?

Russell: Of course a mathematician has his emotions, but his emotions are not concerned with what conclusion he arrives at; they are concerned essentially with the process; the pleasure is in the process of proof, which is a different sort of emotion.

Buchanan: Then it isn't passionless in any cold and rational sense—the way it is so often spoken of.

Russell: If a thing were completely passionless, you wouldn't do it—I mean, nothing but your passions lead you to do anything. So that obviously the mathematician is guided by his passions in doing mathematics; but he is not guided by a passion for arriving at a certain proof of a certain proposition, but by the more general passion of arriving at proofs, no matter what.

Buchanan: Can you find in the third book, where he defines all the emotions, what combination of emotions would go with mathematics? I've tried to do that.

Russell: No. And you can't do that anyhow, because mathematics doesn't count except to people with certain technical skills.

Buchanan: Yes, but they have very special emotions, I've noticed. Mathematicians have very special emotional lives, and I don't mean now their double lives; I mean their emotions in connection with mathematics. There is a unity and an ecstasy about a certain kind of mathematical technique and success which seems to me very characteristic. A lot of people would say that it is the intellectual love of God, wouldn't they? I mean, if you accept the metaphysics here at all.

Russell: It is essentially the thing which he calls that—yes. That emotion you can experience without taking on Spinoza's metaphysics.

Buchanan: Yes, but it wouldn't deny Spinoza's metaphysics either, would it? It wouldn't be incompatible with it. It might even be one of its roots. In fact, this would be what he calls the second kind of knowledge, which leads to the third; that is, the kind of knowledge in which you have demonstration and ratiocination; this has a test of truth inside it and is a stepping-stone to the third kind, which is intuitive. Would you say the kind of thing that is sometimes called mathematical intuition is anywhere near what he's talking about?

Russell: Yes, but I think it applies in all kinds of knowledge. I'm speaking now psychologically, not metaphysically; but in all kinds of knowledge, when you get a certain familiarity, there comes a moment when the imagination seizes upon the total of some body of knowledge that you possess, and suddenly you realize it; you suddenly see it in a kind of vision; and that, I think, is Spinoza's third kind of knowledge. It is not confined by any means to mathematics.

Buchanan: You want to leave God out of it at this point?

Russell: Yes, entirely.

Van Doren: Spinoza is very famous for his God. Many persons are pleased to discover God in this book without the bother of having had to get Him through religion. They don't have to believe in anything except a vastly extended and incessantly thinking universe.

Buchanan: Of course I wouldn't say that this certain kind of knowledge happens only by referring whatever empirical subject you're talking about—individual things, he calls them—to God. That is, you must understand things so as to speak *sub specie aeternitatis.*

Russell: My point about Spinoza is that a great many of the things he says have psychological truth when restated in other language than his, but do not have metaphysical truth so long as you stick to his language. And that, I should say, applies to the third kind of knowledge. I recognize as experience a certain kind of knowledge which he experienced and which he christened the third kind of knowledge; and then he based a lot of metaphysic on that.

Buchanan: Would you say the metaphysics was false or nonsense?

Russell: I should say false, not nonsense.

Buchanan: Then it seems to me that you have shown some incompatibility between the second kind of knowledge and whatever the metaphysic is stating. Do you think they are incompatible? That is, they could be true together, couldn't they?

Russell: Oh, yes, I don't think that his metaphysic is self-contradictory. I just think there is no empirical evidence for it.

Van Doren: And neither, I assume, remembering one of your answers to a question I asked, do you see a necessary connection between it and his ethic.

Russell: No, I think there is no necessary connection, unless you take his ethic as completely satisfactory. Now I don't think his ethic is completely satisfactory; there are ethical problems that can't be dealt with by his method, and that is just where the falsehood of his metaphysic becomes relevant; but a great deal of the moral life, I think, can be dealt with in the way that he suggests.

Van Doren: If there is any defect in his ethic, it might show up in his analysis of the emotions, for I take it that a person could not be excellent in ethic if he were not the master of his emotions—not merely master in the sense of being able to control them, but in the sense of understanding them. Does it strike you, Mr. Buchanan, that his definitions of the emotions are searching, that they hold together and produce evidence of a man who knew man?

Buchanan: It seems to me they are extraordinarily good in that way. The way he systematizes them makes them very clear and takes you a long way toward what he is recommending to you—that is, to try to understand the effects of the external world upon yourself and so work through it.

Van Doren: To me one of the most valuable parts of the book is that series of definitions. It is always startling to hear emotions connected with one another so that each one comes to have only a relative meaning. Pity, for instance, is not for Spinoza something that comes along by itself, a stranger whom we take in overnight and whom we have to value; pity is something to be understood in relation to other things. It is for him an emotion not to be entertained, as a matter of fact.

Russell: I think that's true. I like his definitions of the emotions—they are interesting. But where I think his ethic fails is just in the fact that I can't accept his view of a block universe which, if you understood it, would seem to be all good. The universe seems to me partly good and partly bad, and I think you have to have an attitude toward the bad which doesn't consist of saying, "I don't understand this, but if I did, I should see it to be good." Because there are things that, however well you understand them, will remain bad. Over those I think his ethic fails.

Buchanan: You want to bring some real sin back into this business, don't you?

Russell: Not necessarily sin—sin is only one of the evils. Physical pain is an evil, and it isn't sin.

Buchanan: Physical pain, though, to a great extent can be understood and relieved by understanding alone, don't you think?

Russell: No, I don't. I haven't found that understanding a toothache saved me from going to the dentist.

Buchanan: Well, I have; it seems to me that there is a very interesting psychological phenomena there. If you pay attention to a certain kind of toothache, you can stand it. It doesn't relieve the pain at all, but you find it an interesting, good thing.

Russell: Well, so they've told me, but I've never found it so when I had a toothache, and I've tried very hard.

Buchanan: What do you do with such problems? Is there a radical evil there? Is it an effect of Satan?

Russell: No, certainly not. I mean it is just the way Nature works. But Nature works not only for good, as Spinoza thinks, but also for evil.

Buchanan: What do you do about these evils?

Russell: Go to the dentist.

Buchanan: That is simply submitting it to one of your friends, as he would say, who would understand and do something about it.

Russell: Quite. But understanding isn't what cures it.

Van Doren: As I remember, Spinoza has a paragraph which bears on that point. He instructs you how to behave with reference to those things in the universe which you cannot control. Mr. Buchanan, would you like to read it—in the Fourth Book?

Buchanan: "But human power is considerably limited and infinitely surpassed by the power of external causes, and therefore we have not absolute power of adapting things which are outside us for our usage. But we shall bear with equanimity those things which happen to us contrary to that which a regard for our advantage postulates, if we are conscious that we have performed our duty and cannot extend the power we have to such an extent as to avoid those things, and moreover, that we are a part of Nature as a whole, whose order we follow. If we understand this clearly and distinctly, that part of us which is called our understanding, or, rather intelligence, that is, the best part in us, will acquiesce in this entirely, and will endeavor to persist in that acquiescence. For in so far as we understand we can desire nothing save that which is necessary, nor can we absolutely acquiesce in anything save what is true: and therefore, in so far as we understand this rightly, the endeavor of the best part of us agrees with the order of the whole of Nature."

(1844-1900)

FRIEDRICH NIETZSCHE

Beyond Good and Evil

*F*RIEDRICH NIETZSCHE *incurred the reputation in his own nineteenth century of being a philosopher whose thought was more terrible than true. The terror which it inspired in those who felt their vested beliefs attacked from a source in itself frightening, namely, an attitude icily remote from and apparently superior to the comfortable conventions whereby good and bad were defined, undoubtedly prevented them from even an attempt to investigate its truth. The terror is less felt today, partly because the comedies of Bernard Shaw have transmitted the thought in a medium which, if only through its accompanying laughter, seems to render it more tolerably human. Losing thus his reputation for monstrousness, Nietzsche has lost some of his power; for his books did and do depend, at least on the rhetorical side, upon the success with which they carry the air of being merciless and outrageous in their analysis. But it is possible now to see just*

what it is that he says, and to measure the thing said against the best accumulated wisdom of the race. His excesses trim themselves, leaving it clear that his program of transvaluing values was undertaken at any rate with a profound respect for value. He does not get beyond good and evil; no man can; but he aims at definitions of them which in his mind will square them with reality. His terms "master" and "slave" refer to two kinds of men who in his conviction exist whether we like to think so or not; and "freedom" for him, even if it is not the thing traditionally meant, refers to a state in which humanity perfectly realizes itself. He was a heretic to whom orthodoxy may some day seem not to be without debt.

Friedrich Wilhelm Nietzsche, German philosopher, was professor at Basel, 1869-79. He was devoted to music, and showed some ability as a composer. The two strongest early influences in his life were the writings of Schopenhauer and the friendship of Wagner. But after a period of service in the army, he turned against all that he deemed soft or in any way effeminate and denounced Schopenhauer's "mortality of pity" and the romanticism of Wagner's music. He had long been in poor health when in 1889 he lost his mind. The works of Nietzsche include Birth of Tragedy *(1872);* Human, All Too Human *(1878);* Joyful Wisdom *(1882);* Thus Spake Zarathustra *(1883-85), in which he introduced the concept of the superman; and* The Will to Power *(1888).*

DOROTHY THOMPSON · HENRY HAZLITT · MARK VAN DOREN

Van Doren: We have come to a book by a very influential modern philosopher. No one denies the great influence, the indeed sensational influence of Nietzsche. Mr. Hazlitt, does it occur to you that that is chiefly why he is worth discussing today? Is the reason we are discussing him, in other words, his influence or his wisdom? You see what I mean by that distinction, I hope.

Hazlitt: Yes. His ideas have had tremendous force in giving birth to Fascism, even though some of his statements contradict Fascism, but I think that Nietzsche primarily is a great rhetorician, a great poet. He is a brilliant writer and not a philosopher at all, in the sense at least of a man who puts reason foremost and who thinks his position from point to point, who has coherent position.

Van Doren: You would say then that the outstanding fact about him is his influence rather than his rightness or his wisdom?

Hazlitt: Yes.

Van Doren: Do you agree, Miss Thompson?

Thompson: Well, there is no question about his influence. For instance, he had a direct influence on Mussolini, who quotes Nietzsche and admits his indebtedness to him, and you can trace the same influence in some of the most influential writers of the present day. For instance, in George Bernard Shaw, and in George Moore, who influenced the youth of the late nineteenth century, and in D. H. Lawrence and in Ortega y Gasset whose *Revolt of the Masses* is hardly more than a rewrite of the book we are discussing.

Van Doren: Anybody in America, Miss Thompson?

Thompson: Mencken in Mencken's own paradoxical way. I should say Robinson Jeffers, the West Coast poet, has been influenced by Nietzsche.

Van Doren: This influence is, I suppose, literally everywhere. No one in any country which has contributed to modern thought is totally free from it. But I am interested in the fact that both you and Mr. Hazlitt speak of him almost in the first breath as a man who helped to bring about the state of the world today. A man who either predicted or created what Mr. Hazlitt called the Fascist state of the world. Now perhaps that suggests the question we should address ourselves to today. If it appears from *Beyond Good and Evil* that he helped create that state, does it also appear that he would have liked to see that state had he lived until now?

Thompson: No, he would have detested it. Of that I am certain. But very probably he would have detested most states. He was a perfectionist and he was a paradoxical character; it is very, very difficult to discuss Nietzsche and discuss him accurately because he is so contradictory a writer. In fact, he believes that contradiction is the essence of life, and since he wished to embrace all of life he embraced his own contradictions. Certainly he would have hated Nazism, particularly Nazism, because he would have called it plebeian and he wished to see a new aristocracy rise to lead a united Europe. He described the character of that leadership, and it is certainly not the character of the Nazi leadership.

Van Doren: He wouldn't have recognized Mr. Hitler, then, as one of his noble men?

Thompson: No, but he also predicted Mr. Hitler. He wanted to see a new aristocracy come out of Europe. And he described its characteristics as reticence and reverence, sacrifice and an instinct for quality or rank in others, which instinct he called more than anything else the sign of high rank; he described the nobleman as one who looked out for others not out of pity for them (he thought less than nothing of pity), but out of respect for himself. He quoted Goethe favorably, who said that one can only truly esteem him who doesn't look out for himself. Among the non-aristocratic qualities he considered a love of fatherland and incontinence—political incontinence of every kind. Clumsy self-vaunting he described as the very opposite of the aristocratic ideal. But on the other hand he welcomed an absolute ruler for Europe to weld it together.

Van Doren: Did that ruler have to be in his opinion a German? Many people, I am aware these days, think of Nietzsche as one of those who attempted to call forth a specifically German leadership in Europe.

Thompson: Oh, no! He was very suspicious of the Germans.

Hazlitt: He worshipped Napoleon, for one thing. He thought Napoleon was a bringer of happiness; so he might have thought that Hitler and Stalin were bringers of happiness. And if he liked the slaughter of the Napoleonic wars he probably would have liked still more the slaughter of the present war, because it is a greater slaughter. He demands of the superman and the aristocrat certain fine things which Miss Thompson has spoken of, but he also asks that they be beautifully cruel, for example. He asks, in effect, that they be sadistic; he makes all sorts of demands for evil and wickedness in the rulers.

Van Doren: But is he primarily calling for soldiers, for the sort of leadership that would express itself in war?

Hazlitt: I think he is. Although he sometimes denounces militarism, he for the most part is invoking militarism. But it is part of his contradiction that he never put things together very well.

Thompson: He says that great races and great peoples and great individuals only arrive through danger. He is pro-danger and therefore he is pro-war. Also he greatly admires the soldierly instincts, the soldierly qualities. He doesn't object to slaughter at all. But still he would have hated this world, in my belief; he even warned that it would happen. I said he welcomed an absolute ruler for Europe to weld it together by war—he says it would *have* to be by war, it would have to be by dreadfulness. But he also pointed out that the herd instinct which was growing in Europe would lead the Nazis to follow any fool, that it would be almost impossible to find a really great leader, a really great nobleman in the sense that he uses the word "nobleman," because he said that great noblemen avoided the herd, hated to become herd leaders, and usually would have bad consciences.

Hazlitt: But doesn't the herd leader follow from Nietzscheanism itself? In other words, if there is to be a master morality there has to be a slave morality to complement it; in order that there may be masters there must be slaves; in order that there may be an aristocracy of the Nietzsche sort there must be a herd to follow it. So when he condemns the herd he is condemning the thing that he needs for his own philosophy.

Van Doren: Does he remind you, Mr. Hazlitt, of Plato, or rather of Socrates in the *Republic,* who plays with the idea of a commonwealth which shall be perhaps not perfect yet better ordered than most states have been? In that commonwealth the leaders will be philosophers. You noticed, didn't you, that Nietzsche is always calling for a certain kind of philosopher to exist. He says that when the new philosopher comes along he will be such and such a kind of man and we shall need him. Well, just as he, according to Miss Thompson, foresees that the best men, the men most capable of being philosophers, will least want to lead the herd, so Plato has to grapple with the difficulty that his philosophers will always be reluctant statesmen, that you'll have to drag them out of their studies.

Thompson: It has just occurred to me that probably the only Fascist leader in Europe who would in any degree please Nietzsche would be Salazar of Portugal.

Van Doren: How is that, Miss Thompson?

Thompson: Because he is a philosopher, because he is not a mass leader, because he is reticent and is never seen in public. Far from building up a great *mystique* about himself which would have horrified Nietzsche, as Mein Fuehrer has done and as Stalin has done to an extent, Salazar keeps himself in the background. He is the nearest probably to Nietzsche's idea of a leader. It just occurred to me this moment as you were speaking.

Van Doren: How do you account for the fact that Hitler has written a book? Is *Mein Kampf* in any sense a philosophical work?

Thompson: Oh, it's a terrible parody of Nietzsche.

Van Doren: Of Nietzsche, you say?

Thompson: Yes.

Hazlitt: But it more or less derives from him philosophically.

Thompson: I don't even know whether Hitler has read Nietzsche.

Hazlitt: Well, he could derive indirectly from him.

Thompson: Oh, yes.

Hazlitt: So many people derive indirectly from Marx, for example.

Thompson: Of course Nietzsche loathed the way the German language was usually written, and *Mein Kampf* is probably one of the greatest atrocities ever committed against the German language.

Van Doren: We have a curious situation here, one that I must confess puzzles me. Here is a forward-looking philosopher, or writer if you prefer, who in the 1880's seems to have wanted, seems to have predicted, seems even to have created something like the state that we now have; and yet he is a man who would have been pained by the spectacle of that state once it came into being. What shall we say of such a philosopher? Is he merely the sort that is represented by Rousseau in the century preceding him? One who prevails through his temperament and his eloquence rather than through his rightness or his wisdom?

Hazlitt: I think through his temperament and his eloquence. Nietzsche once called Carlyle, in fact he calls him in this book, a half-actor, a rhetorician, and a muddle-head. That applies to Nietzsche. Carlyle and Nietzsche had a great deal of similarity in their strength and in their defects. Nietzsche for one thing was himself a contradiction of his own philosophy. He was a professor living in boarding houses. He was a constitutional invalid. He avoided suffering as much as possible by going to Italy and the Riviera to regain his health, and yet he demanded that suffering should be. He had no imagination; he didn't know what it meant.

Thompson: Oh, now, I wouldn't say he had no imagination.

Hazlitt: He didn't have the realistic imagination; he had a dreamy imagination; he had a nightmarish imagination.

Thompson: He avoided suffering as much as he could, but he couldn't avoid it after all. He died mad and suffered extremely all his life. I think it might be better or truer to say that he rationalized his own suffering, which he couldn't escape, into something he could use. He believed that suffering creates the human imagination, creates the human being, and he didn't want to see suffering avoided by anybody.

Hazlitt: It never occurred to him that there might be enough suffering in the world, though, without adding to it universally.

Thompson: That's true. But to go back to what you said, Mr. Van Doren, I think you have to make a distinction between what Nietzsche *wanted* and what he *predicted*. Whatever else he is or isn't he was a major prophet. He predicted what was going to happen and what has happened. He predicted the coming to power of mass leaders. He predicted that the kind of democracy which existed at that time and which he hated—he was a great revolter against the democracy of mediocrity—would create mass leaders who would become tyrants and despots. He even predicted that they would be fools, so that you have to see a difference between what he predicted and what he wanted, which has not come to pass and probably never could come to pass. Also between what you said about Plato's philosophers and what actually happened. Nietzsche was a Platonist. He admitted an immense indebtedness to Plato.

Van Doren: He was a student of great literature; as a matter of fact he was a professor of the classics. Now we have here, it seems to me, something really very terrible to contemplate. Or is it terrible? One of the most intelligent, one of the most sensitive, one of the most foreseeing spirits of the nineteenth century foresees in fact a most deplorable world, and a world which he

couldn't help recommend if only in the negative way in which
he did recommend things.

Thompson: I wouldn't say that he recommended it. He saw
it, he *fore*saw it. First of all, he would not have called himself
"intelligent." He distrusted intelligence and he distrusted intellect; in that he has a direct responsibility for Fascism.

Van Doren: It is a curious thing to say about a philosopher,
isn't it, that he did not have respect for intellect?

Hazlitt: That is one reason I don't think he is a philosopher.
As a matter of fact, he gives a furious importance to his own
personal tastes. You realize after you've read a little Nietzsche
that he hardly ever argues at all, he hardly ever reasons with you.
He finds marvelously colorful and abusive phrases for the things
he doesn't like. He finds marvelously attractive phrases for the
things that he does like. A student of semantics could have a
great field day with Nietzsche—and could tear him apart as a
philosopher.

Van Doren: The form of his books is significant, isn't it? Any
book of his tends to be a collection of paragraphs, a collection
of aphorisms.

Hazlitt: Always fragmentary because there is no argument
being built up.

Van Doren: We are more aware of what irritates him and excites him than we are of what he understands and of what he
believes. He is surely not coherent.

Thompson: He is a poet. His whole book is a cry! You're
completely correct, it is not reasoned, it is an anguished cry
against the society in which he found himself and which he thoroughly detested.

Van Doren: By the way, Miss Thompson, do you share with
him any of his contempt for that society? For instance, to use
your own phrase, for the democracy of mediocrity? Is he talking
about something real there?

Thompson: Don't we all share to an extent a contempt for the
emphasis on mediocrity, for the attempt to level everything to
mediocre standards? I share with him his passionate desire that

quality, quality of thought, quality of craft, quality of personality should have more reverence. He himself says that it is not in the masses—and of course he made a definition of the masses which is not a political definition.

Van Doren: Or an economic one either.

Thompson: No. He would have been delighted with Mencken's definition of the masses as the booboisie.

Van Doren: Like so many other valuable men in the nineteenth century he was in search of a society which would recognize great men. Mr. Hazlitt mentioned Carlyle, but Emerson in this country, who certainly was a democrat, nevertheless was always looking for the great democrat, for the democratic gentleman. Perhaps that has been the great political problem, the great social problem of the modern world, the problem of how to create a just society, and therefore to an extent a democratic society, which should nevertheless not obliterate distinctions.

Thompson: It is very important to realize that Nietzsche put an emphasis on reverence for great work in all fields, for the distinguished personality, for the beautifully done piece of work, whether it was in the realm of common work, craft, or anywhere. And he said that such reverence was characteristic of the noble personality. That the noble personality always saw quality. He, like Ortega y Gasset, was in revolt against the mentality of the masses—and he would have counted a lot of people on Park Avenue, and on Long Island, among the masses. Just as y Gasset does. The contempt which they hold for the great artist, for instance. Remember that he was above all an artist, defending the right of the artist in this world.

Hazlitt: He never set a very good example of reverence, because he turned successively upon all his idols, whether it was Schopenhauer, or Wagner, or Goethe, or anyone. He did reverence Wagner for a while, but an inconsistent reverence is really not reverence.

Thompson: It is interesting, though, why he turned on Wagner. He turned on Wagner because he saw him going away from the grand line of Europe to German nationalism. Now that is one thing that doesn't make him a Nazi. He loathed German nationalism. In fact, he loathed nationalism of any sort.

Van Doren: It is clear to me that he is not nationalistic. He is not even Germanic; this leadership which he foresees and which he wants, this aristocratic leadership of Europe, this aristocracy, is curiously international. It is English, it is Italian, it is Spanish, it is Russian—above all things Russian. He seems to foresee the real leadership of Europe some day in Russia. He does not specifically say that it is to be German.

Thompson: Yes, but on the other hand—he is so paradoxical, you always have to say "on the other hand"—he did believe that what he calls the will to power was more inherent in some races than in others. He believed, for instance, that the will to power might be found in Italy because he thought it was young, and he was certain that an enormous will to power was growing in Russia. But he was afraid of Russia. He was afraid of Russia as a menace to Europe; he was so afraid of it that he predicted that it would be necessary for Europe absolutely to unite itself under some leadership in order to defend itself against the Russian will to power. He said that resistance would happen, and at the same time he qualified himself by saying he wasn't sure that he wanted it to happen. It is a very nice question to ask—how, were Nietzsche alive, he would look at this war, on which side he would be. I'm not at all sure. He believed that there was an enormous strength, an enormous will, in North Germany and in Russia. On the other hand, he was himself a passionate European and believed that the really European qualities in Germany came out of the South, and he adored the South. He was pro-French. He said France was the only country that had "the form-creating quality that could really give shape to a culture."

Van Doren: Incidentally he seems to have felt that the Jews were good Europeans too.

Thompson: Oh, yes.

Van Doren: You remember one respect in which he was certainly not like Hitler; he says that the first thing he would do if he were dictator (not that he uses any such word), would be to—

Hazlitt: Chase all the anti-Semites out of Germany.

Van Doren: And out of Europe.

Thompson: He considers anti-Semitism as a pure symptom of plebeianism.

Van Doren: There was a vulgarity about it which was of course extremely painful to him.

Thompson: Yes, and incidentally he greatly admired Mendelssohn. He has a whole passage on Mendelssohn as one of the most purely European of the German composers.

Hazlitt: I think it is important to point out, however, as a part of Nietzsche's inconsistency, that his central doctrine, the will to power, doesn't hold together on any interpretation, because if everybody has the will to power, then nobody has the will to be overpowered, and so you would have in that case continuous warfare, a warfare of extermination until there was no one left. On the other hand, if you take the interpretation that some people are to have the will to power and other people to have the will to submit, then he destroys his own doctrine that the will to power is all-pervasive, and he gets angry at the people who haven't got the will to power because they're not following what he says is all-pervasive. If both of those beliefs are to be allowed to co-exist, if they're necessary to Nietzscheianism, then it means that there is no objective validity to truth at all. And in that case you can't say that the will to power has any truth in it.

Van Doren: Neither does he leave much meaning in the word "leadership." You can hardly imagine what kind of leadership would be taking place if the connection were broken, as you say it is, and as he seems to assume it is, between the master and the slave. The slave is not willingly led.

Thompson: He regretted that the will to power was so weak in those reticent and noble spirits whom he wished to have it. He said somewhere, I can't remember the exact quotation, that the submissiveness of the masses is corrupting the art to command, because they will follow any fool. And the people whom he would have liked to see lead don't lead because they are solitary souls. He was a profound pessimist, was Nietzsche.

Van Doren: He didn't try, as Socrates did in the *Republic,* to bridge that gap between the leader and the herd. Socrates at least sketched a scheme for the education of the slaves and the guardians. He admitted they wouldn't have a very good time in society; nevertheless their education would bring it about that they would make the best of their condition and would bring it about also that they would serve the whole purpose of the state. Nietzsche is not interested, I should say, in the whole purpose of any state. He is interested only in the happiness of the leaders, whose independence he is very jealously guarding.

Hazlitt: And he never sets up any criterion as to who is to become the leaders and who is to become the slaves. Who decides whether a man is fitted to be a leader or fitted to be a slave? If the man makes the decision himself then it depends upon his vanity, but if he doesn't make it, how is it to be made? He never answers that question.

Thompson: No, he doesn't. And really Nietzsche can lead to nihilism, because his own description of what he called the free spirit, the spirit whom he admired most, is a description of someone who never could become a leader of the masses. He has even described that free spirit.

Van Doren: Would you like to read that passage, Miss Thompson?

Thompson: Yes. He is addressing himself to the free spirits, and he says that they must make their own tests. Then he lays down the tests: "Not to cleave to any person, be it even the dearest—every person is a prison and also a recess. Not to cleave to a fatherland—" (Now how can you be a national leader unless you cleave to a fatherland?)—"be it even the most suffering and necessitous—it is even less difficult to detach one's heart from a victorious fatherland. Not to cleave to a sympathy, be it even for higher men, into whose peculiar torture and helplessness chance has given us an insight. Not to cleave to a science, though it tempt one with the most valuable discoveries, apparently specially reserved for *us*. Not to cleave even to one's own liberation, to the voluptuous distance and remoteness of the bird, which always flies further aloft in order always to see more under it—the danger of the flier. Not to cleave to our own virtues, nor become as a whole a victim to any of our specialties."

FICTION

Fables

AESOP

If such a Greek as Aesop lived in the sixth century, B.C., he is now generally supposed to have recited rather than written his fables. There are legends concerning a man of that name who appeared at banquets and in the market place with stories of animals which carried a human meaning. But there is no record that he preserved them in anything better than his memory, and it is certain that the collection of tales now known as Aesop's Fables *cannot be traced back nearer to his time than a thousand years. Far from decreasing the interest of the* Fables, *this adds to their importance; for it is clear that not one man, named Aesop or otherwise, and not even one generation of men invented them. They are the invention of the human race, and their origins are legion. At a particular place and time a particular man may have hit upon the device of the animal tale to render the expression of his ideas more piquant, or more safe; but it is likely that no such thing took place. Fables, like proverbs, cannot be traced to their source. They seem to have been current always and everywhere, just as they are immediately meaningful to any member of the race who hears them for the first time. The wisdom of mankind, and sometimes its cynicism, is imprisoned in these stories as sunlight was once assumed to sleep in gems. The fox and the grapes, the lion and the mouse, the fox and the raven, the town mouse and the country mouse, the ox and the frog— it is hard to imagine how we should get along without them if they were suddenly taken away. Or rather it is not hard. Equivalent stories would be concocted to fill their place. They are necessary to our thought and speech.*

Aesop was reputedly a Greek fabulist, whom legend makes a Samian slave of the sixth century B.C. *The fables bearing his name have come down to us principally through the collections of Babrius (another Greek fabulist of uncertain date), in the Latin verse of Phaedrus (a first-century Macedonian), in the prose of the Greek scholar Planudes Maximus, c.1260-c.1330, and in the French verse of La Fontaine.*

LA FONTAINE *(1621-1695)*

*T*HE IDENTITY *of Jean de la Fontaine, far from being doubtful as Aesop's is, holds one of the firmest and fondest places in the mind of France. No poet of that nation is better known or more popular. Children, long ago it was said, learn the language by reading him, delighting as they do so in the natural gaiety and the unaffected wisdom with which he tells his tales; grown older, they admire the literary art with which he cast the simplest and homeliest of materials into poems of the greatest finish and brilliance; and in their last days they smile and nod over the truth of his observations, not to say the malice of his*

*wit. He retold the fables of Aesop, adding many of his own
invention; and if such things ever can be said to attain final form,
that form was here achieved. La Fontaine was one of the great
writers in France's great century, the seventeenth; he knew his
contemporaries, and he was at home in court. He is to be understood then as a completely sophisticated man, with as few illusions as his friend La Rochefoucauld. And he has sometimes been
charged with an undue cynicism with respect to human manners.
But a sounder reading frees him of the charge. He is simply without illusion; and on the positive side he has a constant interest
in the truth about mankind. His wit is seldom without its warmth,
and his intelligence is always in the service of understanding.
He is one of the great permanent poets of the world, like Horace;
and like Horace he will survive any fashion which has the
effrontery to ignore him.*

    *Jean de la Fontaine was trained for his father's official post at
Château-Thierry. He submitted for a time, yielding to an ar-
ranged marriage and even undertook the study of law, but he
fled his responsibilities and settled in Paris. There Fouquet became his benefactor and patron, and La Fontaine formed the
famous friendship with Molière, Boileau, and Racine. The fall
of Fouquet was the subject of La Fontaine's* Elégie aux Nymphes
de Vaux *(1761). For the next twenty years the poet lived at the
home of Mme de la Sablière. Besides the celebrated fables, he
wrote* Contes Nouvelles en Vers *(1664), resembling the tales of
Boccaccio;* Amours de Psyche et de Cupidon *(1669), a prose
and verse romance; and the entertaining* Voyage en Limousin.

LIN YUTANG · JACQUES BARZUN · MARK VAN DOREN

Van Doren: One of the earliest books I can remember is the *Fables* of Aesop. As a matter of fact, they were read to me before I could read myself. Did you have an experience similar to this in China, Mr. Lin?

Lin: I read them as a child, too, and enjoyed them.

Van Doren: You mean these same stories?

Lin: Yes, Aesop's *Fables*. I read them in Chinese, though.

Van Doren: Later on, were you able to find them in English?

Lin: Oh, yes, but I never cared for them that way. I enjoyed them most in Chinese.

Van Doren: Did you have a similar experience, Mr. Barzun?

Barzun: Similar in general outline, yes. It is the *Fables* of La Fontaine, of course, that most French children are brought up on. They are read to one, and one is generally asked to memorize two or three before one can read—which makes later reading easier.

Van Doren: I know a Portuguese whose children were not learning French under a certain tutor. They failed, year after year, to learn French, until the father hit upon the device of seeing to it that each of his children memorized five fables of La Fontaine—and after that they were able to speak French. I wonder why that is, incidentally. Is La Fontaine particularly valuable for this sort of discipline?

Barzun: In part, yes. The dialogue parts of the fable are very colloquial and simple to understand. But the narrative parts are extremely difficult, and only a dozen or so of La Fontaine's fables are really wholly suited for children as far as easy understanding is concerned.

Van Doren: But the ability to read them all would be an ability to read French, I dare say.

Barzun: Oh, yes, a very highly developed ability. Even for the modern educated French reader, there have to be notes to gloss some of the difficult passages.

Van Doren: Whereas the fables we know as Aesop's, in prose, and found everywhere in the world, do not seem to need such notes.

Barzun: Now that seems to me the fundamental difference between the fable as a popular genre, created by Aesop or dozens of people whose names we don't remember, and the fable as an artificial literary genre, which is what La Fontaine made it. I, for one, prefer the sophisticated genre to the simple one, because it seems to me that the only pleasure that a modern reader can take in a fable is in its dressing up, in its detail, and not in its moral. But I see that you disagree, Mr. Van Doren.

Van Doren: Oh, absolutely. I have never been able to take pleasure in elaborated fables. You probably know that John Gay, the poet who lived only a half century, or even not so much as that, after La Fontaine, wrote a great many poems which he called fables. I have never been able to read them with pleasure. Short as they are, they seem to me almost infinitely long. Mr. Lin, what is your feeling about this? Perhaps I might phrase the question this way: Is the value of fables, considered in their simplest form, for children or for adults? Or do you make any distinction?

Lin: I think that the writer of these fables, whoever he was, really meant them for adults. It was a sly way of taking revenge on mankind by libeling the animals. I feel that all these fables are libels upon our fellow creatures; they are not so sly, so crooked, so hypocritical as man. The man who invented the fable really meant it for adults, I think.

Van Doren: That's interesting. You come to the defense of the animals.

Lin: Yes, definitely.

Van Doren: I think we might all agree there. The animals are being misused. Nevertheless you do say, I gather, that the morals or the points of the fables have an applicability to human life in its mature stages.

Lin: Exactly. That is why they are so universally appreciated, because they are really dissections of human nature, not of animal nature. Remember the story of the sour grapes? Why, it is only man who would do that. The animal just walks away; he doesn't moralize about it. It is we, the crooked men, who do that.

Barzun: I quite agree with you. You are attacking not only the writer of the fable as a libeler, but you are attacking the intelligence of man as a reflective being, aren't you, Mr. Lin?

Lin: Well, not exactly. We do reflect, and the writer of fables himself is reflecting; but he is performing a useful task when he satirizes us by means of animals. It is a good examination of man, I think.

Van Doren: Man is certainly acquainted with his weaknesses, with his vices. Yet he does not like to admit them; or rather, if he is willing to admit them, he is willing to admit them only in the roundabout way of attributing them to the animals—or else to the whole of the human race excluding himself.

Lin: And the readers who are human beings take it more kindly, because it's cloaked in that way, than if the writer of the fable were to say: Men are crooked; men are hypocritical. Human readers wouldn't like that.

Barzun: It is characteristic, it seems to me, of the fable that it flourishes particularly under tyranny or absolutism. Aesop is supposed to have written under the tyrants of Greece. La Fontaine said a good many things by means of animals that he couldn't have said under Louis XIV if he had come out with an essay upon the subject.

Van Doren: I came across a note in the volume I was reading to the effect that the fables of Aesop were very much relished by certain officials of China in some past century—I've forgotten which century. I can never remember, as a matter of fact, any Chinese century by number.

Barzun: They're so different from ours.

Van Doren: Until these same dignitaries began to understand that the stories were against them, were to their disadvantage. Then they suppressed them.

Barzun: Unusual penetration in officialdom.

Van Doren: Perhaps the people, however, kept on reading them.

Barzun: But what bothers me a little bit about the fable is perhaps symbolized in the fact that we call the conclusion of it a moral. Very frequently, don't you think, we ought to call it an *im*moral?

Van Doren: The word "moral" has never pleased me, unless it meant generalization. I should say that that is about all the word means. The text always ends up by saying: Well, what this really means in general is so and so.

Barzun: Still, the pedagogical intent of the fable is very clear, and if you followed in order all the fables of Aesop you would be the most contradictory being in the world; you'd be doing one thing at one time and another at another; you'd be cunning in order to overreach your enemies and your cunning would defeat you. What do you think of that?

Lin: I think Aesop never meant to be systematic. He was a Greek, I believe, and it is an obsession with modern Europeans that they must be systematic; they mustn't contradict themselves. An Oriental or Asiatic doesn't bother himself about it. He wants to observe human nature; he makes a comment here, he makes a comment there, and that is all. Whenever Aesop saw a point about humanity, he recorded it; he didn't work out a system.

Van Doren: Whenever men act this way, this is the way they act. The same objection, Mr. Barzun, could be made, and is often made, against proverbs. There is a proverb, isn't there, a folk-saying, which covers every conceivable circumstance?

Barzun: But at least the proverb is a simple saying; it doesn't pretend to be a literary form and to be useful. What strikes me as particularly unfortunate about the use of Aesop's fables is that for the most part they deal only with the surface aspect of the situation. Take for example the one of the traveler who was taken in by a satyr and who first blew on his hands to make them warm and then blew on his broth to make it cool. This enraged the satyr, who threw him out of his house. That is an absurd moral, isn't it? You should use your breath for exactly those two purposes.

Van Doren: That fable has never struck me as characteristic. The reason we remember it is the phrase "to blow hot and cold." When we now say "to blow hot and cold," we are talking about something that Aesop apparently did not consider. We are finding a moral Aesop did not find. On the other hand, there survive among us at least a half dozen fables which seem to me to have the greatest point—the fox and the grapes, the dog in the manger, the goose that laid the golden eggs, the boy who cried "wolf, wolf."

Barzun: There is a question in my mind, Mr. Van Doren, whether some of these aren't over-simplifications. For example, I should like to defend the fox who said "sour grapes." Isn't it a perfectly sound experience of every one of us that inability to do something makes us reflect on the entire situation and see features in it that we didn't see at first? And it's never been proved that the grapes weren't sour as well as unreachable.

Van Doren: I couldn't help thinking a minute ago—I'm not agreeing with you, by the way, Mr. Barzun; I think you're all wrong—when Mr. Lin remarked that the fox walked off without saying anything—I couldn't help wondering how Mr. Lin knew what the fox was saying or not saying. Possibly the animals have processes which would astonish us.

Lin: But the sophistication of calling it "sour grapes" is distinctly human.

Barzun: Whether animals think or not, they are at our mercy because we are the only ones that write fables.

Van Doren: Of course, the matter of simplification or over-simplification is a very interesting one. To me the whole point of the fables is that they are absolutely simple. No other kind of story can be as short as this and say so much.

Lin: I think so, too. But I should like us to consider whether they are still good today, or whether we should think they are antiquated because they are simple.

Barzun: I'd like to jump into the breach and say that as a strict genre in the form which Aesop bequeathed it to us, it is antiquated. Not in the sense that we can't go back to it and enjoy it as children, or even later, but that anyone who should attempt to add to the number of fables in that simple form would find his labor in vain.

Van Doren: Of course, one reason for that would be that a man making such an attempt would be making it, say, in the year 1942, while thousands of years have gone by during which these fables have grown. Aesop, so far as we can discover, is not the author of any fable that we know, although he may be the origin in some sense of them all. This whole body of literature is of the greatest and slowest growth, so that no one man operating at any time could be expected to add very much to it; just as no individual, even in a lifetime, could create a significant number of proverbs. They are all infinitely old. I quite agree with you that the authority of the fables comes perhaps from their age.

Barzun: Not only that, but granting that they have a real understanding of human nature embodied in them, still that is what you might call rudimentary understanding. It seems to me that the world today and for the past few centuries has needed a deeper understanding, more intelligence than is displayed here, and of a different kind.

Van Doren: Again I must say just the opposite of that. The trouble with the world today may be that it cannot see things as simply as Aesop saw them.

Lin: I agree with you. If we cannot any longer write simple things, the joke is on us. We have lost simplicity of mind; we are too sophisticated, and I think that is a distinct disadvantage rather than an advantage.

Van Doren: Do you happen to know, Mr. Lin, the short stories, many of them in the form of fables, which Tolstoi wrote in his old age? They circulate now in a volume called *Twenty-three Tales*. You know that volume, I dare say, Mr. Barzun?

Barzun: Yes, I do.

Van Doren: That little volume contains almost the best fiction ever written by man. Socrates also, according to the *Phaedo* of Plato, was preparing to spend his last days in prison emulating Aesop. He was going to see if he couldn't say something as simply as Aesop had said it.

Barzun: I should like to say two things to that. One is that it may be a natural desire of old age to seek a simplicity that is impossible. But I would point out also, with respect to Tolstoi, that he wrote these works—and I think two or three other books intended for children—after a religious conversion which implied a much simpler mode of life. I'm a little alarmed by the desire expressed by you two gentlemen for simplicity of this sort. Doesn't it seem to you as if perhaps some of the tyrannical and absolutist attempts of our day are forceful means of bringing about this simplicity that we all desire?

Van Doren: But the lack of this same simplicity, alas, has made it impossible for us to see the very simple things they are doing. Now, the fable in Aesop of the four oxen and the lion is very much to the point. The lion found four oxen grouped in a field, each one facing out from a central point, so that he could do nothing with them. He merely waited until they were separate— each one in a far corner of the field—and then disposed of them one at a time. Our inability to see that the tyrants of today are proceeding on that very theory—one enemy at a time—may be destroying us.

Lin: Simplicity in my mind is synonymous with maturity, true maturity. Mr. Van Doren, you mentioned Tolstoi a moment ago. Tolstoi thought very little of his own novels, and he thought a great deal of his own fables. I think he took that point of view because he had arrived at a certain maturity. You mentioned Socrates, preparing to spend his old age in writing, in emulating Aesop. I remember also that Goethe ended *Faust* with a symbolism about reclaiming land. I think that is the way the human mind works; as it gets mature, it likes to seek for simple symbols that are easy to understand.

Van Doren: Mr. Barzun would say, of course, that that was the weakness of old age.

Lin: No, no, no, no, maturity; don't call it old age.

Barzun: No, a distinction must be made here between what we call simplicity in the sense of clarity—which of course is always desirable—and simplicity in the sense of insufficient provision for difficult situations. The simplest answer in all literature is the one in *Alice in Wonderland*—"Off with her head." It's extraordinarily simple; anybody can understand it, and of course most people can apply it. But it really doesn't solve any problems.

Van Doren: On the other hand, many things for me were illuminated by reading Aesop this time. He has four or five fables which apply directly and with a really terrible conclusiveness to the past ten years of relations between the United States and Japan. In each of them he represents an animal as having betrayed his future—destroyed himself in the end—by having given to an enemy something with which that enemy was to return and finish him. Remember the swallow who asked the other birds in vain to eat up all the seeds of the hemp that was being planted—the hemp that was to be made into nets which would hang them. Our selling of scrap iron and oil to Japan for ten years seems to me to be illuminated here. There is the story also of the woodsman who asked the forest to give him just one little piece of wood. The forest did so, very comfortably, but that little piece of wood turned out to be the wedge which was going to make the head of his ax stay on so that he could cut down the forest.

Barzun: I think, Mr. Van Doren, that that is a very good argument for my side, because here in the fable the situation has been simplified to suggest that if such and such a thing had been done at a certain time, the consequences would not have followed. Now, in the sale of scrap iron and oil to Japan, we always forget that it was predicated upon corresponding advantages, such as

Japan's taking a large part of our cotton supply. At no time is it possible to say Yes or No to abstract proposals without ifs and ands, and the danger of the fable is that you can quote it in just the manner you have done. It convinces, it is simple, it has a certain dramatic force, and only a few people can resist its spell and say "yes, but." It is the "yes, but" that strikes me as important.

Lin: You exactly prove my point. You can defend the selling of oil and scrap iron to Japan only if you have a sophisticated mind; you're bothered by a thousand irrelevancies—how about cotton and silk and all the other things?—where the simple peasant mind would approach the question through a direct moral process: Is it right or wrong?

Barzun: But we're not in a world of peasants. If we were, I might approve.

Lin: That is a disadvantage. Take the question of freedom for India. I think Churchill has a sophisticated mind; he is still bargaining; he is still trying to save what he can of India. He doesn't approach the problem with a simple mind. But Gandhi approaches it with a simple mind. He sees it not as a political problem but as a moral problem. It is a question of right or wrong. You've got to undo the wrong you've done. It is very simple; if we could learn to think in that simple manner—

Barzun: When you say a moral problem, Mr. Lin, do you read an expurgated version of Aesop in which the immoral instances are omitted? Because Aesop preaches cunning and roundabout means and a disregard of moral values on every other page, doesn't he?

Van Doren: Mr. Lin, I don't want to help Mr. Barzun out too much, but what about the story of the tortoise and the hare? The moral of that seems to be, doesn't it, that the tortoise was right— the slow, regular, steady plodder won the race. Which animal in that case do you prefer?

Lin: I prefer the hare. My sympathy is all with the hare. The trick of these fables is that you can turn any of them around any way you like. I would never sympathize with a plodding student; I would sympathize with the man who looks upon learning as an exploration, as a joy, a pleasure, and if I were telling the story I would make the hare symbolize that.

Barzun: But are you willing to have a world in which there are both hares and tortoises, which is my desideratum?

Van Doren: Perhaps the trouble is with the way we are applying the story of the tortoise and the hare. Now, the analogy between a tortoise and a hare who are racing to reach a certain point at a certain time and two students—of whom one is a grind and the other is brilliant and unsteady and erratic—is not perfect, because there is no point at which a student is supposed to arrive. He is supposed to become something on the way.

Barzun: And certainly there are functions in life to be fulfilled by both types of mind. A statistician must be a tortoise, I think.

Lin: But the point about learning, specifically about learning, is that the man who arrives anywhere is the man who enjoys it, not the man who looks upon the process of learning as a torture.

Van Doren: I suppose that is true. One interesting question, it seems to me, has arisen here: Are the findings of Aesop about human nature on the whole unflattering to human nature? Does he seem to be most interested in weakness and vices? Would you call him cynical, Mr. Barzun?

Barzun: The charge is allowable; I think it is even more allowable with respect to La Fontaine, who indicated on several occasions that the moral scheme he had in mind when he wrote many of the fables is that contained in the maxims of La Rochefoucauld. He shows mankind as predominantly evil and selfish, absolutely hopeless as far as improvement is concerned. But there comes up the very interesting question at that point, whether the introspective person—the person who knows himself—is not likely to take a worse view of himself than the unconscious one.

Lin: I think Aesop is essentially cynical; he is a satirist. He wanted to satirize mankind, and any satirist, as you know, takes a rather cynical view of human nature.

Van Doren: I've never been sure that the word "cynical" was quite right. All such men are merely telling you that if you go out among men you will find them in general to be behaving in this way. This is what you can expect to find. But Aesop also understands that you may find something you don't expect, namely, virtue; but virtue is an unpredictable thing; indeed it is an ineffable thing, something about which we can say nothing, something which we have no right to count on.

Lin: He observes human nature very realistically, but we must also say this, that he has a kind of humor; he is able to laugh at human nature. That is the way we all should be.

Barzun: I would say about La Fontaine that he takes less definite stands than Aesop does, and puts the greatest amount of his effort into making the detail significant—you take what view you like. I should like to read the conclusion of La Fontaine's fable of the Wolf and the Dog, the one well fed and the other starving in the woods, as indicative of La Fontaine's technique if of nothing else.

> "But as they ran, he [that is the wolf] spied a curious ring
> Of bald white patch behind his comrade's ears.
> 'What's that?' he asked with dawning fears.
> 'Nothing!' 'How so?' 'Well, hardly anything;
> The collar of my chain, may be,
> Has been the cause of what you see.'
> 'Your chain!' exclaimed the wolf, 'then you're not free
> To run at will?' 'Not quite—but it doesn't matter.'
> 'Doesn't it, indeed? It wouldn't do for me,'
> Replied the starveling. 'You may be the fatter,
> But I prefer my liberty
> To all the riches of your platter.'
> He didn't pause to say good night,
> But ran till he was out of sight."

Van Doren: And here is a very short fable, in prose of course, from Aesop: The Wolf and the Lamb.

"Once upon a time a wolf was lapping at a spring on a hillside, and looking up, what should he see but a lamb just beginning to drink a little lower down. 'There's my supper,' thought he, 'if only I can find some excuse to seize it.' Then he called out to the lamb: 'How dare you muddle the water from which I am drinking?' 'Nay, master, nay,' said the lamb, 'if the water be muddy up there, I cannot be the cause of it, for it runs down from you to me.' 'Well, then,' said the wolf, 'why did you call me bad names this time last year?' 'That cannot be,' said the lamb, 'I am only six months old.' 'I don't care,' snarled the wolf; 'if it was not you, it was your father,' and with that he rushed upon the poor lamb and ate her up, but before she died, she gasped out: 'Any excuse will serve a tyrant.' "

(c. 1494-1553)

FRANÇOIS RABELAIS

Gargantua and
Pantagruel

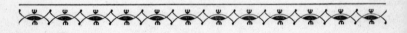

ONE OF THE *many paradoxes concerning Rabelais is that the book by which he everywhere is known is at once strange and natural. It has been denounced as monstrous, both in form and in matter; and there is no question but that any reader, opening it for the first time and beginning to read, will feel as if he were assisting at a literary earthquake, so huge are the mountains of mirth and ribaldry that tumble about him, and so primeval is the laughter that seems to come with an almost impersonal, inhuman roar from somewhere in the hinterland of consciousness. These giants that drink and swagger and carouse, these words that pour along as if in flood, these mockeries of every institution under the sun, are unlike anything the reader has ever encountered or will encounter as long as he lives. Gradually, however, another conclusion will suggest itself, and from seeming merely possible will grow into a certainty. Rabelais is saying something after all,*

and it is this: the world is a good place, and only fools pretend that it isn't—or, even worse, believe that it is a grave, a mourning wall, a closet, a dark room, a draped altar, a schoolhouse, a monk's cell. Rabelais, himself a monk and a medical man, decided in France in the sixteenth century to let himself go. And he did so in one of the most magnificent hymns to nature ever composed. For that is what this tumultuous prose amounts to. Education, medicine, the church, the army, the council chamber: all are submitted to an uproarious review which reveals their pedantry, their inhumanity, their insufficiency for man's plain purposes on earth. So natural a book—perhaps it is no paradox that it should seem so strange.

François Rabelais, French physician, philosopher, and author, began the study of medicine at Montpellier in 1530. He practiced in Lyon and other cities. He found influential friends in the Bishop of Maillezais, Margaret of Navarre, and, especially, the Cardinal du Bellay. His first publications were the Medical Letters *of Giovanni Manardi of Ferrara (1532), and a series of humorous satirical pamphlets. One of the pamphlets was an account of Gargantua; its success led him to compose a sequel, on Gargantua's son Pantagruel. In the five books of this mammoth satire Rabelais sketched the history of civilization. His style was coarse and daring; he employed all manner of devices— puns, enigmas, riddles. In the last three books he dropped adventure to develop his criticism of contemporary life.*

ANDRÉ MAUROIS · JACQUES BARZUN · MARK VAN DOREN

Van Doren: Rabelais' prologue to the book of Gargantua suggests a parallel between that book and the Socrates whom Alcibiades describes in the *Symposium* of Plato. You remember, Alcibiades says that the exterior of Socrates is no index to his true genius. Outwardly he is grotesque, ugly, trivial, commonplace, coarse; but he is like one of those little Grecian boxes, those little packages which have the semblance of a Silenus, and then when opened prove to contain the most precious drugs, perfumes, or what-not. Well, he goes on to say, my book is something like that—it has a gross and formidable exterior, but when opened it will turn out to have some tincture of wisdom in it which will be most precious. Do you suppose, Mr. Barzun, that Rabelais even there is joking with us? Does it seem to you that that is the way to read his book—in other words, to open it for the sake of what is inside it?

Barzun: If it leads to looking for a doctrine or a fixed system, I think it is unfortunate and very misleading. In the same prologue he compares his book also to an onion, and if you applied the obvious lesson of the first suggestion to the onion, you would peel one leaf after another and find nothing at the core. I think the outside is just as important and interesting as the inside.

Van Doren: Do you think something like that, Mr. Maurois?

Maurois: I think that Rabelais chose a subject which from the outside could appeal to the general public. The first two books are the pot-boilers of a man of great culture; but, of course, being a man of great culture, he couldn't help, even in a pot-boiler, showing it.

Van Doren: Are you saying that the two best-known books of Rabelais are pot-boilers?

Maurois: Oh, yes.

Van Doren: And that they prepare us for greater books to come?

Maurois: I think what happened is this: Rabelais was in great need of money at one time, and he knew that the story of Gargantua sold very well, so he thought of writing a sequel. But when the first two books had had a great success and he felt that he had a public, then he went on with the third and fourth books, which are infinitely more profound, because he felt he could do it.

Barzun: I wonder, Mr. Maurois, whether the general public, whatever that may have meant in the sixteenth century, would take the trouble to read through even the first two books—dense, difficult, and learned as they are, at least superficially? Don't you think that a cheaper product, more hasty, more jerry-built, would have been more popular still and would therefore have successfully competed with Rabelais?

Maurois: Yes, probably, but of course Rabelais, being a genius, couldn't write a merely popular book.

Van Doren: You seem to be saying, Mr. Maurois, that the prologue is justified in the point it makes, namely, that if one opens this book deeply enough—let us say, if one turns enough pages—one will finally come to a secret passage or a secret part which will contain wisdom.

Maurois: I think that's much better. I agree with Mr. Barzun that there is no definite philosophy in Rabelais; one couldn't build a system out of Rabelais.

Van Doren: Then it isn't a few truths that you will open upon.

Maurois: No, you will discover a man of great culture who knows all one could know in his time.

Barzun: I wonder, as a matter of fact, whether Rabelais was very much read or *is* very much read. Some English commentator, whose name escapes me now, says that Rabelais certainly is very little read; that he is a name, an expression, perhaps an atmosphere, in our culture, rather than a living force. Does that tally with your experience, Mr. Van Doren?

Van Doren: I doubt very much that any of these five books could now be or ever was in one sense of the term popular. The whole work recommends itself most clearly to a person who already possesses learning. There is no pleasure, I think, to be taken in this book by a mind that isn't well stored with allusions and with a relish for knowledge. A person who buys it in a drug store because he has heard that it is dirty and expects to get pleasure of the sort which is apparently got from dirty books, would be bored almost to death in his search for the thing he was looking for. Of course, what he is looking for he might recognize here and there, but the labor of finding it would be enormous.

Barzun: I should think it would be equally true of even the snobbish intellectuals who own Rabelais and perhaps remember two or three of the famous passages about the Abbey of Theleme, or something of that sort, but who don't go digging into the texture of the prose, which is, to me at any rate, the rewarding thing here—the packing of allusions, of ideas, the burlesque of learning, into a fantastic story which, taken by itself, isn't particularly interesting.

Van Doren: Yes, and the prose must always be good, it seems to me, if one is to keep on reading. As a matter of fact, it always is. I don't know whether the third and fourth books are much profounder than the first and second—they are different, there's no question about that. The climate of them changes, the whole tone of them changes, and the morality seems to be more complex.

Maurois: In France the first and second books are much more read than the third and fourth; there are editions where you find only the first and second. Also—what seems important to me in France from the point of view of knowledge of Rabelais—school children read always a certain number of scenes, and these indeed are known by everybody.

Barzun: Like *Gulliver's Travels*—expurgated and reduced to fairy-tale proportion.

Maurois: Exactly.

Van Doren: But I am worried over the charge which Mr. Maurois seems to level against those two books. I must confess I am terribly fond of them myself. I would hate to admit that they were inferior to the third and fourth, which I also like.

Maurois: I agree with you. I think they are better—the others are more profound.

Van Doren: Oh, I see.

Maurois: Sometimes when you want to write a pot-boiler you write your best book.

Van Doren: You relieve me greatly, because I hadn't understood you to mean that. I had understood you not to despise the first two books by any means, but to feel that they were on a lower level.

Maurois: No, you know how it is. When a man thinks: well, now I am free to express my philosophy, he becomes ponderous.

Barzun: The very fact that the first two books contain giants and a great deal of gross carousing has given rise to the impression that Rabelais himself was a fat, red-nosed, coarse creature, and most people are shocked, I think, when they see the extant portrait of him, in which they see a thin, malicious, mocking-eyed person who seems not at all a carouser, but rather an ascetic monk—which, of course, at one time he was.

Van Doren: He was a monk and a doctor, and he was a man who understood the ascetic life perfectly, wouldn't you suppose? Because only a man who could understand the ascetic way of life could write such a satire against it—could celebrate its opposite so brilliantly.

Barzun: When he was a young monk he had to be kept by his superior from overworking, which doesn't sound at all like the philosophy he later expounded.

Van Doren: Let us come back to the thing. Mr. Barzun spoke of: the way the book is written. Wherever you open it, you find Rabelais writing with apparent carelessness, with a gigantic—or to borrow his own word, "gargantuan"—recklessness, so that he seems to be throwing words into sentences without knowing their effect. Yet he is knowing their effect steadily. The reason I'm sure that a person can read the book right along for no reason at all except the pleasure it may give him—and we must repeat that Rabelais expects him to be learned—is this mastery of the art of writing prose. It is a double art, I take it; the art of pleasing or engrossing the reader with a great design which moves rapidly and swiftly and the elements of which are great, but the art also of pleasing the reader with each sentence, which must be perfect, which must do its detailed work joyfully and rather unobtrusively. Take the end of the thirty-ninth chapter of the first book, when Gargantua has just met the wonderful Friar John and Friar John has been talking for two or three pages with the greatest relish and the greatest coarseness. Panocrates, standing by, suddenly says: "How now, you swear, Friar John." "It is only," said the monk, "but to grace and adorn my speech. They are colors of a Ciceronian rhetoric." There is really a great delicacy about that sentence. I should say that the constant combination of delicacy with coarseness is what pleases us in Rabelais.

Barzun: His fondness for puns is an indication, as it is in all great writers, of that delight in words which is—well, plastic, rather than purely grammatical or literary.

Maurois: That was true, of course, of the sixteenth century in general—the French language was really fluid at that time, and one could invent words.

Van Doren: The same thing was true in Shakespeare's time, which was, after all, not much later than Rabelais'.

Maurois: As a matter of fact, American prose in these days reminds me in a way of Rabelais' prose.

Van Doren: It is inventive in that same way, and it is careless of tradition—or rather, it is free to accept all the elements of tradition.

Maurois: It sometimes delights in coarseness, too.

Van Doren: Yes. And what about Irish prose?

Maurois: Of course Joyce and Rabelais have a great deal in common—*Finnegan's Wake* and *Gargantua* are sometimes the same book.

Van Doren: Something like the same ground prepared them both, I should say. Just as we speak of the French and English Renaissance which Rabelais and Shakespeare represent for us, so the Irish writers of the late nineteenth century and of this century undoubtedly thought of themselves as participating in a renaissance; they actually use that word. There was a special energy with which they sought through all the languages of the world for what they needed to say.

Barzun: To the extent, however, that it was a purist movement and that they wanted Irish or Gaelic as the sole national medium, they were going counter to Rabelais's tendency. If you observe Rabelais' vocabulary, it is full of Greek and Latin compounds that don't occur anywhere else, and his fellow writers in the same period also made their own words which have since dropped out. So there was a cosmopolitan attitude in Rabelais's mind which I don't find in the Irish.

Van Doren: Although you find it in Joyce, don't you, because his words come from every known language? He himself learned about twenty-nine, I believe.

Barzun: Oh, yes. Joyce is an exception. But would you put him in the Irish Renaissance properly so-called?

Van Doren: I suppose not. To say that the Ireland of our times produced Joyce is probably equivalent to saying that the England of Shakespeare's time produced Shakespeare. There is no one remotely like Shakespeare in his time, and perhaps most of what we really mean when we talk about the Elizabethan Age is Shakespeare. So Rabelais has no compeers, wouldn't you say? Do you know of anyone else like him?

Barzun: No, of course.

Van Doren: Then Joyce would be enough. My only point is this: that in periods when you have a great and fertile joy in language, which means that you invent and collect from the corners of the earth the most wonderful words and phrases, at such times also you have a fabulous delicacy of style. For instance, among the Elizabethans there was that thing called "euphuism," which meant that they were pedantically interested in the finest harmonies of prose.

Barzun: And there is euphuism in Rabelais, too.

Van Doren: Oh, yes.

Barzun: But what I've said against the idea of finding a doctrine or system in Rabelais shouldn't prevent us, I suppose, from asking ourselves what Rabelais means, because he's not just writing a book to display his powers of prose. If nothing else he's an author, we've agreed, writing to entertain the multitude. So what is Pantagruelism, if there is such a thing—?

Maurois: Well, is it not chiefly cheerfulness?

Barzun: The cheerfulness deriving its strength from what, Mr. Maurois?

Maurois: Well, to a certain extent from Christianity, because I think that Rabelais is a Christian.

Barzun: Oh, there's no doubt of it, no doubt of that.

Maurois: And also, I think, from the fact that he was a medical student—he had the coarse cheerfulness of the medical student.

Van Doren: I like that phrase very much. Most of the doctors of my acquaintance are coarse and cheerful, and pass for cynical among their friends.

Barzun: Rabelais got his first medical degree in six weeks. I wonder if that has any bearing on the cheerfulness which he developed out of it.

Van Doren: Oh, even very old and wise doctors are likely to have some touch of it—at any rate, a casualness in respect to pain, which of course is important in Rabelais.

Maurois: Then he comes from a province in France which is cheerful; the life is pleasant and the wine good.

Barzun: And the cookery first rate. What about the matter, though, of the doctor's attitude toward bodily functions? It seems to me that Rabelais here is much more a poet than a physician, because functioning in Rabelais goes beyond all bounds of necessity or normality, which are the two criteria that the doctor generally applies.

Van Doren: Yes, but doctors can't help liking children, I imagine, because of their fascination with functions and processes for their own sake. The children speak of them with great exaggeration, also, and act as if life had no other purpose.

Barzun: But what if the doctors say: "Don't drink so much, don't overeat, lead a life of moderation"?

Maurois: Don't you think that a doctor who had also been a monk and had therefore suffered from the ascetic life would exaggerate the importance of functioning because he has seen what it is not to function?

Van Doren: As a matter of fact, the doctors I know spend a good deal of time these days trying to persuade ladies to stop dieting. It seems to them a dreadful thing, this sudden desire of women not to eat.

Barzun: It seems to me that Rabelais' attitude is still something more than that. He is trying to show, through his exaggeration, that we are not individually of much account anyhow.

Van Doren: That's true. I agree that he is endeavoring to shock us into a recognition of the natural things—to remind us of their great importance.

Barzun: And of their unimportance—relatively to our person.

Van Doren: Of their unimportance finally, yes. But first of all we seem to be hearing claims made for their importance, wild claims made for the beauty of drinking, for the almost mystical significance of this or that natural way of life. It is only then— and I think it is now that his parallel between the Silenus and Socrates really has meaning—it is only then, after we have learned about these giants who are so enormously jolly and big and coarse, that we also learn that they are, at the center, very good old boys. They are good-natured giants, gentle giants.

Barzun: Because they are strong.

Van Doren: Yes, it goes along with their strength. But we must have been convinced of their strength first, and their strength must have seemed to have something really quite ruthless about it.

Barzun: But they are, so to speak, corrected by the personality of Panurge, who is a natural force, unlimited, unconstrained by any moral consideration, and Rabelais makes a pretty horrifying spectacle of that.

Van Doren: That is why I was wondering about the distinction Mr. Maurois made between the first two and the second two books. Now the gigantic good nature, gentleness, sweetness, and charity of the first two heroes, Grandgousier and· Gargantua— and Pantagruel, for that matter—are sharply contrasted in our minds as we finish the book with the very different sort of power which is in Panurge. It is not a physical power, is it?

Maurois: The good point about Rabelais' giants is that they have no inferiority complex.

Van Doren: That's true, they have nothing to worry them. Since they don't have to prove their greatness, they don't have to prove their superiority.

Maurois: Because it's obvious.

Barzun: Well, do you think that Panurge has an inferiority complex?

Maurois: No, because Panurge is so—well, is unconscious.

Barzun: He doesn't think.

Maurois: He doesn't think at all.

Barzun: He acts, and he's so full of impulses that half of them are good and half of them are bad—by virtue of statistical average.

Maurois: He has the human instincts without the human mind. Or rather, without the human conscience.

Van Doren: I would deny that he had no mind. He is using his mind very expertly all along to prove this or that evil thing, is he not?

Barzun: Yes, but on the spur of the moment—there's no continuity, there's no comparison between two ideas or two goals.

Van Doren: That's true—there's no system of ideas. He has no plan. He would prove anything, wouldn't he, against anybody?

Maurois: Don't you think that any great writer who wants to express himself completely has to create at least two characters, because there are always two sides to human nature? Molière writes a dialogue between Alceste and Philinte, but I think it's a dialogue between Molière and Molière. Rabelais was probably partly Panurge and partly a giant.

Van Doren: Let us say, he was in Panurge a very, very bad boy, and in Grandgousier and Gargantua and Pantagruel he was a very good old boy.

Barzun: There's one thing he was not and that was Picrochole—the man of deliberate wickedness.

Van Doren: The Picrochole, you mean, who invades the territories of Grandgousier without any reason at all?

Barzan: Well, with only a pretext. His egotism and vanity are, it seems to me, especially hateful to Rabelais.

Van Doren: I suppose the point at which we can see the relation, if any, between the giants and Panurge is the attitude of Pantagruel in particular toward him. Now you might expect Pantagruel not to like Panurge; but he does seem to, very much.

Barzun: He's a source of inspiration in a sense—the things that we do not think of, because we are conventional and institutional creatures, Panurge finds natural.

Van Doren: It is something like the admiration of Gargantua for Friar John, who again is someone, I suppose, Gargantua should not approve of and yet totally loves.

Barzun: The emancipated are a source of social progress.

Maurois: What I think is very important in what you said is that Friar John and Panurge are not wicked. That is extremely important. Rabelais doesn't hate vice; he hates wickedness.

Van Doren: All these men are absolutely free. They are free men, but, as you say, they do not use their freedom toward any private end.

Barzun: And you can see in the Abbey of Theleme, about which so much has been written and said, that it is Panurge reduced to rules; therefore it ceases to be wild and impossible and becomes a civilized society.

Van Doren: It was conceived by an author who thought of his own society as worrying too much, as having what Mr. Maurois perhaps meant by inferiority complex. Most of the troubles of the world come from distrust, both of ourselves and others.

Maurois: And from attaching too much importance to things over which we have no control. Rabelais' philosophy, if any, is a sort of wide sympathy for human affairs together with a comprehension of their vanity.

Barzun: Yes, but there is a very important part which we haven't yet brought into this general survey, and that is the institutions Rabelais makes fun of. He doesn't say we must have no institutions, but he thinks that most of those he sees around him are ridiculous and false.

Van Doren: What about the institutions of education?

Barzun: He comes back to those again and again.

Van Doren: One of the most important parts of the first book is surely the education of Gargantua, isn't it?

Barzun: Yes.

Van Doren: What sort of education does he finally seem to recommend as good?

Barzun: I suppose the progressive education of the whole man, to use the jargon of our own day.

Van Doren: The jargon of our own day, but he himself does not use jargon, does he, in describing the education—I mean the good education—of Gargantua? He is fresh and first in recommending it.

Barzun: To be sure he has his pupil do everything as if there were forty-eight hours a day instead of twenty-four; yet even on the subject of education he puts limits and reservations—as when more important things come along. Perhaps it would be apt at this point to read a letter which Grandgousier writes to his son Gargantua at the time when Gargantua is being educated.

"The fervency of thy studies did require," says Grandgousier, "that I should not in a long time recall thee from that philosophical rest thou now enjoyest, if the confidence reposed in our friends and ancient confederates had not at this present disappointed the assurance of my old age. But seeing such is my fatal destiny, that I should be now disquieted by those in whom I trusted most, I am forced to call thee back to help the people and goods which by the right of nature belong unto thee. For even as arms are weak abroad, if there be not counsel at home, so is that study and counsel unprofitable which in a due and convenient time is not by virtue executed and put into effect. My deliberation is not to provoke, but to appease; not to assault, but to defend; not to conquer, but to preserve my faithful subjects and hereditary dominions, into which Picrochole has entered in a hostile manner without any ground or cause, and from day to day pursues his furious enterprise with that height of insolence which is intolerable to free-born spirits. I have endeavored to moderate his tyrannical choler, offering him all that which I thought might give him satisfaction; and oftentimes have I sent lovingly unto him, to understand wherein, by whom, and how he found himself to be wronged. But of him could I obtain no other answer but a mere defiance, and that in my lands he did pretend only to the right of a civil correspondency and good behavior, whereby I knew that the eternal God hath left him to the disposure of his own free will and sensual appetite—which cannot choose but be wicked, if by divine grace it be not continually guided—and to contain him within his duty, and to bring him to know himself, hath sent him hither to me by a grievous token. Therefore, my beloved son, as soon as thou canst, upon sight of these letters, repair hither with all diligence to succor not me so much, which nevertheless by natural piety thou oughtest to do, as thine own people, which by reason thou mayest save and preserve. The exploit shall be done with as little effusion of blood as may be. And, if possible, by means far more expedient, such as military policy, devices and stratagems of war, we shall save all souls and send them home as merry as crickets unto their own houses. My dear son, the peace of Jesus Christ, our Redeemer, be with thee. Salute from me Panocrates, Gymnastes, and Eudemon. The 20th of September. Thy father, Grandgousier."

CERVANTES

Don Quixote

IF DON QUIXOTE *is the world's comic masterpiece, and it is,
it becomes the clearest explanation of what must have been in
the mind of Socrates when he remarked that the genius of comedy
is the same as the genius of tragedy. For the one book by which
everybody knows Cervantes is both ludicrous and sad. It is, in
other words, truly profound: so much so, in fact, that the irony
in it has never been traced to its bottom. Its hero is a foolish old
man who sets out from home in the belief, or under the delusion,
that the world is the ideal place which romancers have described:
a place where virtue and vice will appear plainly marked, and
where the first will always, after heroic effort on the part of its
champions, be recognized as triumphant over the second. Don
Quixote's first adventure would have been sufficient evidence to
the contrary for any ordinary man. But the Don was no ordinary
man. He was a hero; which is where he suggests tragedy. He*

Don Quixote to see the world as it is. I suppose Mr. Bishop would understand that an obligation to see the world as it is might include the obligation to see it as Don Quixote sees it. Perhaps the world as it is is among other things the world that Don Quixote sees.

Bishop: I don't think that seeing the world as it is is sufficient. I think that is just the point brought out here, because, after all, we cannot see the world without forming a conception of it. The world is not merely something that is outside us; it is also something in us which we form judgments on—moral judgments above all.

Van Doren: The very act of seeing the world involves seeing it through an idea.

Bishop: Yes, and it is the relation of ideas to what we see, particularly as they affect our conduct, which is the subject of this book, as of all great books.

Barzun: But, Mr. Bishop, Don Quixote has a perfectly good inner scheme of conduct. He is interested in righting wrongs, he will not break his word, he will behave in all occasions as we would want any man to behave. Then why does he fail?

Bishop: He in one sense very conspicuously fails. Every attempt that he makes to right a wrong, every attempt that he makes to beautify the world and to make it appear to be the world that chivalry dreams of its being, is most brutally frustrated. He is beaten for nine hundred pages; he is dragged around over the Spanish desert, he is deceived, he is mocked—

Barzun: He does harm to a lot of people.

Van Doren: And actually, as so many mechanical reformers do, he brings into the world as much injustice perhaps as he ever cures.

Bishop: Yes. The point is made by Cervantes again and again. Now isn't that actually the weakness of the reformer? He sees certain things before him; he has a concept of justice, of generosity, of honor; he is particularly concerned with questions of injustice. But what does he do? He takes injustice at a particular point without seeing the surrounding circumstances, without understanding what is behind it. We get this again and again in Don Quixote, as we get it in all reformers. One can bring up a modern instance in *The Grapes of Wrath*. Steinbeck is essentially of the same race as Don Quixote. He takes up his story of the people in *The Grapes of Wrath* at the point where their own responsibility for what has happened to them is not allowed to appear. Exactly the same thing happens all the way through *Don Quixote*. The hero sees wrongs, but he doesn't inquire into them.

Van Doren: If he sees a corpse being carried to its grave, he assumes that it is a victim of men's cruelty and so starts to punish the carriers of the corpse.

Barzun: In contemporary Spain there might have been some warrant for feeling that. Doesn't the existence of a Don Quixote imply that things have got to such a pass that everything is an act of cruelty and persons are not responsible for the difficulties they get into—the convicts, for instance?

Bishop: I think it's a point of view more prevalent in our own day, with our belief in economic fatalism, which relieves the individual of responsibility for his own misfortunes.

Van Doren: Of course, Don Quixote himself is referred to in the book, not only by everyone else in it but by the author, as mad—as a man incapable of seeing the world as it should be seen.

Barzun: Still, that's no test. All the people whom we credit with great discoveries and ideas have been called mad. We have to go to a further test in order to find out those that are and those that aren't.

Van Doren: This book is especially interesting to me because it explores that situation—the situation of an excellent man being set down by the world as mad—more completely than any other book. There is a great literature of the misunderstood, of the hero who is persecuted by his inferiors. Socrates was not only persecuted but put to death by his inferiors. And so was Jesus Christ. The theme is of primary importance. It is not an accident perhaps that one of the most successful of recent motion pictures, *Mr. Deeds Goes to Town,* was the story of a man whose purity of heart and whose disinterestedness of mind and whose love of nothing at all except the truth made the whole world call him mad.

Barzun: And whose incapacity to carry out his own ideas is also present.

Van Doren: Quite right. But there is this difference between Cervantes's book and all the other books that make our best literature. In the other books the reader is left with the impression finally that the world—even if the world is represented only by himself and the author—does understand somehow or other the superiority of the hero. Now in this book we have an extra dimension added. The author himself seems to be against the hero, because at the end you remember Cervantes forces Don Quixote to recant, to say that he is sorry he ever started on his crusade. Cervantes, in other words, seems to add his vote to the otherwise universal vote of the world; the only question finally being: What is the whole and exact truth? What has Cervantes done, even if he didn't know he was doing it? What has he done to the idea, to the situation? Has he not made Don Quixote after all a great gentleman, after all a man, even if mad, who must be loved?

Bishop: That is true, but I don't know but what we are reading something into this that Cervantes did not intend. The thing that puts me off the book all the way through is that Cervantes seems not only to be deriding Don Quixote as a lunatic, at least on this particular subject of knight-errantry, but to be throwing the ideals of knight-errantry into the realm of lunacy. Throughout he has taken the point of view of the man in the street, the middle point of view. And he does represent Don Quixote as sane in other things. Yet the thing that actually makes Don Quixote superior is his very definite belief in the principles of honor, of trustworthiness, of kindness to those who cannot help themselves.

Barzun: But, Mr. Bishop, aren't you somewhat misrepresenting the point of view in the book? Sancho Panza is the man in the street, or even a little lower than that, and there is no one more devoted, more admiring toward Don Quixote than he. He really appreciates his master.

Bishop: Without quite knowing why, don't you think?

Van Doren: Well, so do we. That is the real reason for the charm of the book. We have no reason to love this man, and yet I think we love him as much as any man who ever lived.

Bishop: Yes, almost from the very beginning. But I do not feel that one can altogether love Cervantes.

Van Doren: Mr. Bishop, I find a certain inconsistency in you. You say that Don Quixote as created by Cervantes—because no one else created him—admirably illustrates the limitations of the reformer, the man who proceeds mechanically, automatically, to assume that wherever there is injustice a certain thing needs to be done about it. You seem to say that such a man would be mad, and now you berate Cervantes for calling him so. Which of course he is, because I quite agree with you that the idealist who expects to find the world ideal is mad. The world by definition would not be ideal.

Barzun: Very possibly, Mr. Van Doren. The point of the whole book is that every man who is not a Sancho Panza is mad. Don Quixote devotes himself to one object after another, and being mad devotes himself mechanically. On his deathbed he discovers that he has been wrong-headed and entirely vain.

Van Doren: And gives up.

Barzun: He gives up and becomes sane as he dies.

Van Doren: Because it is only then that he is ready for death. While he was alive he should not have given up.

Barzun: No, he is an example of something, whatever he does.

Bishop: I think you're quite right, Mr. Van Doren, in saying that I'm inconsistent. I don't see what else one can be in regard to the reformer and the idealist, because our whole attitude toward them is necessarily equivocal. That is, we must believe in certain ideals of conduct. Even on the most practical grounds one must believe in them. I was thinking, in connection with this book and also as a result of having seen *The Wookey* the other night, that one of the differences between England today and

France at the time that it fell has to do with the question of the English being able to trust each other, even though they mistrusted their government, while the French no longer were able to trust each other. Now, it is very easy to take the realistic point of view and say no man is trustworthy; but the world won't run that way.

Van Doren: Another way of saying that would be this: The world does keep on running because there are a certain number of persons, I dare say a majority, who believe in something that does not exist. Would you put it that way?

Bishop: Not if they believe in it undoubtingly.

Van Doren: I really mean that of course. I said "does not exist" ironically.

Bishop: You take the ideal of knight-errantry which Cervantes tends to ridicule. After all, that whole ideal was a literary creation. It was not created by the knights; it was created originally by the poets. And that ideal must have done an enormous amount to mitigate the natural ferocity of those who were at the top in the feudal system.

Van Doren: Would you say, as a historian, Mr. Barzun, that that is true?

Barzun: Quite true, and there is a love of playing up to any idea if strongly put forward which we see in this book. Half of the characters play up to Don Quixote and believe in what he believes, and go to great trouble to make their acts conform to his beliefs.

Van Doren: The real difference of opinion between them and him is often over the question of whether or not he is realistic. There are many who say: Well, we are very happy to think about knights, knights are an extremely good thing to think about, just as honor is a good thing to think about, but we don't agree with you that knights ever existed or could exist now. Whereas he quite madly insists that they did and do exist.

Barzun: Shouldn't we on this question also look at Sancho Panza? What about him? Is he educated through the book by the adventures that befall his master?

Van Doren: You remember once, when the two of them are brought back home to their native village through misfortune, he insists to his wife that after all he has been living a really wonderful life. He says: In spite of the fact that my master is mad, I have after all traveled, I've seen the world, I've had all sorts of things happen to me, and it's never cost me a penny.

Barzun: And he gets an island to govern. Which is a wonderful thing.

Bishop: What kind of a governor does he become?

Barzun: A very good one.

Van Doren: He settles certain matters of law very wisely.

Barzun: Yes, and his island is like everything else in the book—wonderful because it is on dry land.

Van Doren: In other words, Sancho Panza, who in the beginning is nothing but an animal, does in some sense, some peculiar sense, become humanized through his contact with a man who was trying to be more than human.

Bishop: I don't quite agree with you, Mr. Van Doren, that he's nothing but an animal, and I'll tell you why: Cervantes everywhere makes him the inheritor of accumulated folk-wisdom of the race.

Van Doren: You are referring to his proverbs?

Bishop: You perhaps will make the point that he doesn't, again like Don Quixote, know how to carry them out properly into action. Sancho Panza is personally something of a fool, just as Don Quixote is something of a lunatic. Nevertheless, what keeps Sancho Panza from being an animal or a complete fool is that he has inherited the enormous wisdom which is expressed, rather haphazardly to be true, in these proverbs, these old songs, and so on.

Van Doren: Both men are inheritors, are they not? Don Quixote has inherited a tradition of idealism.

Bishop: An upper-class tradition.

Van Doren: That's right.

Barzun: But, Mr. Bishop, the character of Sancho Panza is not so much that of a fool as that of a man who is limited. He sees perfectly well that there are windmills where Don Quixote sees giants. But windmills are commonplace; they don't interest him; in fact, all the moral problems that Don Quixote is interested in leave him cold until he sees through his master's behavior that they exist. So he is not deficient in understanding; he is deficient in imagination.

Van Doren: As Don Quixote is deficient in the inability to see the world—

Bishop: Concretely. He has an excess of the imagination. You have all kinds of contrasts in this book, of course, and that is a very interesting one: Don Quixote suffers from an excess of imagination and Sancho Panza from a deficiency of it.

Van Doren: And it is only through two men who are as wrong as these two men are, that a world so real and so wisely understood is created. Because my own final impression is that almost the whole of the world is in this book, the whole of the world as anyone will ever know it.

Barzun: The combination of the two men resembles, let us say, the combination of Sherlock Holmes and Dr. Watson—Watson, who sees nothing except what is in front of him, and Holmes who sees the solution to things that perhaps do not really exist as problems.

Bishop: That is very interesting about Holmes. Holmes sees the solution because he sees the connection between things apparent to the eye which the ordinary man doesn't see; and that is exactly what the reformer, the typical reformer if we use Don Quixote as example, does not see.

Barzun: He jumps to a false conclusion.

Van Doren: I am delighted, Mr. Barzun, that you mentioned Mr. Holmes and Dr. Watson, because in doing so you suggest how good Cervantes' instinct as a story-teller was. He hit upon perhaps the perfect formula for this kind of narrative. The formula is nothing more than the travels of two men about the world, two men who differ in the way that you suggest. Can you think of any other examples?

Bishop: I can think of one other which seems to me very

apropos, and that is *Tristram Shandy*. There you get Mr. Shandy who, like Don Quixote, has had his mind filled entirely by books; he sees the world entirely in terms of his learning. Then you've got Uncle Tobey, who's the old soldier, who has learned the world through action and through being buffeted by the world.

Van Doren: And I can think of another example: Huckleberry Finn and Tom Sawyer.

Barzun: Mutt and Jeff, as far as that goes.

Van Doren: Can you think of any examples out of literature before Cervantes? I am interested in the question whether Cervantes invented the formula. I'm almost certain that he didn't.

Barzun: I think it's an eternal formula. In Greek tragedy one thinks of Orestes who does all the thinking and doing and Pylades who carries out the suggestions of his friend.

Bishop: I wonder if Cervantes didn't get it from the stage, where the hero, who is always of the aristocracy with very highfalutin notions of action and feeling, is accompanied usually by a servant or a confidant who comes from the lower class and is much more realistic.

Barzun: From the knight and the squire. He got it from romance.

Van Doren: And of course in an author who is strictly contemporaneous with Cervantes, Shakespeare, you find Hamlet and Horatio. Again the brilliant and if you like deluded man and his commonplace friend, Horatio. I can't remember myself any really satisfactory pair out of ancient literature. There must be such a pair, but my difficulty in thinking of any such pair makes me wonder to what extent Cervantes did really here create the perfect formula, the formula which Fielding, his servant in literature, took over in *Tom Jones,* giving us Tom and Partridge.

Barzun: It is probably a feudal relationship anyhow, because Cervantes does mention Achilles and Patroclus, and though the characters of the men are different the relation is the same. Which leads me to ask you, Mr. Van Doren, do you really think that this book started or remained a literary parody of the romances?

Van Doren: I am very much interested in the opinion of J. B.

Trend, with which I recently became familiar. He says the most sensible thing I have ever heard about the legend that *Don Quixote* destroyed the literature of chivalry which Cervantes says he was writing it to destroy. The literature of chivalry in Spain ceased to be produced and reproduced at about this time, but Mr. Trend says that this might very well be because after all the whole of it was contained in *Don Quixote*. And there was a great deal more too. *Don Quixote,* curiously enough, was more romantic and remains more romantic than most of the literature of romance; the essence of chivalry is here surrounded and put in perspective by a view of the world which most romantic writers never had. That would make Cervantes for another reason a great writer. A great satirist loves his subject; paradoxically, he prefers that subject to any other, although he can discuss it in nothing except the reverse language of scorn.

Barzun: It strikes me, too, that the book belongs in Spain because Spain had had even by the time of Cervantes such a long tradition of crusade for no real practical purpose, crusade that really destroyed the country and has left it in the state in which we see it today.

Van Doren: A few years ago it lost one out of every twenty of its inhabitants in a civil war.

Barzun: And of course what Don Quixote is doing is carrying on a civil war in violation of all the laws of the realm.

Van Doren: One further question occurs to me. Is the book too long? Some of my acquaintances think it is too long. I can simply say that I didn't find it so this time.

Bishop: It is wonderfully written. The immediate success of it, like its continued success, bears that out. You're carried from one incident to another in a wonderful way, and the actual pages are those of a born writer. Cervantes, whatever his training may have been, is a born writer; you can't get around it. He manages to sustain your interest throughout, and he does not let any given episode run too long.

Van Doren: He has a perfect sense of time, of the reader's notion of time. Just as soon as the reader is beginning to find something too long, it stops.

Bishop: But it does not break down. His whole book, I think, holds together extremely well.

Barzun: Yes, but, Mr. Bishop, if he was a born writer, he must have been born late in life, because his earlier works are quite unreadable.

Van Doren: It is a very curious thing, he did in this book somehow find his element. Every writer perhaps could write a great book if he found his element; it may be only accident that permits one to do so. Most writers never become really successful because they never discover that the thing they should write about is the thing closest to themselves; they never are able to see that. Cervantes must have seen it. His writing is always joyful. He seems to relish his job.

Barzun: Yes, and his humor is in what he says by the way rather than in the slapstick incidents.

Bishop: But there is one passage which I think brings out quite clearly the weakness of Don Quixote and the whole idealistic point of view, or if you will the reformer's point of view, and that is where he breaks up the funeral procession. Remember, he runs into this funeral procession and at once decides that the corpse has been unjustly killed; and that he must avenge this wrong.

Van Doren: He decides on no evidence.

Bishop: On no evidence whatsoever. Then, after having created great havoc among the mourners, he decides to inquire, and the clergyman who is in charge tells him: "We were going to Segovia to bury the corpse of a gentleman of that town, who died a baker and lies now in yonder hearse. And who killed him, asked Dan Quixote? Heaven with a pestilential fever, answered the other. If it be so, said Don Quixote, I'm discharged of avenging his death. Since heaven did it, there is no more to be said. Had it been its pleasure to take me off so, I, too, must have submitted. I would have you informed, reverend sir, that I am a Knight of La Mancha, my name Don Quixote, my employment to visit all parts of the world in quest of adventures, to right and relieve injured innocence, and punish oppression. Truly said, replied the clergyman, I do not understand how you can call that to right and relieve men when you break their legs. You have made that crooked which was right and straight before, and heaven knows whether it can ever be set right as long as I live. Instead of relieving the injured, I fear you have injured me past relief, and while you seek adventures, you have made me meet with a very great misadventure."

VOLTAIRE

Candide

THE WHIRLWIND satirical romance which Voltaire composed in three incredible days has made it difficult ever since for any knowing person to say, with the optimists whom Voltaire so brilliantly despised, that this is the best of all possible worlds. The book was written, indeed, to render further repetition of the commonplace impossible. And if it has become so, the reason is not at all that Voltaire demonstrated its untruth. One is still free to believe what Pangloss believed; or, to make the doctrine respectable, what the great Leibnitz believed. But no one again will be free from the threat of ridicule which Voltaire's glittering pages continue to shake. This grinning prince of pamphleteers did not argue the doctrine down; he laughed it away, and the laughter has not ceased. Voltaire's method was so simple as to be absurd. He threw his hero into such a series of misadventures, he filled the world with such a fantastic heap of stupidities and

*cruelties, that the imagination of any reader must stagger and col-
lapse. This, the book says without pausing to take breath, is your
"best" world; like it if you can. An answer, if one cares to make it,
is that nevertheless there is no better world; bad as this one is, it
is the only one, and doubtless therefore the necessary one. But
one does not care to answer thus. For the response would surely
be a cackling so loud from Voltaire's ghost that words henceforth
must seem to lose their efficacy. Whatever the truth of the matter
is, the brilliance of this little book remains indisputable. It is satire
at its diabolical best.*

*François Marie Arouet de Voltaire, French philosopher, was
the son of a Paris notary. Young Voltaire (he himself added the
"de Voltaire" to his original name) early evinced the facility at
caustic satire which was to send him to the Bastille for a year and
ultimately into permanent exile. His stay of more than two years
in England resulted in the* Letters Concerning the English Nation
(1734, later published as Lettres Philosophiques*), which was
banned in France for its attack on French institutions. Voltaire
lived at Cirey, 1734-49, with Mme. du Châtelet, made a two-year
visit to Frederick the Great (terminated by a quarrel), and from
1758 lived at Ferney near Geneva. His works include the dramas*
Zaire *(1732) and* Mérope *(1743); a history of Charles XII of
Sweden;* La Pucelle, *a satire, offensive to many, on the Joan of Arc
legends; a treatise on tolerance (1763); and the satirical romances*
Zadig *(1747) and* Candide *(1759).*

Fiction

IRWIN EDMAN · ANDRÉ MAUROIS · MARK VAN DOREN

Van Doren: Candide seemed to me upon this reading to be especially interesting because the events of our own time had provided a background for its crazy events such as I had never thought possible. It is a story which tries to disprove the proposition that this is the best of all possible worlds, and the way it proceeds is simple enough. It gives you a set of adventurers for its hero and its heroine which would seem to indicate that this is the worst of all possible worlds. The world we live in is, to say the least of it, disagreeable. Does it seem to you, Mr. Maurois, that the book is especially applicable to our predicament?

Maurois: Yes. And it seems to me a very healthy book to read today, because it gives one the impression that what we are going through is, after all, what men have been through always.

Van Doren: The book seems healthy, then if, only because it encourages you not to think too hopelessly about contemporary events?

Maurois: Exactly. It is a pessimistic book in a way because, of course, it implies that all men are mad, cruel, cheats, liars, and so on; but it is encouraging too because it proves that even amid all this cruelty you can find the possibility of working and cultivating your garden, as Candide says.

Van Doren: Well, Mr. Edman, did it strike you as pessimistic or as optimistic? What was the tone of the book as you encountered it this past week?

Edman: I was very much struck, in rereading *Candide* by neither its optimism nor its pessimism, but by the serene gaiety of it. Voltaire seems to be trying to prove this is the worst of all possible worlds and that anyone is an idiot who insists it is the best of all possible worlds. And he gives his hero and heroine, and practically everyone in the book, all the worst possible disasters. But at the end he suggests that for reasonable people, even in this infinitely bad world, you can at least cultivate your garden and so avoid either boredom or anguish. That isn't altogether pessimistic, really, is it?

Van Doren: No, it isn't. I suppose the thing that would most surprise anyone who had merely heard about the book is the very gaiety of which you speak. Of all books it is surely one of the most abounding in its vitality. The most dreadful things are described as happening to the hero and the heroine and their friends, and yet somehow those blows of fate seem to glance off of them, and they continue able to talk and able to reason and able to amuse themselves.

Maurois: To think that this book, which is so gay, as you say, was written by a man who was sixty-five at the time!

Van Doren: Perhaps that is an encouraging thought.

Maurois: It contains the philosophy of an old man.

Van Doren: I should say it was the book of an old man because it seems never to blink at a reality.

Edman: Not only does it not blink at realities; it goes out of its way to think up every conceivable kind of disaster that could possibly happen to anyone. Leibnitz may have been wrong in saying that this is the best of all possible worlds, but statistically the chances that all these dreadful things could happen to any one person are pretty small.

Maurois: Well, they were pretty small up to two years ago.

Edman: Mr. Maurois, I am interested to have you suggest that. In the Bulgarian War, where all sorts of atrocities emerged, Voltaire thought he was thinking up things just about as bad as could have been imagined, but he's really an amateur now; we've had much better work in boorishness and brutality since.

Van Doren: I wonder, Mr. Edman, if right there a question couldn't be asked about the pessimism or optimism of the book. One reason perhaps—this is a rather discouraging thought—one reason that Voltaire is able to be so gay about these calamities and about these brutalities is that he seems able to imagine some corner in the world where they could be escaped. At the end, as you have said, all of our people have found a garden in the east where they can settle down and raise their vegetables and do their spinning and weaving and what not and eat the nice food that Cunegonde cooks for them, in the assurance that somehow or other nothing more is going to happen to them. In this one place, at any rate, they are safe, and they can say: Well, no matter what this government or that government is doing, no matter what Bulgaria or Turkey or England or France or Germany is doing, we are going to be safe here. The rather disquieting question occurs to me whether any such corner of the world, any such garden, is now conceivable.

Maurois: Of course that was Voltaire's impression, because he himself had such a garden at Ferney where he couldn't be reached by the French King or by anyone.

Van Doren: Why couldn't he?

Maurois: Because he was outside the limits of France, you see. He said that he had three frontiers around his château, so that if anyone was after him, he could always in one jump be in another country.

Van Doren: But I am again disquieted by the thought that it is extremely difficult to imagine any such point of vantage now; to be sure, one might live on the border of one country in which dreadful things were going on, but equally dreadful things either are going on in all the neighboring countries or are about to begin there.

Edman: That last single phrase suggested to me a curious thing. We have been pressed by the universal disaster in the world, in which we're all involved, to the understanding that you can't cultivate your own garden, or even have a garden, unless you begin seriously to think about the possible garden of the whole world. It seems to me one might almost extend Voltaire's phrase and say that you've got to cultivate the garden of the world to make private gardens possible. Moral isolationism, as Mr. Van Doren points out, is really impossible. It struck me as ironic while Mr. Van Doren was speaking just a moment ago that perhaps there is a kind of symbolism in the fact that Switzerland has been maintained for generations in Europe as a kind of refuge and garden for the world. It too is now closed. I don't imagine Voltaire in Switzerland today could have been very happy; after all, he would have heard the news every day over the radio.

Van Doren: If Switzerland is a garden, it's a rock garden, isn't it?

Maurois: I suppose there is one garden we can still cultivate. It is an inner garden; the kingdom of God is within us.

Van Doren: That is what Mr. Edman was suggesting, perhaps, when he suggested that the garden is not a geographical but a philosophical place.

Edman: I really meant two things. One of the things people used to retreat to we were calling a few years ago the ivory tower, which has badly crashed of late. One of the things people thought was that you could retire to an inner solitude and fortress, and in bad times philosophers, especially stoics, have always done that. But I think also that Voltaire himself didn't quite mean that cultivating one's private garden is enough. He never would have written this book, so savagely, if gaily, attacking the stupidities and cruelties of the world, if he hadn't had the kind of hope which in our generation H. G. Wells has had, for instance: the hope that through a kind of sensible reasonableness you can make a world like that Eldorado where his hero finds himself for a short time.

Van Doren: On the other hand, does it strike you that he believes there is sufficient reason in man to make us count upon any particular philosophical proposition ever being able to prove itself? I get the impression, and I think Mr. Maurois has that impression, too, that Voltaire finds the world to be largely inhabited by madmen; the belief that some generalizer may be comfortable and pleasant to have, but at best it has very little bearing on what is actually going to occur.

Maurois: At one moment Candide asked Martin the other

philosopher: "Do you think that men have always been and will always be liars, cheats, weak, cowardly, bloody, back-biting, fanatical, hypocritical, and silly?" "Do you not think," answers Martin, "that hawks have always eaten the pigeons they came across?" The answer to this would be a League of Pigeons.

Van Doren: You think they might be able to keep the hawks away?

Maurois: It might be possible.

Van Doren: And that that was in Voltaire's mind?

Maurois: I think so. Voltaire was not always very consistent, because if he had accepted the philosophy of *Candide* altogether, then why fight as he did? Why take all this trouble about the trial of Calas, or about those other men who were wrongly accused? After all, he knew nothing about them, but all the same he fought for them. And that means that he believed that one could fight for them and that it was useful to do it.

Van Doren: I have no doubt that he personally lived the life which would imply such a belief. In this book, however, he strikes me as being very restless and very impatient with propositions in general. He is so acutely aware—and this might be because he is an old man—that any one thing that can be said describing the world is possibly wrong, because something immediately will happen in the world to disprove it, or at any rate to make it ridiculous.

Edman: There is just one proposition he himself seems to subscribe to, though, one general principle: that somehow what is wrong with the world is due to the madness, cruelty, deceit, lust, villainies of men, but that somehow men could be reasonable and that there is a possible general reasonableness in men. As a matter of fact, isn't that the point of his hero's brief vacation from villainies and so on in the land of Eldorado?

Van Doren: Now what do you think about that utopia in the mountains which is so inaccessible and so extremely difficult to leave? In this book Voltaire seems to be making fun of almost everything under the sun. Is he also making fun of utopias? Eldorado is a perfectly typical utopia, is it not? It is a place where there are no lawyers because people do not hate one another, where there are no doctors because people live rationally and eat rationally, and where there are no priests to ask that one another be burned because the people have a rational religion—a sort of deist's religion. Does it strike you that the very perfection of his statement there suggests parody?

Edman: Well, at the same time that he is satirizing the corruptions of European civilization by pointing out this perfect and reasonable society of Eldorado, it struck me as very interesting that when his hero is warned that if he leaves it will be extremely difficult to get out, and that if he goes back to Europe it will be much worse, he recognizes the difficulty, and recognizes the corruption of Europe, yet goes back nonetheless.

Maurois: Voltaire tells you that man can choose between the convulsions of anxiety and the lethargy of boredom. Probably he was bored in Eldorado.

Edman: To that extent it is a parody. You have a feeling that Voltaire, if he got a perfectly reasonable society, would miss the amusing absurdities of human beings as well as their cruel ones. But one point I'd like to raise is this: The book seems to me, gay and instructive about human folly as it is, to do one thing that I found extremely annoying. It is supposed to be, among other things, a satire on philosophy, and if you read just this book and no other book about philosophy, you would quite properly get the impression that philosophers were systematic idiots, that they simply tried to organize optimism into a foolish kind of logic. Now, I think it ought to be pointed out to anybody reading the book, or to any of us rereading it, that this was after all just one kind of philosophy that was epidemic in Voltaire's time, a philosophy of optimism and a philosophy that insisted that everything that happened was the effect of a cause just as every cause has an effect; no matter what happened, it all added up to something perfectly reasonable in the sense of being attractive and good.

Van Doren: Attractive and good because necessary.

Edman: Because necessary. Just because things happened in a certain order, they somehow were good. Now, philosophers say many foolish things. Voltaire himself in another book says: "In metaphysics there are two kinds of things. The first kind is what everybody knows and the second kind is what nobody will ever know." He apparently regarded metaphysicians as moving in a kind of foolish fog. Obviously Voltaire had a philosophy himself, and I was wondering what Mr. Maurois, for example, would say it was.

Maurois: I think you can say he had one philosophy. He liked to explain things; and he believed that things were true when they were perfectly intelligible, which is after all not true in itself, for it is just as absurd as Leibnitz's contention that all is for the best in this best of all possible worlds. I had a master of philosophy who said: "All general ideas are false and this is a general idea." This applies to Voltaire. The old Empress Eugénie used to say: "Oh, Voltaire, I'll never forgive him; this man makes me understand things I shall never understand!"

Van Doren: Yes, Voltaire has the theory that you can live without theorizing. You remember that at the end Martin says: "Very well, let us sit down here in our gardens and cultivate them and live without theorizing." To me that is a theory in itself. Martin says that only life without theorizing is endurable. But you can offer the proposition also that life without theorizing would be unendurable.

Maurois: Yes, and he wrote, after all, the *Dictionnaire Philosophique,* which is nothing but theorizing.

Van Doren: He was constantly acting as if one thing were more important than another, wasn't he? He was very much engaged in controversies; he could be outraged by an act of injustice.

Edman: You might almost say that Voltaire's complaint about the world was, despite his satire on one kind of philosophy, that people weren't philosophical enough; if they only learned what the principles of an ordered society and an ordered life were, they would get rid of all these lusts and superstitions and cruelties. It seems to me everything Voltaire attacked, he attacked not so much because it was cruel or because it destroyed human life or human feeling and paralyzed people, but because it reminded him that there was so much needless and gratuitous stupidity in the world which could be cured by reason.

Maurois: I think that is quite true. And I think that *Candide* is just a mood; it was written in three days. Well, during these three days, Voltaire was like that; he was impressed by the stupidity of the world.

Van Doren: No one can object to his proposition that a philosopher is to be honored only if he is proved to be a man who knows the world. After all, no one wants philosophy, does he, from someone who is ignorant of the world—innocent, in the bad sense of the word? Would you agree with that?

Edman: I would agree with that, and I think his objection to Pangloss proves it; whenever there is an earthquake it is perfectly good, and whenever anybody is shipwrecked it is perfectly fine—in the long run. What he is complaining about is not that Pangloss is a philosopher but that he is a foolish man.

Van Doren: Put it this way—he is a bad philosopher. This is a satire upon bad philosophy, not upon philosophy. Incidentally, can the book be said to disprove anything? It certainly makes so much fun of those who say all is for the best in this best of all possible worlds that I should think anyone now would be ashamed to say it, but would he necessarily have to proceed to the belief that the proposition was untrue? For instance, what could be made now of Leibnitz's proposition? Leibnitz was a great man, wasn't he?

Edman: Oh, yes, he was a great system maker and he had a very clear head; given his assumptions, he was probably as clear-headed a philosopher as ever lived.

Van Doren: Would you say then that Voltaire either had misunderstood the proposition or was being somehow unfair in his ridicule of it? What about the proposition? Can it be supported?

Edman: The proposition that this is the best of all possible worlds, considered in a context very different from that of the rather vulgar optimism which Voltaire satirizes could be maintained. Given the possibility out of which this present world came, it couldn't be any better. Given those conditions, that is, we have done as well as we could do—it came out this way. That is quite different from saying it's the ideal world, the one we would have preferred; it's just the best one possible.

Van Doren: Yes, or put it this way: It is the only actual world. Many other worlds perhaps had been possible, but this is the only world that we have, and to say that you would want some other world would be to say that you would have no world at all.

Maurois: It is not the best of possible worlds, but what does it matter? It is the one we have and we've got to live in it.

Edman: It is a poor thing, but our own.

Van Doren: One way of understanding the proposition and what it might mean is to ask yourself whether, if you had the power to alter the past—let's say the past which has produced the present—if you had the power to erase Napoleon out of it, or Cromwell, or Shakespeare, or Plato—someone that you either liked or disliked—whether you would accept that responsibility and produce a world which couldn't exist at all, because no world would be imaginable which did not contain the past that we know.

Maurois: Well, a book was published at one time—it was called "If"—which asked us to imagine that certain great events had been different. Each event was represented as entirely different, and yet it wasn't necessarily better. I mean, man would have been the same.

Van Doren: That's the question. If the world were different from what it is now, wouldn't it be either just as bad, or would it be in some curious way the same after all?

Maurois: The same, probably.

Edman: I seem to remember, Mr. Maurois, an old French expression: The more it changes, the more it remains the same thing. That's exactly what Voltaire was trying to prove, it seems to me. As a matter of fact, without being too—as we say in this country—Pollyanna, I think one can find in any situation a disastrous train of events that led up to something very pleasant. The fall of France gave me a chance to talk with you and Mr. Van Doren this morning. Now you could make a whole philosophy out of that.

Maurois: Would it be worth while?

Edman: Possibly not, I admit; but if we had changed one thing, maybe we would have made a totally different world in which we would have had the fall of everything in the universe. We can't tell, and I think the only point is that given this world, this is what you have; and to guess what another world might have been is pure speculation. This is the actual world.

Van Doren: And of course given the world that we have, we have a world in which there are all sorts of good people lamenting evil and doing all they can to remove it. After all, the world which we do have, which was necessary perhaps in a sense that it is the only actual one, is a world which contains men who want to fight evil. After all, the optimism of Leibnitz does not need to be the complacency of the idiot whom Voltaire is satirizing, does it? The complacent man merely says: "Very well, we must sit back and let things be as they are." But things are as they are only because there are all sorts of people competing with one another to prevail.

Edman: Mr. Van Doren, you took the word "complacency" out of my mouth. I was going to say that what Voltaire is objecting to, and what he is making so absurd, is that in the face of a great many evils, some of which people couldn't change, there are people who quietly sit about insisting that this is all for the best and therefore don't try to improve it. Don't you think that's true?

Van Doren: Yes. And those are the persons he most despises.

Maurois: Let us cultivate our gardens means, let us start from the world as it is and try to improve it.

Edman: And perhaps make a garden of the whole world, instead of some little corner of Turkey where we happen to be shipwrecked.

Van Doren: In other words, it isn't the Epicurean garden, strictly speaking. It is not a garden into which one merely retires.

Maurois: What Voltaire did himself at Ferney was to try to make happy the small colony of people he had around him. He had 300 or 400 workmen; he found work for them and really made his little kingdom very happy.

Edman: The garden that was a kingdom, in other words. He was trying in a sense to make it a little Eldorado.

Van Doren: And he was very active there. The gaiety of the book has been mentioned a number of times; I want to come back to it for a moment. We must recognize how difficult it is to communicate a sense of it to anyone who has not read it. What one does as one reads the book is rather regularly to laugh, is it not? And what is it that one laughs at? Isn't it the suddenness and brilliance with which things are accomplished? The book moves at almost incredible speed.

Maurois: Yes, its tempo is wonderful.

Edman: Voltaire is constantly making points that you've realized almost before he's made them. And, incidentally, he maintains a running, swift satire at lots of incidental things, such as pretentious literary criticism, such as pretentious officialdom. He satirizes all the ways in which people have failed to be reasonable. At the end there is perhaps just a little note of despair, for in a world that's so full of absurdity he thinks the only thing you can be certain of is your own garden and its cultivation. The book closes, do you remember, on a little sermon almost, a moral, which I should like to read:

"I also know," said Candide, "that we should cultivate our gardens." "You are right," said Pangloss, "for, when man was placed in the Garden of Eden, he was placed there to dress it and to keep it; which proves that man was not born for idleness." "Let us work without theorizing," said Martin; " 'tis the only way to make life endurable." The whole small fraternity entered into this praiseworthy plan, and each started to make use of his talents. The little farm yielded well. Cunegonde was indeed very ugly, but she became an excellent pastry-cook; Paquette embroidered; the old woman took care of the linen. Even Friar Giroflée performed some service; he was a very good carpenter and even became a man of honor; and Pangloss sometimes said to Candide: "All events are linked up in this best of all possible worlds; for, if you had not been expelled from the noble castle, by hard kicks in your backside for love of Mademoiselle Cunegonde, if you had not been clapped into the Inquisition, if you had not wandered about America on foot, if you had not stuck your sword in the Baron, if you had not lost all your sheep from the land of Eldorado, you would not be eating candied citrons and pistachios here." " 'Tis well said," replied Candide, "but we must cultivate our gardens."

(1707-1754)

HENRY FIELDING

Tom Jones

THE EMINENCE among novels which Tom Jones *continues to enjoy is explained by other things than the interest of its theme and the superb skill of its narrative. The identity of a foundling is something which can arouse any reader's curiosity; and all readers of Fielding's masterpiece recognize the artistry with which their curiosity is coaxed to sustain itself through hundreds of pages. But more than that is entertaining them as they proceed. For they are in the company of a huge and human spirit. The way Fielding writes his book is fully as important as the story he has to tell. His is an amply ventilated mind, miraculously free from meanness of any kind, and dedicated always to the praise of generosity, good nature, honor, love.* Tom Jones *has many imperfections, and some of his misdeeds continue in our day to shock the unwary reader. But Tom is readier than such a reader to pass the appropriate judgment; and he is likelier to benefit from the*

*experience of error. For his heart is always right, as we are sure
that Fielding's is. Neither, in other words, remotely resembles a
prig; though both are inveterately moral. Fielding leaves behind
him the strongest impression of moral and intellectual health at
the same time that he neglects no accent or aspect of reality. The
conversation of Squire Western is as veritable as that of Fallstaff,
and he himself is accepted by Fielding with no desire that he
change himself from the obstinate old boor he is. Fielding perfectly reports the world that is without ceasing to suggest the one
it might be. He is both Olympian and witty: the rarest of com-
binations, and perhaps the most attractive.*

*Henry Fielding, English novelist and dramatist, was trained
for the law. He was admitted to the bar in 1740 and in 1748 was
appointed justice of the peace for Westminster. Before his legal
career began he had produced twenty-eight comedies, farces, and
burlesques. His first novel,* Joseph Andrews *(1743), began as a
burlesque of Richardson's* Pamela, *but assumed a career and a
comedy of its own. After his masterpiece (1748), he wrote*
Amelia *(1751) and the posthumously published* Journal of a
Voyage to London. Jonathan Wild *appeared in Fielding's* Mis-
cellanies *of 1743. Fielding died at Lisbon, where he had gone in
search of health.*

Fiction

KATHERINE ANNE PORTER · ALLEN TATE · MARK VAN DOREN

Van Doren: Fielding had a great rival in the eighteenth century among novelists, and that was Samuel Richardson, whose works, *Pamela, Clarissa* and *Sir Charles Grandison,* he despised. Many persons have been in the habit of supposing that he was right in so despising them. Nevertheless, I was interested the other day to encounter in a British literary journal the remark, very casually made, that the fiction of our time tends to be Richardsonian rathen than Fieldingesque. Does it seem to you that this is true, Miss Porter?

Porter: Yes, I do, but the work of Fielding in the picturesque novel is almost a freak. There are only about half a dozen really celebrated examples of the type in the world, and they are scattered over almost as many countries. It has almost no tradition, no descendants; it is like a company of illegitimate brothers.

Van Doren: You seem to indicate that it is easier to write a Richardsonian novel than a Fieldingesque novel—easier, that is, to write a novel which is subtle and interested in the refinements of sex than to furnish broad, outdoor fare like *Tom Jones.* Do you think it is?

Tate: I think, Mr. Van Doren, it is possibly easier to write a novel in the Richardson tradition than it is to write one in the comic tradition that Fielding seems to think he invented. But at the same time I think it is much more difficult to write a great novel in the Richardson tradition than it is to write a comic novel. In other words, the really great novels of the world are much nearer to Richardson than they are to Fielding. I don't mean to say that I don't admire Fielding tremendously, but I do feel that

[194]

Fielding: Tom Jones

the greatest novels, like *The Brothers Karamazov* or *Madame Bovary,* would be closer to Richardson.

Van Doren: Perhaps this means no more than that the comic genius, as we shall inquire whether Fielding is one, is almost the rarest of men.

Tate: Take a late nineteenth-century novelist like George Meredith, who described himself as a writer in the comic tradition. Yet the vigor that Fielding had is lost and the pure comedy tends to go off into painstaking analysis of motive, and intricate feeling for human relations, which Fielding lacks.

Van Doren: Meredith is subtle, whereas the sort of comedy we associate with Fielding is the sort that doesn't seem to be aware of subtle distinctions between human characters and human feelings.

Porter: If he stopped to make subtle distinctions in human feelings, then his characters could never behave as they do. They wouldn't be what they are if there were any subtle distinctions or any fine shades of feeling in their minds or their emotions. They couldn't, they wouldn't do what they do, because they would not be what they are.

Tate: Miss Porter, couldn't we say something like this, that Fielding's realism—that is, realism in the sense that realism is supposed to convey the more brutal aspects of life, and to communicate an ordinary impression of reality—has to be limited because of the demands of the picaresque plot? It's all got to work out in the end so that Tom gets Sophia and Squire Western is satisfied, so that if there were too much analysis of motive in the course of the story the plot might be wrecked. All has to be subordinated to this great sweep of action which leads toward the conclusion.

Porter: Yes, it is first of all a novel of action, and that is the important thing about *Tom Jones;* it is most marvelously made; it is perfectly constructed. Everything happens just as it should, and the author keeps also the loose air of accident, as if these creatures were all the creatures of fate; whereas of course they are his own creatures and he sees them as children. They all get to the inn at

Upton, you remember, at precisely the right time, you might say, for everything to go wrong, and they're all thrown out into the road again, by the maddest but most necessary logic, in order that the plot may succeed. It's a perfect plot, and that is, I think, the beauty of the book; it is a very rare thing.

Van Doren: Of course it is rare.

Porter: It is all very gay, outdoor, hardy, full of action, and of perfect construction.

Van Doren: It is an especially rare thing, is it not, in a picaresque novel? I suggest by "picaresque" not much more than incessant travel—the hero always on the move, tramping from one town, one inn, to another. It is unusual to find a picaresque novel which has an intensely ordered plot. Spanish, French, and English novels of the sort tend to be really loose in their structure.

Tate: Well, *Don Quixote* is not so well constructed as *Tom Jones*. But it's a much richer book; there's a great deal more in it. And it doesn't have the symmetrical plot that this novel has.

Van Doren: I am glad that you mentioned *Don Quixote,* because Fielding himself would be sorry if we had not mentioned his literary hero. He is always paying homage to him as to a master. He must have taken from Cervantes, too, one of the simplest and yet one of the finest formulas for the novel of adventure, that is to say, the travels of two men through the world. Just as Cervantes has his Don Quixote and his Sancho Panza, so we have here Tom and Partridge, and so Mark Twain had his Huckleberry Finn and his Tom Sawyer. It is a great formula, although an extremely simple one.

Tate: It is one that will work all the time. It's foolproof. It's good in any age.

Van Doren: Foolproof if you take the trouble to distinguish between the two men. One is usually of a different social station from that of the other, and one is usually more intelligent than the other—or at any rate his intelligence works in a different way.

Porter: One is also supposed to be of superior morals to the other, but that is not true of this book. That is where Fielding makes his own contribution.

Tate: I was going to say, Miss Porter, that it is one of the few subtle distinctions of character which we find in *Tom Jones*—the difference between Tom and Partridge, his Sancho Panza. Partridge, of course, comes from an inferior social station, but at the same time, Tom is an illegitimate child. Their social relations are complex. Partridge has his Latin and he also has his superstition. Tom has his weaknesses of character. The distinction is rather subtly drawn, and I don't believe it is possible for novelists to make that kind of distinction today, because it was based on some reality in the social organization of eighteenth-century England.

Van Doren: Tom is also inferior to Partridge on one level: intelligence, or at least education. Partridge read. Tom didn't read because Tom was an English barbarian, to use Matthew Arnold's term. He was too proud to read, too proud to have ideas.

Tate: At the same time, Tom quotes a little Latin occasionally. And it has a sort of aptness. Partridge has only a few tags from Virgil like *"Jubes renovare dolorem,"* and occasionally Tom's education is sufficient to remind Partridge that what he says doesn't fit. Now I'd like to ask Miss Porter a question. How much realism is there in Fielding? As we know, Fielding began to write *Joseph Andrews* in order to show up Richardson, to prove that Richardson was all wrong in his delineation of human nature. To what extent do you think that even *Tom Jones* still shows the effects of an almost polemical spirit? I think it does to some extent. That was the fashion in fiction at the time, because Fielding was very, very conscious of the fact that he was likely to be unfashionable, that people wouldn't like him.

Porter: When you said realism, my mind went off on an entirely different track. Fielding in this book, it seems to me, is very determinedly combating something, something that he hated and which was popular in his time. He himself was often detested. I believe this book was published serially; four times in the course of the story you realize that parts of it have already appeared, and the critics have all snapped him up again. He goes into four different fits of anger against critics, just as he regularly attacks the style of fiction popular in his time, without mentioning any names. He defends his hero, and all of his characters, as being much more near to real life than the characters of fiction then popular, and perhaps they were nearer to the life that Fielding knew. We have to realize that Fielding was the only member of the nobility, you might say, who was also a man of letters. He was a cousin of the Duke of Kingston, father of Lady Wortley Montagu, and that was the world he really knew. He lived in a society of extraordinarily cynical worldliness, intelligence, and wit, and of extraordinarily bad behavior. That was an extremely tough and hardy-spirited age in all classes, but the nobility were perhaps the toughest of all.

Van Doren: His moral argument against Richardson comes down to his disbelief that a single act by a person proves him good or bad. Richardson's novels are all based upon the theory that one act must not be committed by the heroine, one thing must not happen to her. Of course the century was all agog over the thousands of pages during which the temptations of the heroine were described. Fielding very roughly brushed that aside and said: "Nonsense, a person is good not in terms of a single thing he does, but in terms of his nature, in terms of his heart, in terms of the sort of person he generally is." That is why he was so willing to let Tom do all sorts of bad things if Tom had a good heart—which Fielding kept on insisting he had.

Porter: Which I doubt to the end.

Tate: I, too, can imagine a sequel to *Tom Jones* in which Tom and Sophia reach the age of forty and Tom will become very much like Sophia's father, swearing every other breath, and using metaphors from the field in discussing affairs of love; and I can imagine Sophia becoming more and more like her aunt, Mistress Western, and using a very rich vocabulary. I agree with you, Miss Porter, that in some fundamental sense, both Tom and Sophia tend to be incredible.

Van Doren: Well, Mr. Tate, what would be the future of Clarissa if Clarissa had lived? It is rather difficult, isn't it, to imagine the futures of persons in fiction?

Tate: Yes. You can't imagine any future for Clarissa. I can't see it.

Van Doren: I would say then that Fielding was more real than Richardson, because at least you can imagine a commonplace future for his hero and heroine. Those other persons cannot be imagined as living at all outside of the very subtle brain of Richardson himself, which created them.

Porter: Richardson probably realized that there was no future for his heroine and so there was nothing to speculate about. Her natural end was death in the last chapter, or whenever it occurred. But it is true, I find that there really is a future for Tom and Sophia because of their strong family relationship, their strong family resemblance to their parents, and also to the world in which they lived, to that society which produced them. By these signs you can see really very clearly what they will be, miracles barred, and there aren't any miracles in this kind of book.

Van Doren: No, Fielding would not have been aghast at all, I think, if he heard us say that Tom and Sophia would settle down to be ordinary people. On the whole, I assume, he thought it extremely important that the world continue to be populated by their kind of people. He does, after all, have the comic view of life, which means, I think, that he wants life to keep its center; the tendency of such a mind is always to draw persons back from the extremes, and he would be more content to live in a commonplace world than he would in a world of geniuses, even though he himself were a genius. Now that doesn't mean that he himself has a commonplace mind. He does here one of the most extraordinarily difficult things, it seems to me, for any novelist. He gives you the adventures of a dozen people very simply, indeed very roughly, and he seems to take no account of the subtle distinctions of character and feeling of which, as you know, capital is made in our time, yet nowhere in his book do you lose the sense that he is a wise man. He knows a great deal more than he mentions. He understands a great deal more than he explains.

Porter: He is an extraordinarily worldly wise man, too. He had worldly wisdom to a degree that almost no author had at the time, and also he had a very fine moral sense. He reveals himself as a very good moralist in his own private beliefs. I think he wrote this book with his tongue in his cheek. He gets in quite a nice number of very improving little sermons, and he makes them witty, so that you read them in perfect good humor and agree with him, you know. That is very adroit.

Tate: I agree with you, Miss Porter, but I think that on the whole some of the minor characters tend to be more credible than the main characters. For example, Lady Bellaston, though we don't see a great deal of her. The fortunes of Squire Western's sister, Mistress Western, are not of primary concern in the novel. You get a character like Mrs. Waters, who is important to the mechanics of the plot but not as a character in the novel. All these people seem to me to be extremely real, to have a reality which convinces me much more completely than the reality of Sophia or Tom, and I think it is simply because we get only glimpses of them. We see them in situations in which they behave as we expect such people to behave, and we don't have to see them extricate themselves from impossible situations; they tend to remain fixed in their possible situations. The people who have to be extricated are Tom and Sophia, and the way in which they are extricated is not credible. It seems to me that the Richardson tradition, which is more realistic psychologically, tended to produce a tradition in the novel which was more useful because it could be continued. The plot doesn't dominate; character dominates.

Porter: That is quite true, but this, I think, was never Fielding's intention. After all, it is a different kind of thing and has a different end in view. He was writing something meant to be amusing; you're right, he pulls his two main characters about in some improbable situations in order to get them out of the predicament they are in. I do think that his minor characters are the most realistic, most interesting, and the most amusing, and besides, the book is so charmingly and uproariously funny. Do you remember that free-for-all fight in the kitchen at the inn? Everybody gets into it sooner or later, just everybody joins in for his own reasons. That strikes me as quite marvelous comedy; it could be played on a stage. It seems to me it ought at least to be made into a moving picture. But don't you think he really meant to write a comic book, something amusing, and let the moral implications fall where they might?

Tate: Oh, very much so. Yet he says in his preface that he had some moral improvement in view.

Van Doren: Yes, but he says in his dedication to George Littleton, whom, by the way, Lord Chesterfield described as the "awkwardest man" in England, that it is easier to make good men wise than it is to make bad men good. He makes an effort in this book to show that Blifil, for instance, couldn't ever have been made good. Blifil had a small and mean heart to begin with, but Tom or anyone else who was naturally good might become wise. Now, Fielding goes on to say that the only thing that can make good men wise is laughter, which is why he has written a comic book. I don't think that is the real reason. The real reason is that he was that sort of man.

Porter: He wanted to write a comic book.

Van Doren: I wonder what we mean by comic in this case, if it's anything more than a certain distance at which he stands from all of his persons and all of their actions. There is a condescension in Fielding even toward his hero and heroine, whom he admires and adores. There is nothing to which he cannot condescend.

Tate: He never tries to establish them as great people, as characters of great proportions.

Van Doren: But the spirit in which he puts them down is in itself affectionate, and finally very powerful. The general effect of this book, I think, is that even though the author seems to be smiling at everybody in it, he does love some and hate others. And the result is that we somehow find life to be quite good as we read along, because a man who is so sure of his attitude, so sure of his ethics, so sure of his own soundness of position, can afford to smile even at heroes and heroines.

Porter: I reread the book after a good many years, and I found it a very gay and happy kind of book to read, really, where once I had found it a little dull, perhaps, or even a little crude. But I saw then a different thing from what I see now. This time I saw only the extraordinary health and gaiety, the perfectly irresponsible comic attitude toward life which after all we have lost; it's refreshing to find it again in the record of human life. Besides, Fielding lived comfortably in his society. He never quarreled with the politics of his country; he enjoyed all the prejudices, you know, of his time; he was a completely loyal Englishman.

Van Doren: Like Shakespeare, for instance.

Porter: He was perfectly unself-conscious.

Van Doren: In other words, he had that sense of security without which you cannot laugh.

Porter: Every kind of security.

Tate: He had moral security, which seems to me to be the main thing. I should think that while tragedy at its best is much more important than comedy, much greater, having a wider dimension of life, it takes a greater degree of maturity to appreciate comedy. When I was a boy I couldn't have read Fielding at all. I tried to and I was bored by him, but at the same time, when I was very young, I was trying to read the most serious novels.

Van Doren: I don't agree, Mr. Tate, that tragedy is more important or comprehensive than comedy. It seems to me that they are precisely equal in their range. Comedy is rarer than tragedy, although both at the top are very rare.

Tate: But wouldn't you agree that Shakespearian tragedy includes comedy also?

Van Doren: Yes, but the comic view does not dominate, say, *Hamlet,* whereas the comic view does dominate the plays in which Falstaff appears. Both comedy and tragedy require a great wisdom, and I should add also a great sense of security in the author. We get successful tragedy only in an age which knows what it thinks, and likewise we get successful comedy only in an age which knows what it thinks.

Tate: I'm not so sure that I'd agree with you, Mr. Van Doren.

I don't think Shakespeare's age knew what it thought as clearly as Fielding's did.

Van Doren: It knew what man could be. At least Shakespeare had a very clear idea of the utmost human capacities. His tragic heroes are always trying to go beyond their capacities.

Tate: I was thinking of the comedy of humor of which Fielding would be a late example. That is, the kind of comedy in which each character tends to represent what we would call some particular trait, which they called a "humor." Squire Western's humor is choleric. Squire Allworthy has only one humor, which is benevolent.

Porter: Squire Western has anger, and then he has a roaring drunken humor, I mean his own kind of humor that isn't funny to anybody else.

Tate: Shakespeare's characters are a little bit more complicated.

Van Doren: I wasn't thinking of Fielding as a comic genius in terms of the various kinds of humor you get in him. I was thinking of himself as the center of this comedy; of his attitude toward everything.

Tate: Fielding as a man participates in his works to a much greater degree than most novelists do, much more than Richardson does, for example. Yes, that is why his style is so important.

Van Doren: The style of this book is one of its essential things.

Tate: Very much so. The style is like a man walking a tight rope. If he slips once the whole thing collapses. But he never slips. It has this beautiful tone, the same bright level, and he never deviates.

Porter: But the two things the book has are style and plot. And they really are both perfect. But about the comedy. It is quite true almost any real comedy with just a half-turn could become tragedy. I feel there is not a character in this book who could possibly have a tragic experience; no matter what happened to any character in *Tom Jones,* it couldn't possibly be tragic. It would be sad maybe, it would be pathetic, it might be a great pity, but it wouldn't be tragic.

Tate: At that one place in the story, where Tom is in jail after running his sword through Mr. Fitzpatrick, Mr. Fielding pauses to remind us that Tom is in a very desperate plight. He uses the word "tragic," and says in substance: "If I were a tragic writer, I could do justice to this, I could elaborate it, but since this is comedy, I won't." As a matter of fact, Tom's position is not actually a tragic one. It is merely a pathetic one, one due to circumstance, and we are perfectly confident that as soon as the circumstances change, Tom will be all right. Now in tragedy that won't work, because change of circumstance doesn't do the hero any good. He is doomed anyhow.

Van Doren: No reader at that point worries about Tom, I should think.

Porter: Not at all, because even if he were hanged it wouldn't be tragic.

Van Doren: Now, this book is so long, and has so wide a comic range, that I wonder whether I shouldn't ask you two to read a passage each from him, because I can't think of any single passage which would represent the book.

Tate: We have two very good passages here—and we are fortunate in finding two that don't have to be censored. This passage is about Squire Western. It shows one characteristic thing about him without giving us a close view.

"Contiguous to Mr. Allworthy's estate was the manor of one of those gentlemen who are called 'preservers of the game.' This species of men, from the great severity with which they revenge the death of a hare or partridge, might be thought to cultivate the same superstition with the Bannians in India; many of whom, we are told, dedicate their whole lives to the preservation and protection of certain animals; was it not that our English Bannians, while they preserve them from other enemies, will most unmercifully slaughter whole horseloads themselves; so that they stand clearly acquitted of any such heathenish superstition."

I think, Miss Porter, we'll let you read a passage about love.

Porter: This is the last part of the first love scene between

Sophia Western and Tom Jones, and it is very, very symptomatic, because nothing could exceed the delicacy of these lovers from the first page to the last:

"Jones, who was hardly able to support himself, offered her his arm, which she condescended to accept, but begged that he would not mention a word more to her of this nature at present. He promised he would not, insisting only on her forgiveness of what love without the leave of his will had forced from him. This, she told him, he knew how to obtain by his future behavior. And thus this young pair tottered and trembled along, the lover not once daring to squeeze the hand of his mistress, though it was locked in his."

(1832-1898)

LEWIS CARROLL

Alice in Wonderland

*L*EWIS *CARROLL (Charles Lutwidge Dodgson) was a lecturer in mathematics at Oxford and he loved children. These two
circumstances, whether or not they would have had a significant
relation in any other life, became one circumstance in his when
he wrote, it is said for the amusement of a little girl, the daughter
of a friend, his best-known book.* Alice in Wonderland *could
scarcely have been conceived by one who was not at home in logic
and mathematics; but neither could it have been made as mys-
teriously charming as it is by one who lacked an understanding
of children. It established itself at once, and it has remained, one
of the few books capable of delighting in equal measure the
young and the old, the uninitiated and the sophisticated. A child
may wander forever through its fantastically logical landscape,
and listen with inexplicable pleasure to its preposterously plausible talk. But neither do philosophers tire of the exercises it so*

gently forces their minds to take. Alice in Wonderland *continues to be one of the most quotable books in the world, because Lewis Carroll in writing it never strayed from the essentials of thought. To the question "Why?" the indignant answer "Why not?" is still one of the best possible answers that can be returned to those, whether six or sixty, who have not thought far enough. Lewis Carroll laughed in his own Victorian way at the smallness of the Victorian world. But his way has not lost its rightness in a world which has grown no larger. There is no sign of age anywhere in his unpretentious masterpiece. For clarity can never be out of date, nor can wit lose its savor.*

Lewis Carroll is the pseudonym of Charles Lutwidge Dodgson. Eldest of the eleven children of an English clergyman and himself destined for the ministry, he never took holy orders, although he was ordained deacon in 1861. In 1850 Dodgson went to Oxford and was thereafter at Christ Church College, a lecturer in mathematics from 1855 to 1881. As Dodgson, he wrote scholarly books on mathematics and a record of a journey to Russia (his only travel abroad) and as Dodgson he discounted Lewis Carroll— but Carroll is the name he is remembered by.

KATHERINE ANNE PORTER · BERTRAND RUSSELL
MARK VAN DOREN

Van Doren: Miss Porter, you may wonder why you were asked to come this morning to discuss *Alice in Wonderland.* One reason I might give you is this: I was curious to know whether you, like other women of my acquaintance, were horrified by this book rather than made happy by it when you were a little girl.

Porter: I was. It was a horror-story to me; it frightened me so much, and I didn't know then whether it was the pictures or the text. Rereading it, I should think it was the text.

Van Doren: Even without Tenniel's drawings you would have been scared?

Porter: Oh, yes. It was a terrible mixture of suffering and cruelty and rudeness and false logic and traps for the innocent— in fact, awful.

Van Doren: This must have been partly because you believed the story.

Porter: I believed it entirely. The difference between it, I think, and the other fairy stories (because we had an appetite for the most grim and grisly horrors; nearly all stories written for children in the old times were horrible and we loved them, because we knew they weren't true; they couldn't happen, they were mere stories) is, that all this takes place in a setting of everyday life. The little glass table with the key on it, and the furniture and the gardens and the flowers, the clock—they were all things we knew, you see, familiar things dreadfully out of place, and they frightened me.

Van Doren: Well, Mr. Russell, you also might wonder why

you are here, and the reason might be another reason altogether. But I'm tempted to ask you whether anything like this was your experience.

Russell: No, I never had any feeling of horror about it. I have heard other women say the same thing, that they felt a horror about it. The reason I didn't was that after all it was a girl who had all these troubles, and boys don't mind the troubles of girls.

Porter: I'm afraid that's true.

Van Doren: You mean that boys don't mind if girls are treated rudely?

Russell: They don't mind a bit. No, they think it's what they deserve.

Van Doren: I wonder if that is because boys themselves are in the habit of being treated rudely by girls with no ability to strike back. Did you read the book at an early age?

Russell: Oh, yes. I was brought up on the two books, both *Alice in Wonderland* and *Through the Looking-Glass*. *Through the Looking-Glass* was published the year I was born, and they were still comparatively recent books when I was young. I was brought up on the first editions, which I had in the nursery. It didn't occur to anybody that they had any value and I just had them to wear out. I knew them by heart from an early age.

Van Doren: That was true of other children in your generation, I dare say.

Russell: Yes, they all knew them by heart. And I don't think that I can remember any of them being horrified. I'm a little surprised by what Miss Porter said. I don't remember any of them thinking of the stories as possibly true.

Van Doren: I was talking recently to an acquaintance of mine —a man—who said that he now feels a horror in reading the book which he did not feel as a boy. You remember the occasion when Alice is growing in the little house and she has grown so large that she has to have one arm out of the window and one leg up the chimney. Well, little Bill, you know, who comes down the chimney to see if he can do something about it, is suddenly kicked by her so that he flies out and is badly hurt, and she hears everyone outside say: "There goes Bill." Now this friend of mine, as a boy, roared with laughter over that. He and his brothers thought it was the funniest thing in the world. But now it doesn't seem funny to him that Bill was hurt. So apparently conversions can take place.

Russell: That is true. I think people are more merciful than they used to be, and I think old fun often strikes us now as rather brutal; anyway, it didn't in those days.

Porter: It is curious about cruelty, because Bill didn't seem to worry me much. A thing I accepted, which I know now is extremely unkind, was putting the dormouse in a teapot headfirst. But I remember reasoning to myself even then that the dormouse was asleep anyhow and didn't care.

Van Doren: No. And the dormouse seems on the whole to want to be some place where it is warm and wet.

Russell: It never occurred to me that the dormouse minded. The only thing that occurred to me was that the teapot was too small.

Van Doren: The dormouse when he was pinched and squealed didn't hurt you, then, vicariously? Does all this mean that the book for you was a perfectly satisfactory children's book? And that it perhaps is still?

Russell: It was then. I don't regard it now as a perfectly satisfactory children's book. I've been rereading it with a view to this broadcast, and I think there are many objections to it as a children's book. In fact, I should like to label it "For Adults Only." I don't think it's a suitable book for the young.

Van Doren: I wonder if the young these days actually do like it as much as children used to like it.

Russell: My experience with them is they don't, and I think this is because there are so many more children's books now and because, when I was young, it was the only children's book that hadn't got a moral. We all got very tired of the morals in books.

Van Doren: This very book makes fun of books that have morals, doesn't it? Remember, the Queen is always going about saying: "The moral of this is—" and then some preposterous statement comes out such as "Take care of the sense and the sounds will take care of themselves."

Porter: But don't you think, too, that it is because children really seem to be much more realistic; that is, they do like a graphic, factual kind of story? Even the fantasies written for children now are nearly always something grotesque and not deep, something that doesn't touch their emotions. Like the comic papers, you know. And then their stories all seem to be about quite ordinary living children. Rather extraordinary but not fabulous adventures occur, which might very well occur to any child.

Van Doren: To me that is highly unfortunate. I am aware of the truth of what you say, that children prefer these days, or at any rate are assumed to prefer, matter-of-fact stories. But every now and then a story which is not matter-of-fact has a great success among children, such as the books about Mary Poppins. Have you read those?

Porter: Yes. Well I would never know whether the children really like that sort of thing or not. Perhaps like grown-ups, they take what is given them because they aren't given anything better.

Van Doren: Do we really mean that *Alice in Wonderland* has declined as a children's book because of its cruelty?

Russell: Partly, I think, but partly also from competition with other books. Grown-ups always tend to think of children with a certain contempt as dear little things, and when a child feels that element in a book he resents it. If he can get a book that doesn't regard him as a dear little thing he's very pleased. But grown-ups will always buy that sort of book and give it to children unless the children educate them.

Van Doren: Are you implying, Mr. Russell, that *Alice in Wonderland* assumes children to be dear little things? Alice is pretty well kicked around, isn't she? And she's rudely treated, she's interrupted, she's rebuffed.

Russell: Yes, but she's always treated rather as a figure of fun, and nobody quite likes to be treated that way.

Van Doren: Yes, she is assumed to be absurd because she has a little habit of talking to herself, reasoning with herself, holding conversations with herself, because she remembers her homework and tries to bring that into this new world she finds herself in. Remember when she meets the mouse. She doesn't know how to address the mouse except by saying "O Mouse," because she had learned the vocative case in Latin.

Russell: All that, I think, is a little absurd, because as a matter of fact she's an extremely Victorian child and very different from most modern children that I know, and certainly no modern child would think of saying "O Mouse." It wouldn't occur to it. All the lessons that she has had at home are different lessons from those the children have now.

Van Doren: That is true. And I'm admitting that occasionally, perhaps regularly, she is treated like a little prig, a little girl who has no ability whatever to imagine other experiences than those she has had. But I suppose the interest of the book to lie very largely there, either for children or for adults. It is a rebuke to those who cannot imagine as possible other experience than that which they have had.

Porter: You've spoken of the children being fed so much realism today; never being given any experience beyond something that might possibly happen to them.

Van Doren: Yes. Now, for instance, to me a very salutary answer to the proverbial question of a child's "Why?" is the answer once given to Alice: "Why not?"—without any explanation at all. It seems to me one learns a great deal by that.

Russell: May I come back to what I said a moment ago, that this book ought to be labeled "For Adults Only"? What you're recommending is a very suitable education for adults, but much too difficult for children. The whole book is much too difficult for the young. It raises metaphysical points, very interesting logical points, that are good for the older ponderer, but for the young produce only confusion.

Van Doren: Of course Alice was always confused. But you imply, Mr. Russell, that adults, these days or perhaps any day, stand in need of metaphysical instruction and logical sanitation.

Russell: I'm professionally bound to think so.

Van Doren: I agree with you heartily, as a matter of fact. Does the book still seem to you of interest on that level?

Russell: It provides, of course, the sort of things a philosophical lecturer can bring in when he wants to seem light. It is very useful to a philosophical lecturer who wants to liven up his stuff; it is full of philosophical jokes which are quite good for philosophical students. But I think you oughtn't to read the book before you're fifteen.

Porter: I wonder. Probably that's true. You were talking about the sentimental Victorian attitude toward children as dear little things. I think Lewis Carroll quite definitely made a bow in the direction of the dear-little-creature attitude in his poems of dedication to Alice and the other children. In the story I think he said what he really believed and what he really meant—and it was pretty grim!

Van Doren: Neither one of you would agree with me, perhaps, that the best children's book is always a book which should be labeled "For Adults Only." My own experience with children, my own children included, is that they really enjoy most those books which they don't wholly understand, which leave them perhaps only slightly bewildered, but nevertheless bewildered.

Russell: Well, I think the young should read some books that adults think of as for adults only, but that's because the adults are always wrong about it. The books the adults think suitable for the young are certainly not.

Van Doren: I'm glad to hear you say that.

Porter: I've always believed that children should read adult literature, should read far beyond their years, and perhaps not read anything that was cold-bloodedly written for them.

Van Doren: Yes, because it has never been clear enough that adults do know what children are like; they're always merely assuming that they know what they're like. I quite agree with you that when they're most sure they're most likely to be wrong. Mr. Russell, I want to come back to that question of the value of the book, if any, on the metaphysical and mathematical level.

I was interested in your saying that philosophers quoted it only when they wanted to introduce a light touch. Now, that after all wouldn't be saying much for the book, would it? Or would it?

Russell: Yes, I think most of the most instructive things are jokes. Quite a number of important things have originated as jokes because if you can put it in that form it isn't so painful. Now, for instance, when they discuss whether they're all parts of the Red King's dream and will cease to exist if the Red King wakes—

Van Doren: This is in *Through the Looking-Glass.*

Russell: Yes, it is. Well, that is a very instructive discussion from a philosophical point of view. But if it were not put humorously, we should find it too painful.

Van Doren: But you really mean that it is instructive?

Russell: I think it is worth considering, yes.

Van Doren: It is more than just an illustration of a point? It contains a point of its own?

Russell. Yes. I think he was very good at inventing puzzles in pure logic. When he was quite an old man, he invented two puzzles which he published in a learned periodical, *Mind,* to which he didn't provide answers. And the providing of answers was a job, at least so I found it.

Van Doren: Do you remember either of those puzzles?

Russell: I remember one of them very well. A boy is going with his two uncles, and one of the uncles says he's going to be shaved, and he's going to a shop that is kept by Allen, Brown, and Carr. And he says: "I shall get shaved by Allen." And the other uncle says: "How do you know Allen will be in?" And he says: "Oh, I can prove it by logic." "Nonsense," says the man. "How can you do that?" "Well," he says, "you know there has to be always one man to mind the shop, so if Allen is out, then, if Brown is out, Carr will be in. But Brown has lately been ill, and so he can't go out alone, and he's quarreled with Allen, so he only goes out with Carr. So if Brown is out, Carr is out. Now if Allen goes out, if Brown is out, Carr is out, and if Brown is out Carr is in. That's impossible, so Allen can never go out."

Van Doren: That sounds like a syllogism, doesn't it?

Russell: Of course it's a fallacy, but showing up the fallacy is difficult.

Porter: A lovely illustration of all this extraordinary, oblique, fallacious logic that was a trap for Alice all the way through two books.

Van Doren: There are many outrageous syllogisms here, such as this in skeleton form: "Alice, you like eggs; serpents like eggs, therefore you are a serpent." And there is another form of logical fun which seems to me important here; I think you would call it a conversion, would you not? That is to say, Lewis Carroll was constantly playing with a subject and predicate converted. Alice is asked why she doesn't say what she means. And she says: "Well, at least I always mean what I say." So she converts the terms cats and rats. Do cats eat rats? Perhaps rats eat cats. Which is true? And she finally forgets which is the important question to ask. She says she has often seen a cat without a grin, but never a grin without a cat. I'm not at all sure that that doesn't lead us to a conversion which it is possible to make on the title of the book. The title of the book is *Alice in Wonderland.* Possibly it should be *Wonderland in Alice,* because Alice is constantly in a state of wonder at something which, in this particular world where she is, she shouldn't wonder at at all. For instance, she eats a piece of cake—after twenty or thirty pages—and she suddenly says to herself: "Isn't it strange that I don't get any bigger from eating this cake?" Lewis Carroll very gravely remarks: "That is what usually happens when you eat cake." She is never able to adjust herself; she is never able to remember the relations which exist in this new life.

Russell: That is quite true, but I still think there is a great deal in his books that is meant to be suitable to the young and isn't. Like when they say "threaten a snark with a railway-share." No child has the vaguest idea of what that means.

Van Doren: But again I wonder if children don't like to read books—if they don't today, that's all there is to it, but my own experience as a child, and my experience of children these days, is that they often do—which they don't totally understand. They come to a railway-share. Well, they want to know what it is, and find out; or they develop in their mind some grotesque notion of what it is, which is quite charming. Students in colleges like best on the whole those lectures which, as we say, are a little over their heads.

Russell: That is perfectly true, but then what puzzles them ought to be something serious that when they understand it they will see to be serious. It ought not to be a mere joke.

Van Doren: But, if, as you say, these jokes are oftentimes cloaks for philosophical, even metaphysical, points, then the book at bottom is serious. I think I've been trying to say that the book is at bottom quite serious and quite edifying. Alice is always learning—her experience is less than it might be—she is always learning that something that she has supposed to be grotesque is not, as a matter of fact, grotesque. She says to the caterpillar once, you remember, on the mushroom: "It's really dreadful always to be changing one's shape." He says: "It isn't dreadful at all." And we immediately remember that the caterpillar changes his shape at least three times in his life.

Porter: And of course she really changes hers too, not into an entirely different form, not from one thing to another, but she's changing and growing all the time; she's not the same person today that she was yesterday by any means. But she doesn't understand that.

Van Doren: As when she is carrying the Duchess's baby. For a while she thinks the baby is ugly because it has a nose like a pig. Then when she determines that the baby *is* a pig, she thinks the nose is quite beautiful.

Porter: The nose is very becoming, and she's glad it's a handsome pig. But I was thinking her confusion was due to the setting aside of all the logic of experience. Because there is a certain sort of progression of experience that I think we can depend upon a little, and this is all removed, you see, from her when she falls into this Wonderland. There isn't anything that she can refer to as a certainty. And then there's another thing that's very important: Alice's state of mind is a fine example of the terrific sense of uncertainty and insecurity of childhood trying to understand an adult world in which very little provision is made for the young. This was true in those days much more than now. I think now perhaps that the family plans are made a little bit too much around the child.

Van Doren: I think so myself.

Porter: But Alice was at a terrible disadvantage, struggling with an adult, alien, and apparently hostile world, which had set traps for her, or so it appeared, purposely to trip her up.

Russell: Perhaps that is why the book was better liked then than now. That particular kind of bafflement was one to which children were accustomed, and it didn't strike them as it does now. But now, I think, the modern child is simply bewildered by all this and feels: oh, this is horrid! At least some do.

Van Doren: I wonder which is the better procedure for the human race—to endeavor to make children understand adults or to endeavor to make adults understand children.

Porter: Do you know, I think one of the great troubles is that too many persons are going around painfully trying too hard to understand. I wish we could relax a little.

Russell: I quite agree. If you could take children more naturally and spontaneously and not bother so much about child psychology, it would be very much better I think.

Van Doren: Certainly. And likewise children should be relieved of the necessity of understanding adult psychology.

Porter: Well, I think one of the most sinister things I ever heard was a little boy, a small child about four years old, weeping bitterly by himself. His parents found him and tried to discover what had happened to him. He wept for a while and finally he blurted out: "Oh, I do want to be happy."

Van Doren: Mr. Russell, I should like to ask you, because of your own distinction in the field of logic and mathematics, whether Carroll is thought actually to have any importance in that field today.

Russell: His works were just what you would expect: comparatively good at producing puzzles and very ingenious and rather pleasant, but not important. For instance, he produced a book of formal logic which is much pleasanter than most because, instead of saying things like "all men are mortal," which is very dull, it says, things like "most hungry crocodiles are disagreeable," which is amusing, and that makes the subject more agreeable. Then he wrote a book of geometry which is pleasant in a way, but not important. None of his work was important. The best work he ever did in that line was the two puzzles that I spoke of.

Van Doren: And are those better in that line than anything in either *Alice in Wonderland* or *Through the Looking-Glass*—I mean to say, considered as contributions?

Russell: Oh, certainly, because there is nothing in *Alice in Wonderland* or *Through the Looking-Glass* that could conceivably be thought a contribution. They offer only pleasant illustrations for those who don't want to be thought too heavy.

Van Doren: But for children perhaps? I mean, could one seriously say that a child might learn a little bit to be logical from reading these books?

Russell: I shouldn't have thought so.

Van Doren: That was a very heavy question, and you should have rebuked me for it. But the famous error that is made (I don't know whether this is a logical error or not) when it is said that butter should not have been used in the works of a watch and the answer is: "but it was the best butter"—is that amusing to a child?

Porter: That was frightfully amusing. That was funny always.

Van Doren: Or the demonstration that, since a dog is not mad because when he is happy he wags his tail and when he is unhappy he growls with his throat, therefore a cat which when it is happy moves its tail and growls *is* mad.

Porter: I think we understood that all very well, don't you?

Russell: How about the treacle well?

Porter: Yes, I liked the treacle well.

Russell: Do you remember, they drew treacle out of the treacle well? "But I don't understand," said Alice, "they were in the well." "So they were," said the dormouse, "well in."

Porter: That was funny, too.

Van Doren: They were drawing treacle from the well, and the dormouse explains: "Well, we were just learning to draw; we didn't draw very well." And suddenly they're talking about drawing pictures—drawing pictures of things the names of which begin with the letter M. "Why with the letter M?" "Why not?"

Porter: But do you remember the lessons they had? Was it the eel, or some underseas creature, who had lessons in drawling and stretching and fainting in coils? You know, we were never told how to translate that and we didn't need to. We thought those tricks were funny in themselves.

Van Doren: And the exercises in reeling and writhing.

Porter: We didn't get on to that for a long time.

Russell: I found the only thing that my boy really liked, my small boy, was the poem about Father William. He looked at me with a grave face and said: "Father William was very clever *although* he was old."

Van Doren: How old is the boy, by the way?

Russell: Four and a half.

Van Doren: A shrewd remark. Now we have not referred often enough in our conversation to the presence in this book of some very famous poems which are of course parodies. I think the poem about Father William is the most interesting. Would you agree?

Russell: I agree—yes.

Van Doren: Miss Porter, would you like to read that?

Porter: I'll swing along as we used to when we read it as children.

> *"You are old, Father William," the young man said,*
> *"And your hair has become very white;*
> *And yet you incessantly stand on your head—*
> *Do you think, at your age, it is right?"*

Fiction

"In my youth," Father William replied to his son,
"I feared it might injure the brain;
But, now that I'm perfectly sure I have none,
Why, I do it again and again."

"You are old," said the youth, "as I mentioned before,
And have grown most uncommonly fat;
Yet you turned a back somersault in at the door—
Pray, what is the reason of that?"

"In my youth," said the sage, as he shook his gray locks,
"I kept all my limbs very supple
By the use of this ointment—one shilling the box,—
Allow me to sell you a couple?"

"You are old," said the youth, "and your jaws are too weak
For anything tougher than suet.
Yet you finished the goose, with the bones and the beak—
Pray, how did you manage to do it?"

"In my youth," said his father, "I took to the law,
And argued each case with my wife;
And the muscular strength which it gave to my jaw
Has lasted the rest of my life."

"You are old," said the youth, "one would hardly suppose
That your eye was as steady as ever;
Yet you balanced an eel on the end of your nose—
What made you so awfully clever?"

"I've answered three questions, and that is enough,"
Said his father. "Don't give yourself airs!
Do you think I can listen all day to such stuff?
Be off, or I'll kick you downstairs!"

(1843-1916)

HENRY JAMES

The Turn of the Screw

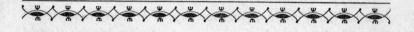

THE ART *of fiction as Henry James practiced it through a long, solitary, and devoted life was the art not so much of telling stories as of suggesting them; of assembling, arranging, and analyzing materials, of maneuvering them at the right speed and in the right order toward the reader's attention, and of leaving them then to produce the effect which, thus shaded and controlled, they were bound in logic and nature to produce. All this means that he became one of the subtlest writers ever to deal with the human situation. It also explains why many readers continue to prefer the simpler method of direct, unequivocal statement. James did not like to make statements about anything, and the dislike grew on him until in his old age he went to fantastic lengths to avoid even the semi-obvious. He so much preferred to see life making its own statements, and as a writer to assist it in the process. But the statements of life are richly ambiguous. No one knew this better*

[221]

than he who had explored so many ambiguities. He was never willing, for instance, to answer questions about his famous tale, The Turn of the Screw. *Had he had in mind real ghosts? Did those two evil persons ever exist in the flesh? Just what did the children know or see? His answer might have been to the first question: What is a real ghost? And to the second and third: You as reader have as much knowledge as I have. This is the way I saw these things, and no one can see them more clearly, for this is the way they were. With such answers we must be content; and with a story which few others have matched for delicacy of touch and authenticity of terror.*

Henry James, brother of William James, the psychologist, was born in New York, but from the days of his early education in Europe he found on the Continent and in England his intellectual home. (He lived in London from 1876 and became a British subject in 1915.) His first literary attempts were essays for the reviews; his first novel, A Passionate Pilgrim *(1871) appeared serially in the* Atlantic. *Many of James's novels have for theme an American character placed in a European scene; the contrast between the English and the American leisure class repeatedly recurs. Among his chief novels are* Roderick Hudson *(1875);* Daisy Miller *(1878);* Portrait of a Lady *(1881);* The Awkward Age *(1899);* The Ambassadors *(1903); and* The Golden Bowl *(1904). The autobiographical* Middle Years *was published in 1917.*

KATHERINE ANNE PORTER · ALLEN TATE · MARK VAN DOREN

Van Doren: This great and famous story is told by a governess, who lets us know how she saw two children under her charge, a little boy and a little girl, in an English house of indeterminate antiquity and solitude, corrupted by the ghosts of two evil servants, recently dead. Now the first question we shall be expected to settle, if we can, is the question whether all that happens, all that is seen, is in the mind of the governess, or whether—or to what extent—there are objective existences here over which she has no control.

Tate: Mr. Van Doren, if you mean by "objective existences" only those existences which can be seen visually, I would say no, except in so far as the governess sees them; but I think there are objective existences which don't manifest themselves visually. Again, I think that these apparitions, in so far as they become agents in the action affecting human lives, are just as real as if they were people in the sense that we are people around a table. I don't want to quibble about it, but I think that a discussion along that line is the way to get at it.

Van Doren: Is that true for you, Miss Porter? Does it seem to you a false problem if I state it by asking whether everything happens in the mind of the governess or nothing does?

Porter: When I first read this story, I accepted the governess's visions as real, that is, the ghosts were real in themselves, and not only the governess, perhaps, but others might have seen them; they had a life of their own. But as I went on reading the story and studying it through the years, and I read Henry James's notes on it, I decided that the ghosts were a projection of the governess's imagination and were part of her plot.

[223]

Tate: It is evident, Miss Porter, isn't it, that nobody actually sees these people but the governess?

Porter: Nobody.

Tate: James is very adroit in convincing the readers that perhaps they can be seen by other people, or have been, but if you look closely it is perfectly evident that nobody sees them as physical existences but the governess. I don't say that that destroys their reality.

Porter: Not at all.

Van Doren: And, of course, there's no possible doubt that she does see them. The statement "the governess sees the ghosts" is a true statement.

Tate: Oh, there's no question of that.

Van Doren: Not only does she have no doubt herself, but it never occurs to her that anyone else could question their presence.

Tate: She has a momentary doubt of a certain kind, Mr. Van Doren. Doesn't she say toward the end that if Flora goes out into the world and people come in from outside—for example, her employer, the uncle of the children—and look at the situation and find that the apparitions don't visually exist, then she will have to say: "Where am I?" Those are her exact words.

Van Doren: Yes, and there is one moment when Mrs. Grose, the housekeeper, the plain and simple woman of the story, fails to see Miss Jessel, the evil governess who has died.

Tate: That is one of the most interesting moments in the whole story.

Van Doren: The present governess even then, as you say, seems to understand that she may be lost if she can't make Mrs. Grose see this woman who is "as big as a blazing fire," for then she has no case. She does seem, at that moment, to think of herself as one having a case.

Tate: She has been so hard-pressed that she feels she must build the case herself even at the expense of the children. That is the sinister note which enters the second half of the story.

Porter: In her attempt to vindicate herself she's doing the whole thing really at the expense of the children—I have always believed for the sake of destroying them, of putting them out of the way in some manner or other in order to clear a road to the master.

Tate: I agree with Miss Porter. But does the governess realize that consciously?

Porter: No, never.

Van Doren: Well, this is the question then that frames itself in my mind: are we to take the story as a piece of psychology, as an exploration of a peculiar temperament, namely, the governess', suffering under illusions and hallucinations? I prefer not to take it that way. It seems to me that the story would shrink a great deal in power and significance if it were merely a story which psychoanalyzed an old maid.

Tate: I think we've got to take it that way and the other way, too—both at once—and perhaps if we take it both ways, we've got to take it in a third way which will explain the fact that the story is a unified thing, a single thing which is neither psychological wholly nor a mere naive attempt on the part of this governess to protect her children.

Van Doren: You see, I am interested in Miss Porter's statement that the first time she read the story she believed the governess. This is certainly true for me.

Tate: And for me, too.

Van Doren: And it still is. The first time Miss Porter read the story, it never occurred to her that the evil personified in these two persons—at least these two, because Miss Porter would add a third, or . . .

Porter: Even a fourth, perhaps—

Van Doren: . . . all right, that the evil somehow was there. Now, I think we must take that as a fact. If the story were merely —I'm agreeing with you, Mr. Tate—if the story were merely a clever piece of psychology, no reader, even a child, would feel in it the powerful presence of evil.

Tate: That's absolutely right. It seems to me that given the time in which James lived and the growing interest then in the processes of the mind, we have to see James as taking that peculiar interest as a medium through which to set forth the reality of evil; because the reality of evil in this story is not destroyed, or made a false issue, by explaining it psychologically. In James's time the psychological basis was necessary. In the past, treatment of ghosts, the material projection of evil in earlier literature, didn't follow a psychological bent; it wasn't done psychologically; the evil creatures were presented in their full physical body and the public accepted them at their face value. We have become more sophisticated, and perhaps a little more decadent in our literature—certainly more critical. Don't we demand that all of these allegorical effects, all of these realities of evil, be set forth on some level that will also satisfy the critical point of view?

Porter: Yes, that is important. James himself confessed that he wished to catch those not easily caught.

Van Doren: Exactly.

Porter: And he made in effect booby-traps of a very high order, with a great deal of wit and a great deal of good humor. But I was thinking that one of the really interesting levels of analysis in this story is theological, admitting the existence of original sin, of the fact that we really are conceived in sin, brought forth in iniquity. I think that is a very interesting point in the study of this story.

Tate: Wasn't James always preoccupied with evil?

Porter: Yes.

Van Doren: That is one reason we call him a great writer.

Tate: But wasn't his problem then to make that evil as dramatically convincing as possible?

Van Doren: Yes, but I think of him as suffering under the limitations which modern literature and the critical mind imposed upon him. He wasn't able to ask us to believe that anything like Furies or devils existed. Aeschylus could put the Furies on his stage, and even Shakespeare could put on a ghost. All James was able to do was to ask us to believe in the return—somehow—of two very evil individuals. They are not devils; they don't represent evil; they simply *are* evil. A very bad man, Peter Quint.

Porter: Known to have been bad, yes. And the woman, known to have been bad.

Van Doren: A very tragic and dishonored woman, Miss Jessel.

Tate: Now, are they described as necessarily evil during their lives? My feeling is that they were merely "bad." Couldn't we make this distinction: that this story is not about good and bad, but about good and evil? The question of the way in which James makes evil dramatic and convincing has always fascinated me in this book. If you will remember, Quint first appears dressed in the master's clothes; it is the first thing the governess notices about him. Then she notices that he has red hair, and strange pointed eyebrows, and . . .

Porter: All the physical attributes of the legendary devil.

Tate: Exactly.

Porter: The evil eye.

Tate: Precisely. And I think James is playing with us a little there—bringing in an additional dimension of the imagination. But when she tells Mrs. Grose about Quint, it seems to me that James's dramatic powers, his powers as a writer of fiction, are at their very highest, because his job is to insert Quint into the scene and make him an actor in it, and that is very difficult. In order to do that, he must have the governess get some objective verification for her vision, and the way in which the governess makes the simple Mrs. Grose identify Quint establishes him in the scene. Well, that is—if you wish—a trick of fiction. It is the novelist's technique. Actually, at the same time, it doesn't invalidate Quint as an evil person. That's the ambivalent thing in the story.

Van Doren: And of course there are some wonderful strokes as Quint is painted. Remember, his first two appearances do not reveal anything except the upper half of him. Once he is standing behind a sort of balustrade on top of the tower; another time he is merely looking in a window, but the lower half of him is not there—it is as if he were in some ghastly way truncated. I am also interested in the fact that he is pale—that he has a pale face with light hair. If he is the devil, at least he is a very special sort of devil; he's not swarthy or grimacing; his face is rigid. He has a thin face and light curly red hair.

Tate: He never changes his expression. I recall something that James says in his preface to this book about the presentation of supernatural creatures in fiction. We must remember that neither Quint nor Miss Jessel ever does much of anything; they just appear; they just stand there and look—and their mere appearance is enough to set all this machinery of horror into motion.

Van Doren: That's enough, incidentally.

Tate: Yes. He says supernatural creatures should do as little as possible, as little as is "consistent with their consenting to appear at all."

Van Doren: Exactly. The awful thing is that they should appear.

Porter: The one thing we haven't talked about yet is the role of the children in this story. This, I think, is terribly important, because the governess persistently tries to fix upon the children evil motives and base actions, and takes seriously an accusation made against the little boy by the head-master of the school when he is sent home with a note saying that he had been an immoral influence. She was using this accusation as a weapon against the little boy—a kind of moral blackmail. The girl, who was in some ways a simpler nature, I think, and of a more positive mind than the little boy, was uncomplicated by the fact that she had had no sad experiences. Well, their simplest and most natural acts are interpreted by the governess as being of a suspicious nature, even when they got up in the night and went out to look at the moonlight, and that sort of thing. The governess constantly attempts to draw the children into her orbit of evil and force them to share it and prove them guilty. She transfers her guilty motives to them, making them accomplices to justify herself. But it seems to me that their conduct is perfectly simple and intuitive. They surmise the purpose and the enormous threat to them . . .

Tate: But the threat was real, wasn't it, Miss Porter?

Porter: Very real. The children were frightened for good reasons, though they did not understand anything; they acted with the curious reserved defensiveness of children who don't know what is happening to them. They surmised evil, surmised the threat and were trying to escape. They even tried to get together to confide in each other, but the governess made constant efforts to keep them separate so that they would never be able to work up a common defense against her.

Van Doren: She assumes that when they are together they talk unspeakably evil things.

Porter: Yes.

Van Doren: But I wonder if we're not a bit misleading about the governess. I quite agree that the children are in some sense innocent, beautiful and clear. But so is the governess. We are suggesting that she is more sinister than she ever, at any rate, knows herself as being.

Tate: She never knows herself as being sinister.

Van Doren: We almost have imputed to her a plot to corrupt the children herself. Now I'm willing to believe that it is she who corrupts the children and brings about the death of the little boy. Nevertheless, that is precisely my way of understanding how potent the evil in this story is. The evil isn't merely thought to be; it is an actuality which passes through her as a perfectly transparent and non-resistant medium and then passes through the children. The evil is somehow there.

Porter: And finally it is projected to an immense distance.

Van Doren: Yes, for she has great power. If it were merely a story of what she thought, of what she could fool herself into seeing, she wouldn't have the power she has over us as readers; she wouldn't be able, as you say, to project Quint and Miss Jessel to great distances, across lakes, to the tops of towers, and so on.

Tate: Mr. Van Doren, couldn't we put it this way? The governess doesn't invent these apparitions; they merely use her as a medium. Because, obviously, the monstrous proportions of the evil are so great that they are beyond the power of any individual imagination to invent. There is something much stronger than the governess operating through her. She has her own innocent later existence, as is proved, I think, by the prologue of the story, where we learn that after this terrible incident had passed, she went on to other posts and nothing like it occurred again. It was some peculiar conjunction of forces which permitted this evil to emerge through her here.

Van Doren: That is extremely interesting, Mr. Tate. You suggest to me another reason why James is a great writer. Living as he did in our time, which usually does not take stock in either good or evil, he was able to construct in the governess a creature almost like Cassandra, through whom evil tears its way without any instigation on her part at all—without, so to speak, her permission.

Tate: Don't you feel then that the governess, at the end of the story, in spite of the fact that you see what she's done, has a certain dignity of her own, that she is a person of great proportions? She is not in the least an insignificant creature.

Van Doren: She is no such creature as a story-teller makes his victim when he wants to deal in mere delusion. She is not ridiculous or trivial. As a matter of fact, she becomes tragic.

Tate: Exactly. It's her tragedy.

Van Doren: Of course, individual creatures can be the vehicles or channels of great good also. Just as Cassandra is a person through whom evil tears, so a saint may be a person through whom good pours in floods.

Porter: An illuminant is not always an illuminant for good. The most dangerous people in the world are the illuminated ones through whom forces act when they themselves are unconscious of their own motives. And yet, no force has ever acted through either a saint or an evil person that wasn't somehow directed to further the ends and the ambitions and the hopes of that person, which makes me feel that the instrument is not altogether so innocent and so helpless as we have been saying. Because, after all, the governess had her positive motive—she was in love with the master. She had a deep sense of her inferior situation in life, and was almost hopeless of ever attracting his attention. And I do think that this love, which was quite hopeless, which was an ingrown thing, took this form; she herself, in her imagination—

yes, unconscious of her motives—designed all this drama to make the desired situation possible—that she would arrive somewhere at a level with the man she loved and create some sort of communication with him.

Tate: I agree with you, Miss Porter, but it has always seemed to me that that level of the governess's experience—that is, her personal motivation, what she expected to get out of it and all that—has a perfectly naturalistic basis. Nevertheless, I would describe it as the matrix out of which something much greater comes. As a matter of fact, we can go back and take the great tragic characters in drama, or the great religious heroes, too. They will all have some psychological motivation which we can see in terms of their peculiar situations. At the same time, are we agreed that in the case of the true saints, of the great tragic heroes, possibly in the case of the governess here, the psychological basis doesn't explain it all?

Porter: The popular psychological explanation is too superficial.

Van Doren: Otherwise we should be aware that an explanation is ready and easy as we read along, whereas the truth is—we all grant this—that as we read along we're not explaining anything to ourselves at all. We're not saying: Well, a dreadful, dreadful thing is happening, yet we know the reason. In a very important sense we don't know the reason. Something is loose here in the world, if only in the mind of a woman. Something is loose in the world which is very powerful and beyond the control of any human being.

Porter: I would say quite beyond the Freudian explanation.

Van Doren: Oh, decidedly.

Porter: Here is one place where I find Freud completely defeated.

Tate: James knew substantially all that Freud knew before Freud came on the scene.

Porter: All major artists do.

Van Doren: Any great story-teller has to, because a great story-teller has for his subject good and evil.

[231]

Tate: There is an aspect of this story which has always interested me very much. It is what we might call the technical aspects. I should think readers of the story would be very much interested in how James established the realities of these things which would otherwise be incredible. Consider the fact that the story is told by a governess and the fact that, as Mr. Van Doren said some time ago, in reading it we tend to forget that the governess is telling it; we think we are actually participating. That is due, I think, to the great art of James. Isn't it true that one trouble with the first-person narrative, the story told by somebody in the story, is that the authority of that person is usually not quite established? We say usually of such a person: she is participating in it, you can't expect her to give us an unbiased version of it; she's not sufficiently detached; she's not disinterested. But, while that's a liability in most first-person narratives, it seems to me that James's triumph consists in the fact that he has been able to take the defect of the method and use it for a positive purpose. The very fact that the governess is biased becomes a dramatic factor. The bias becomes a part of the story.

Porter: Yes, and because she has no understanding at all of her real motive, she gives herself away completely and constantly.

Tate: Constantly. There are two levels: the level at which she sees the action and the level at which the reader can see it, and this creates an irony of which the governess is not aware.

Van Doren: She is not aware, for instance, of how much it is against her own nature and her own desire to plague the little boy at the end, to make him tell more and more and more about the bad things he has done. They turn out to be rather slight things, don't you think? No reader assumes that the little boy has done anything very bad.

Tate: Nothing bad at all.

Porter: Some vague little offense against Victorian morality, no doubt.

Van Doren: Yet the governess all along has wanted to spare the children. Indeed, her declared intention was to protect, to shield them. Here she is forced by the irony of her character and fate to torture this little boy into confessions which he doesn't want to make, which he doesn't even know how to make because he has nothing to confess.

Tate: Isn't that a wonderful scene in Miles's room at night? The governess comes—it bears out just what you were saying, Mr. Van Doren—she comes to have a talk with him, as you will remember, and to try to get out of him what he did at school. It's a general stock-taking of Miles's situation. It is one of the most powerful pieces of irony I've ever read, because the governess is actually making love to the little boy and she doesn't know it. But he knows it in a curious instinctive way; he blows the candle out to get rid of her.

Porter: And the scene is wonderfully written—his terror at this visit in the night, with what for him was ghost or devil, all evil in fact, everything that he had reason to be terrified of, coming into his room with that unpardonable invasion of his privacy —this is all projected with such admirable simplicity and directness that the reader forgets the words and shares the impression.

Van Doren: His very childish understanding of the fact that she is in love with him comes out, it seems to me, in the conversation in which he suggests that he should be going back to school now, because, after all, he's just a "fellow," and has no right to spend all of his time with a lady.

Tate: He shows something perfectly wonderful there. It is so simple that the implications are sometimes lost on the reader. He is sitting with her and there's a silence. The governess says, "Well, here we are." And Miles says, "Yes, we're here." Just like that.

Van Doren: That's right. But again it seems to me that the fame of this story among all of James's stories is justified by the fact that the evil in it somehow remains pure and general, remains undefined. All of the attempts on the part of the governess to find out what it is, after all, are frustrated. There is never any danger that evil will shrink here into vice, into misdemeanor.

Tate: James says that evil is never credible in fiction if it is presented in "weak specifications."

Van Doren: We have all had the experience of reading a story about some villain whom we can believe to be unspeakable—we like to believe in unspeakable villains—and then of being shocked by the discovery that all he did was murder his grandmother. That never is enough.

Porter: Yes, nearly always the specific act, the crime, does seem inadequate compared to the great force of evil which produces it.

Van Doren: I am reminded of Iago, whose evil is never explained by the specific motives he is said to have, and even himself thinks he has. Iago thinks that he is jealous of Othello, but it isn't jealousy, it isn't ambition, it isn't anything you can name at all. That is why Iago is a force. He is one of these figures who are being used.

Tate: But he's an evil figure, not merely a bad one. There's a fundamental difference between the evil and the bad.

Van Doren: Good and evil is the distinction. I wonder if everyone agrees with us that the great theme is good and evil. We keep saying so.

Porter: Yes, or rather the conflict between them in the minds of men.

Van Doren: Do you suppose anyone doubts us?

Tate: Otherwise we get merely social literature, the literature of social problems, political and economic literature.

Porter: I think that during the nineteenth century, when the perfectibility of man was an accepted doctrine, James was one of the few who had this genuine knowledge of good and evil, and the courage to take it as his theme.

Tate: I would like to read the very last paragraph of this story. It is the moment after Miles has died. He is lying there dead and the governess is looking at him.

"But he had already jerked straight round, stared, glared again and seen but the quiet day. With the stroke of the loss I was so proud of, he uttered a cry of a creature hurled over an abyss, and the grasp with which I recovered him might have been that of catching him in his fall. I caught him; yes, I held him, it may be imagined with what a passion. But at the end of a minute I began to feel what it truly was that I held. We were alone with the quiet day and his little heart, dispossessed, had stopped."

(1859-1930)

A. CONAN DOYLE

The Adventures of
Sherlock Holmes

A LITERARY *form may produce its classic in the early stages of its career, and indeed the thing can happen at the very moment of birth, a book which is the first of its kind proving also to be the best. This is not strictly true in the case of the form known as the detective story; for Edgar Allan Poe, who is credited with its invention, died well before Conan Doyle was born. But with Sherlock Holmes the detective story took a new turn and became almost a new form; and in any event the wizard of Baker Street can be said never to have been surpassed by his successors, or never to have been displaced from his position as type and symbol of the detective hero. Rich and various as the literature he fathered has been, comparison still must be made between any new-born expert in crime and the strange, keen, mysterious fellow with his pipe and cap who controlled a wide world from obscure London chambers. It is the world of Holmes that interests us so much,*

and rightly interests us. For the detective story came when it was needed. Fiction had ceased to consider that its chief business was to tell stories; it had become history rather than poetry, to revive Aristotle's distinction, and above all it had lost speed. And it had deserted the field of fancy. Conan Doyle revived the techniques of celerity and economy in narrative; and he peopled a delightful world with his fancy. The charm of Holmes is not so much in his solutions; it is in the position he occupies at the center of a universe where anything can happen, and where all sorts of odd yet plausible things do happen. It is the happenings that enchant us, along with an atmosphere which is always promising more. Sherlock Holmes's Adventures *are truly adventures, and therefore unique in modern story.*

Sir Arthur Conan Doyle was born in Edinburgh. He studied medicine and served as a physician in the Boer War. For his patriotic pamphlets The Great Boer War *and* The Cause and the Conflict of the War *he was knighted. Doyle's literary career is signalized by the creation of Holmes and his adventures, but he also wrote historical novels and romances and plays, including a Henry Irving success,* The Story of Waterloo. *In his later years he was an ardent student of spiritualism, conducting experiments and research in psychic phenomena and writing a* History of Spiritualism.

REX STOUT   •   ELMER DAVIS   •   JACQUES BARZUN
MARK VAN DOREN

Van Doren: Personally, gentlemen, I approach the discussion of this masterpiece with particular pleasure. It is a modern masterpiece of not much more than a half century's life, so far. In view of its short life, but in view also of the fact that Conan Doyle has had so many imitators and followers, possibly the first question we should consider is whether Sherlock Holmes is in any sense dated. Does it seem to you, Mr. Davis, that the stories about Holmes, considered as a collection—either the small collection that we are officially dealing with today or all of them together—have lost anything?

Davis: On the technical side I am not competent to discuss that; Mr. Stout can tell you far more about the technique of mystery-story writing than I can. But it seems to me that the great merit of these stories—the entire Sherlock Holmes corpus, the complete writings of John H. Watson, M.D.—is that it certainly provides the best picture ever set down of the focal point of the world at one of the high points of human history.

Van Doren: That was London?

Davis: That was London, and London at the time when England was definitely the predominant nation in the world—had been for almost a century. So you have a period here comparable, say, to late eighteenth-century Paris, or let us say second-century Rome, or Alexandria in the first century B.C.; and this is the only case in which we have such an absolutely complete contemporary account of the whole thing.

Van Doren: That capital of the world was the one Oscar Wilde referred to, I suppose, when he had a character in one of his plays remark: "The man who dominates a London dinner table dominates the world."

Barzun: Mr. Van Doren, since Mr. Davis has made the historical point, may I exchange places with him and make the literary one? Not only does it seem to me that the stories do just what Mr. Davis has said, but I think that we mustn't forget about Sherlock Holmes. Chesterton said he was the only character in fiction that had been created in the last fifty years, and I think there is a great deal to be said for that.

Van Doren: You make the literary point that Sherlock Holmes is a character. In looking over the stories again I was very much impressed by the skill manifested in the making of this character. Sherlock Holmes is what few persons in contemporary fiction are—limited or defined. He is absolutely clear. You know what he is, you know what he isn't. One of the first things Doyle, or rather Watson, does is explain what it is that Holmes does not know, what it is that he cannot do, what it is that he isn't.

Stout: I'm beginning to get mad already, because Baker Street Irregulars don't agree that Holmes is a character. Holmes is a man! Holmes is a great man! One of our rules is, you know, that you're not allowed to mention the name of A. Conan Doyle in the Irregulars because there just wasn't any such person. Sherlock Holmes lived, Dr. Watson lived—or Mrs. Watson, whatever you want to call her.

Barzun: To come back to your point, Mr. Stout, I agree with you that Holmes is a great man, but I should say he is a character in a special sense. He is unique in fiction. He is the only genius in fiction who is successful. I don't mean whose work is successful, but who comes off as a genius.

Van Doren: Whom you can believe.

Barzun: Yes. You hear in other books of great painters and great poets and statesmen, but you never see them performing.

Van Doren: As a matter of fact, Mr. Barzun, wouldn't you admit one exception there? Hamlet is a genius whom you can believe. To be sure, we don't see him accomplishing anything, but no one doubts his superlative intellectual qualities.

Barzun: That is true.

Stout: Genius at what? Poisoning swords, or what?

Van Doren: No—genius as a man. He is a great gentleman, obviously a very distinguished person. He is always referred to as distinguished, and you can believe it.

Barzun: Yet there are others in Hamlet's category—Ralph Touchett in Henry James, for example—but here is an artist whose works are laid before the public at the same time that his qualities are praised.

Van Doren: You see him performing.

Barzun: Yes, you do.

Stout: That's the whole point of the detective story—in Doyle's hands.

Van Doren: Mr. Stout, I think—if I may mention Doyle once more, then perhaps we should bury him—pays him a great compliment, it seems to me, when he says that the Irregulars never think of Doyle. That is the compliment to an author which consists of saying that his character has really been created. Holmes moves under his own power. You believe him, do you not?

Stout: Indeed you do. That's why you re-read him about every month. But since we're mentioning Doyle, which we're not allowed to do in our own meetings, let me say that we can never in our meetings bring up one of the best things Doyle ever wrote, which wasn't a Sherlock Holmes story at all. It was when he was a starving young doctor and sent in his income tax to the government and it was very incomplete, to say the least, and he got it back about two weeks later with a notation on it: "Unsatisfactory." Doyle wrote on it, "I thoroughly agree," and sent it back.

Davis: Now that was very characteristic of this gentleman whose name may not hereafter be mentioned, but it certainly was not characteristic of Dr. John H. Watson. You speak of Sherlock Holmes as a living character. Surely Dr. Watson is a much more complex character than Holmes and just as alive. No question about his reality.

Van Doren: Very much alive.

Barzun: Why do you say "much more complex"?

Van Doren: Because he has scruples?

Davis: No. I need not cite to you the tremendous amount of historical and scholarly research that has been done into the life of Dr. Watson, a life as to which he himself was extremely reticent. We have discovered that there were all sorts of psychological depths in this man which he thoroughly and successfully endeavored to conceal.

Barzun: Couldn't you explain it this way—that Watson was a man of good capacities in the presence of a great genius, and when that relation occurs the genius is baffling to the ordinary man. Mr. Van Doren referred to the fact that very early in the "Study in Scarlet" we hear what Holmes knows and doesn't know. That turns out to be wholly fallacious. Holmes was always upsetting Watson's calculations, not only about crime but about himself, so that I think the complexity of Watson is somewhat like the imprint of a metal in wax. It's the work of Holmes.

Stout: I think I agree with Mr. Davis, though in one way Watson was certainly very complex. It is the only case in detective-story writing where the stooge to the detective is made, in story after story, to tag along behind the detective with his tongue hanging out, but is never made to appear ridiculous. No modern writer of detective stories has been able to create a Watson as stooge without making him ridiculous, but Doyle did that.

Van Doren: Well, Watson is ourselves, is he not? And that is why Mr. Davis said that Watson is complex. He was only saying what we all like to think about ourselves. I think the reader, curiously, identifies himself with Watson, and therefore Holmes is as marvelous to the reader as he was to Watson.

Stout: Oh, no, I don't think one identifies oneself with Watson. I think they're both thoroughly objective up there in Baker Street and one couldn't be either of them. You couldn't stand Holmes and you couldn't be Holmes.

Van Doren: I must confess I'm much more like Watson than
I am like Holmes, though I would give both my arms to be
Holmes.

Stout: Who are you, Mr. Davis, when you read a Holmes
story? Aren't you Holmes?

Davis: No, I am the customer who is hearing about Holmes
and Watson.

Barzun: Mr. Davis, just as you can't identify yourself with
Watson, you couldn't be snubbed that many times a day and
survive.

Van Doren: Well, I think I have a poorer opinion of myself
than any of you gentlemen has of yourself. I'm very simple-
minded; I'm extremely simple-minded. I can never guess the end
of a detective story. I'm always surprised at the things I should
be surprised at. My gullibility is somewhat like Watson's.

Davis: Well, now, Watson was gullible to a certain extent,
but he was also a pretty good guller. The man had a marvelous
automatic capacity for glossing over the difficulties in his own
life. Consider the very first sentence in the writings of Dr. Watson that have been preserved. "In the year 1878 I took my Degree
of Doctor of Medicine at the University of London and proceeded directly to go through the course prescribed for surgeons
in the Army." Now there is a very simple declarative sentence,
but the researches of Miss Helen Simpson have disclosed that in
between the first and second clauses there lies the sudden termi-
nation of what seemed to be an extremely promising career in
the medical service of the Army, which at that time was definitely a step down. In short, Watson has simply glossed over
what must have been a great tragedy in his own personal life.

Van Doren: And here you are talking about Watson as if he
existed.

Stout: But of course he did.

Van Doren: We're paying Doyle (I'm sorry I mentioned his
name) the supreme literary compliment: we are believing his
creations, assuming them to be much more important than he is
and willing to read any story he tells us about them.

Barzun: That describes popular literature in the strict sense of the term, doesn't it? As in Beowulf and Roland and so on.

Van Doren: Yes, and we are reminded that any story must be believed to be good.

Barzun: Yes, and believed in a very special way. After all, we're saying here that this has happened in no other book and no other character in recent times. It's a phenomenon.

Van Doren: All right. Then let us go back to our original question about the difference, if any, between these stories and millions of other detective stories, some of which of course are much better than others. Would you say that there is some kind of absolute difference between these and the others? Are these more believable, Mr. Barzun? Even in your special sense of the term?

Barzun: Yes, I think that these are the model of the classic genre. For one thing, most of them are short stories rather than long stories, and I still adhere to the belief that the short story is the natural form of the detective tale. In the second place, they're not mystery stories—they're *detective* stories, and that means simply that what is interesting is the process and not the result. And in the third place it seems to me that the whole literary atmosphere which surrounds these stories is an offshoot of great literature—in particular, Dickens.

Stout: I don't get all this stuff about offshoot and popular—not with a sneer but maybe with quotes—and with the introduction to this program asking people if they wondered why we included Sherlock Holmes among the masterpieces. Is there any question about its being a masterpiece, Mr. Davis?

Davis: I certainly think not, Mr. Stout.

Van Doren: There is no question in my mind—or in yours, Mr. Barzun?

Barzun: No, not in the least.

Van Doren: But right there, I should say, comes in an important literary question. We all believe Holmes and Watson. These stories, I think, have been believed by everyone who ever read them. But what are we saying when we say we believe them? We are saying we believe things which if given us by any other author we would deny as incredible. I would develop the paradox that we love Sherlock Holmes so much, we love the stories so much, because their author is able to make us believe things that no one else could make us believe.

Stout: Well, I don't think a Dickens character is ever as real as Sherlock Holmes is.

Barzun: Pickwick doesn't live for you like Holmes?

Stout: Not in the sense that Holmes does. Pickwick amuses me. Pickwick lives for me in the same way that Harpo Marx does when I see him on the stage, but Sherlock Holmes lives for me in the sense that Harpo Marx does when I'm permitted to be at a dinner party with him, which is a very different thing.

Barzun: I shouldn't go as far as that, though it is not one of the effects, I suppose, of the book, but shall I say of the religious attitude which is present in these pages? I mean the religion of science.

Stout: You may say that. We'll discuss that out behind the barn after we're through, Mr. Barzun. I don't think it's that at all. I really mean what I say. A Dickens character to me is a theatrical projection of a character. Not that it isn't real. It's real, but in that removed sense. But Sherlock Holmes is simply there. I would be astonished if I went to 221½B Baker Street and didn't find him.

Barzun: You would? I'm afraid I went there in the same hope and was disappointed.

Stout: He was out on a case.

Van Doren: Did you even find the number?

Barzun: No, the number isn't there.

Davis: The numbering has been changed.

Van Doren: I want to ask you once more whether the very great and deep pleasure we take in reading these stories isn't the pleasure in seeing romantic things happen. The stories are surely wildly romantic, and in such a way that we don't need to say to ourselves that we are reading romance. Now Holmes himself, you know, scorns the romantic touch. He always does. Whenever he reads the stories that Watson has written he says: "But

son had manners too. The least gentlemanly thing that one can do is to assume that other persons are not gentle. That is where their manners will come from—from your assumption. Chesterfield constantly breaks this rule by referring to his son's defects, and by never being more than grudging in his praise.

Krutch: Again and again he says, almost literally: Now, while you are at the court in Germany or at the court in Turin, I want you to be gay, I want you to be charming, I want you to lose all self-consciousness; and remember that I will have plenty of spies there to report to me just how gay and how unself-conscious you have been.

Van Doren: He was doomed to failure when he took the attitude: I will love you if you deserve it. The only way in which manners can grow in a youth, it seems to me, is for him to understand that he will be loved by his father whether or not he deserves that love. That is the thing which makes persons gentle.

Krutch: You don't need love to feel warmly toward a person who deserves it.

Van Doren: Exactly!

Krutch: You need only justice, and love is something beyond justice. But would you agree with me that anyone may have manners if he is conscious of being loved?

Barzun: And there is the further overarching question: Should a boy be a gentleman in the complete sense in which Chesterfield expected that this infant would be?

Van Doren: You mean he started too soon? He began too early to heap upon him rules and injunctions?

Barzun: Yes. At the age of seven he was already thinking of the future diplomat. Now that violates two rules—precocity and the possible choice of another career that the boy might have made.

Van Doren: That is a mistake which parents are always making, isn't it? The mistake of trying to teach their children something before they can learn it? My own experience among fathers —insofar as they confess their errors—is just that. Particularly with their first child. They tried to teach him everything too soon.

They gave him toys to play with at six that he could not understand before he was ten.

Krutch: Chesterfield gives himself away a number of times by saying that he is living again, through the boy, not his own life but his own missed life, the experiences he didn't have, the wisdom he acquired only slowly.

Van Doren: I was interested in your suggesting, Mr. Barzun, that if the boy had had his father about to imitate, none of these letters and, therefore, none of these injunctions, would have been necessary.

Barzun: I think that is probably true. Lord Chesterfield was, I think, generally recognized to have beautiful manners and to be a gracious and courtly gentleman. Even though Dr. Johnson could despise him, yet Dr. Johnson had to admit that the man had manners. If the son had been at home and if the son could have heard his father speak to other men, perhaps the thing could have succeeded.

Krutch: It would have helped also if the son had been legitimate. There was a psychological hindrance there which the son must have felt very keenly, and which Lord Chesterfield never seems to take into account.

Barzun: Doesn't all this lead us to one consideration of the book which perhaps does a little more justice to Lord Chesterfield? As an educational experiment we agree it's a failure; it couldn't have succeeded. But the book can be turned inside out and made to reveal and express very felicitously one attitude toward the world and society. Which is what has happened.

Van Doren: Yes, but it has happened rather to Chesterfield's detriment. People have said that he had very frivolous manners and no morals, and I think that is very unfair.

Krutch: I was just going to bring that question up, in a slightly different form. I was about to remark that no one had yet mentioned the fact that a great many of Chesterfield's own contemporaries professed to be shocked by the book—notably the poet Cowper, for example, who called Chesterfield "the graybeard corrupter of our listening youth." Many people were shocked, and I think we ought to talk about what shocked them, and whether or not they had a right to be shocked.

Van Doren: Yes, that is the final question. The son can very happily drop out of view at this moment, as he was always wanting to drop out of view. My own notion is that if manners are important to you, this book immediately becomes valuable because its author has a very nice understanding of the importance of manners.

Barzun: He makes one suggestion which I think perhaps answers your question, Mr. Krutch. He says that good breeding is closely allied to good nature. Now we can take them for granted if we want to, but there always comes a point where good nature must cease in order to provide for other qualities, such as honesty, self-assertion, individuality, and it may be that his contemporaries thought Chesterfield wanted good nature to go so far as to become flattery and servility and fickle fancy.

Krutch: That is exactly the question. Manners go just so far. There comes a point when you have to ask whether or not they should be sacrificed to honesty. You have to ask at what point good manners become dishonesty, and many people thought that Chesterfield passed that point. For instance, he is accused, quite truly, of recommending flattery. He says: "If you see a beautiful woman, compliment her on her brains. She probably hasn't any. At least she is not as sure of her brains as she is of her good looks, so compliment her on her brains. If she is a learned woman, compliment her on her looks." Again and again, he pushes the art of pleasing straight into flattery and straight into insincerity.

Van Doren: And sometimes he is cynical. He says: Learn the weakness of each individual—of Sir Robert Walpole, for instance, who was competent in statecraft but who had an absurd desire to be thought gallant. Chesterfield says: If you want to benefit by Sir Robert Walpole, flatter him for the quality which he doesn't have—which, as a matter of fact, he has less than any man alive. There he is quite cynical. But I have a reservation to suggest. I have great belief myself in the art, not of flattery, but of compliment or praise. I can respect no man who is unable to praise. I have a few acquaintances who are utterly lacking in the gift of praise, and for those persons I have neither love nor respect, because it is through the more-than-willingness to recognize a friend's merits that we learn who our friends are—that they reveal their actual virtues to us.

Barzun: It is amusing to imagine what would happen if two perfect Chesterfieldians were to meet. Chesterfield recommends, for example, that you should talk not about yourself but about the other person; not about what interests you but what interests the other person. Now, supposing two perfect gentlemen, trained in this way, meet. They get nowhere at all. Each insists on talking about the other and they finally have to relapse into complete silence.

Van Doren: But what would happen in the world of men— this is an old question—if suddenly all persons started telling the truth? Obviously, society would collapse, would shatter in an instant. The world is familiar with that problem, and I think we are familiar with the answer. The importance of manners comes in just there.

Barzun: Ease in social relations is the essence of Chesterfield's manners; presumably, we need all that we can get to go around; they act as a lubricant to all the friction that society necessarily generates.

Krutch: There is a scarcity of manners. I'm not sure that I would accept the apparent implication that there is a super-abundance of truth, though.

Van Doren: Mr. Krutch has sketched the metaphysics of the problem. Clearly you can't have a society in which there is nothing except persons flattering and complimenting one another and assuming honesty in one another and agreeing with one another, taking one another's tone. Clearly there must be a point every now and then when honesty saves the world. My only point was that honesty alone can destroy the world, too. There must be a constant balance between respect for others and a respect for oneself.

Barzun: Yes, and that suggests something about the book—indeed about any book which pretends to give receipts for behaving in a certain way. Things are much worse when put down in print than they are when carried out in life. For example, the Duke of Marlborough, whom Chesterfield cites again and again as a model of good manners, was universally loved and admired. Now, he may have thought some of the things Chesterfield says, but he never wrote them down; so he gets the credit for the finished article and Chesterfield gets the discredit for giving the game away, so to speak.

Krutch: I think that's very true. Any worldly author labors under a disadvantage for the reason that you have given. Heroics always sound well, but even those bits of worldly wisdom which we ourselves are proud to be able to practice are likely to appear a little shocking when given as advice.

Barzun: Polonius is despised, isn't he, because he gives advice to his son? And yet it is perfectly good advice—of a commonplace sort.

Van Doren: Chesterfield at several points is a perfect Polonius. But once more we must remember that Chesterfield is talking only about those things that can be taught. You remember, he says once to his son: "So far as I know, God has not made you a poet, and personally I am glad that he hasn't made you one"—meaning, I dare say, that a poet would have been a nuisance. "And no man can be made a poet. A man, nevertheless, can be made an orator, and the following rules are rules laid down for your success in speech."

Barzun: I rather doubted, didn't you, Mr. Van Doren, that effort can make one an orator?

Van Doren: Yes, but Chesterfield is perfectly convinced.

Krutch: Of course, it is also only fair to mention the obvious fact that Chesterfield continually himself specifies that he is talking about manners, not about morals, and that he considers morals equally important. I'm not sure that he did, but at least he says so.

Van Doren: There is a metaphysical area where manners and morals are difficult to distinguish, don't you think?

Krutch: Yes.

Van Doren: Manners, in the profoundest sense of the term, are morals because they are based upon love; they are based upon the capacity to love others.

Krutch: Yes, and there is always the implication that in manners as well as in morals you are dealing with your fellow creature and setting a value upon him. There is one subject which Chesterfield comes back to again and again, and which struck me as perhaps the most important in his book. It is the subject of attention and inattention. He says that a person who is inattentive is not fit to live.

Van Doren: I think we can all agree with him there.

Barzun: Here in one of his later letters he summarizes the whole subject, and I'd like to read him if I may. He says: "I know no one thing more offensive to a company than inattention and distraction. It is showing them the utmost contempt, and people never forgive contempt. No man is distrait with a man he fears or the woman he loves, which is a proof that every man can get the better of that distraction when he thinks it worth while to do so, and, take my word for it, it is always worth while. For my own part, I would rather be in company with a dead man than with an absent one, for if a dead man gives me no pleasure, at least he shows me no contempt, whereas the absent man, silently indeed but very plainly, tells me that he does not think me worth his attention. Likewise, can an absent man make any observations upon the characters, customs, and manners of the company? No! He may be in the best companies all his lifetime, if they will admit him, which if I were they I would not, and never be one jot the wiser. I never will converse with an absent man—one may as well talk to a dead one. It is in truth a practical blunder to address ourselves to a man who, we see plainly, neither hears, minds, nor understands us. Moreover, I have heard that no man is in any degree fit for either business or conversation who cannot, and does not, direct and command his attention to the present object, be that what it will."

(1740-1795)

JAMES BOSWELL

The Life of Samuel Johnson

JAMES BOSWELL has given his name to the type of biography he created when he set down, after years of personal acquaintance with his subject, the truest and most intimate possible account of that subject's life in the London of the eighteenth century. To be someone's Boswell has meant ever since to be the one unquestioned and unquestionable authority that curiosity can consult concerning his genius and his manners. Yet in the full sense there has never been another Boswell. For it takes more than patience, good memory, and stenographic skill to report a man as Boswell reported Johnson. It takes genius too, and a love for the subject which is more than adoration. Boswell, notwithstanding his reputation as a toady, as nobody in his own right, was actually very much of a person. For one thing, he was capable of recognizing when he did the singular fascination of Johnson's character. And then he was capable of working over his voluminous notes *until they yielded the unique portrait we find there. It is unique because it is absolutely lifelike. Dr. Johnson talks in these pages with his own voice, and moves under his own power. There was never, of course, anyone like the great lexicographer; to know him is almost in itself to understand what is meant by the word individual. But another biographer might have failed to do what Boswell did. Boswell not only saw this individual plain, he made him plain to all who came and will come after. For once a personality was preserved with all its accent and its flavor. And if such an achievement seems easy, the answer is a question. In what other book to date has it occurred?*

James Boswell studied law in his native Edinburgh and was admitted to the Scottish bar. His ambition, however, lay in letters, an ambition stimulated by meeting Voltaire, Rousseau, and Paoli, in Europe, and Johnson, in 1763 in London. Law and letters met in Boswell's Dorando, A Spanish Tale *and* Essence of the Douglas Case, *both published in 1767 and dealing with the same celebrated suit. His* Account of Corsica *appeared in 1768. Boswell visited Johnson frequently, and shortly after their first meeting began work on the great biography. His* Journal of a Tour to the Hebrides with Samuel Johnson, LL.D., *recounted a journey taken in 1773.*

RALPH H. ISHAM · JOSEPH WOOD KRUTCH · MARK VAN DOREN

Van Doren: Gentlemen, we have as a subject for our conversation today the biography which most people agree is the greatest of all biographies. A good old question about Boswell's *Life of Johnson*—a question that was asked at the very beginning, in the late eighteenth century, and that Macaulay thought he answered finally in the nineteenth century—is this: whether the greatness of the book is to be explained by the nature of its subject or by the nature of its author. Is it Johnson himself, he having been what he was, who makes this book so great, or is it the artistry of Boswell? Mr. Krutch, have you an answer offhand?

Krutch: I have only the answer that it was a very happy conjunction of two things. Macaulay's famous paradox that Boswell wrote a great book because he was a fool is, of course, absurd; folly cannot be great. Boswell often did foolish things, very foolish things. He often said foolish things. But it was his wisdom, not his folly, that made the *Life of Johnson* a great book.

Van Doren: Colonel Isham, since you possess the wonderful collection known as the Boswell Papers you might have a special answer. Or do you think it's an outmoded question?

Isham: The question is often asked: which is the greater man? Certainly one must say that Johnson was the greater man: greater in caliber, greater in learning, greater in philosophy. But I think one can safely say that Boswell was the greater genius. He had a great, unconscious intellectual talent, which one finds, for example, in the fact that in his journal, which was his confessional as well as his repository for the people he collected—

Van Doren: It is one of the items among your papers.

Isham: Yes, we have his notes or journal from 1761 to 1794, just before he died. In it he wrote so frankly, so honestly, and so simply, that when he came to write the *Life of Johnson,* perhaps on fifteen occasions he tore pages out of this journal and, with some minor corrections, sent them to the printer as printer's manuscript. I think that's a testimony of his unconscious intellectual talents.

Van Doren: These were pages that he had written immediately after conversations?

Isham: Very shortly after, yes.

Van Doren: His habit was, if he had been with Johnson, to go home as quickly as possible, I take it, and set down what had been said.

Isham: Well, not always as quickly as possible, because Boswell liked a good time, and if he was having a good time, he didn't go home early. But as soon as he regained consciousness, shall we say, he made at least short, rough notes of these things —anyway, from one day to a few weeks after—and then expanded them into his journals without any sacrifice of accuracy.

Krutch: Nevertheless, the fact remains that when we are reading Boswell's *Johnson* it is Johnson that we are aware of. That is one of the proofs, perhaps, of Boswell's genius. He knows that we are interested in Johnson, not in Boswell; it is part of his art to retire himself from the pages so that we seem to be coming in almost direct contact with Johnson. It isn't really direct. If it were, it wouldn't be so interesting or so pointed; but Boswell creates the illusion that he is of little importance, of less importance than he really is.

Van Doren: And that is a very profound tribute to him, as it would be to any artist. One reason, I suppose, that we adore Shakespeare is that he never makes us think of him while we are reading one of his plays. Boswell does this very subtly—I imagine you would agree, Mr. Krutch—because sometimes he does it by putting himself apparently in the foreground, but only as an object from which our glance can be thrown to Johnson himself.

Krutch: He admitted, of course, that he was perfectly willing to appear as a fool in the pages, if by appearing as a fool he could draw from Johnson one of the remarks that delighted the reader.

Van Doren: There is a very interesting paragraph, at the conclusion of his introduction, in which he says that he is not going to do that quite as often as he had in his *Tour to the Hebrides.* The world had misunderstood him, and the world was a fool; it had not been able to recognize that it was artistry oftentimes which compelled him so to behave.

Isham: Well, sir, Boswell was always willing to take a rebuff from Johnson, and Johnson's rebuffs were wholehearted.

Van Doren: Yes, they were.

Isham: To draw him out, you see. And I can give an example of that. He writes in the *Life*—he does not disclose that it was himself; he just says "a gentleman," but it *was* Boswell, we find from the *Journal*—he writes: "A gentleman, using some of the usual arguments for drinking, added this: 'You know, sir, drinking drives away care and makes us forget whatever is disagreeable. Would you not allow a man to drink for that reason?' Johnson: 'Yes, sir, if he sat next to you.' "

Van Doren: You mean next to Boswell?

Isham: Boswell. But he does not disclose it in the *Life*. He was always glad to take a rebuff if it drew the old boy out.

Van Doren: But on another occasion he might very well have made it clear that it was himself, if to do so had served an artistic purpose.

Isham: An *artistic* purpose, yes.

Krutch: Now, those who go to the opposite extreme and think Boswell completely a genius rather than a fool sometimes speak as though Dr. Johnson were Boswell's creation. It is often said that Johnson is remembered only because of Boswell. I think that is absurd for several reasons. One of them is that, after all, various other people did leave accounts of Johnson. Not one of these is so good, not one of these is so vivid, as the Johnson of Mrs. Thrale or of Fanny Burney. But all of them present the same Johnson. In other words, Boswell's *Johnson* is more of a portrait than a creation.

Van Doren: I dare say it is. That merely brings up the metaphysical question where, in the case of any portrait, say by a great painter, credit lies for the greatness of the result: in the subject who had a soul to be discovered or in the man who was capable of discovering that soul? It is a question to which I suppose you never find the answer.

Krutch: Boswell's Johnson is more continuously and perfectly Johnson than Johnson ever was himself, but it is still the essence of Johnson, not something else.

Van Doren: Boswell had a great capacity for recognizing interesting people and for devoting himself to them, not at all as a toady or a sycophant, I take it, but as one whom, incidentally, they welcomed in their presence. It is important to remember, when we hear it said that Boswell was the toady of Johnson, that Johnson almost from the beginning liked Boswell, and a short time after he met him insisted on accompanying him to Harwich when he was going to the Continent.

Isham: Yes, sir. And Boswell recorded it with, I imagine, great satisfaction. He says as his boat drew away from Harwich that he watched Johnson standing on the shore rolling his great bulk until finally he turned and disappeared into the town.

Krutch: It is worth remembering that one of the things Johnson scolded Boswell for was Boswell's continual demand that Johnson should reassure him concerning his feelings for Boswell. On one occasion I remember Johnson said: "I love you. Write that down in your notebook and don't ask me about it again."

Isham: I can explain that, I think, psychologically, sir. Boswell was always suffering from hypochondria; he had what we would call today a great inferiority complex, and he needed Johnson. Johnson was his strength, almost his religion. The strong moral philosophy of Johnson saved Boswell from his weaknesses, undoubtedly, and you find very often in his *Journal:* "Be like Johnson. Remember you are his friend." That was a constant strength to him; he worshipped Johnson. The theory that he was a sycophant, that he was just trying to shine in reflected glory, is not true—he really worshipped Johnson. You find that before he ever meets him he is recording in his *Journal* how he is strengthened by reading *The Rambler*.

Van Doren: As a matter of fact, that was the reason he wanted to meet Johnson, wasn't it?

Isham: It was the chief reason.

Van Doren: And not the purely professional reason, either, that he some day wanted to write a biography of this man.

Isham: Exactly, sir. It was as if a man wanted to meet the god he believed in.

Van Doren: That accounts, I think, for the extremely dramatic character of those pages in which Boswell, who up till now has been writing a biography of a man he had not known, describes his first meeting with him. It is almost as if an annunciation, a visitation, were occurring. The front door of a shop opens and in comes, at last, the great man. It is very exciting.

Krutch: I remember also that Boswell in his own *Journals* rather frequently asks whether or not something he has done or is about to do is worthy of James Boswell—which is, of course, the vanity of a man who distrusts himself rather than the vanity of a man who is sure of himself.

Isham: I find that an excellent observation.

Van Doren: It is. We have today, of course, to talk about another question which is directly related to this, a question which hypothetical strangers to the biography might want answered. We have to answer this question, if possible; I admit that it's probably impossible. What sort of man was Dr. Johnson? What can we say about him either in terms of himself as we know him from other sources than Boswell or, more properly, in the terms of Boswell? Mr. Krutch—because this new book about Dr. Johnson that you are writing must mean that you are greatly engaged with the question—does it seem to you that three men in a few minutes can say anything essential about the character of the man?

Krutch: Maybe a few essential things, but they would certainly be scraps. If I were asked to say one thing about Johnson, I would say something that, at first sight, seems commonplace but I think isn't: I should stress the point that Dr. Johnson was a great man. Most people think of Johnson as a curious man, perhaps as a perverse man, as an amusing man, as a witty man, as a man of prejudice. He was all of those things, but he was also much more than the average person realizes who knows only the funny anecdotes about Johnson. He was a great man, a great character, a courageous and wise man, as well as an interesting and a funny man.

Van Doren: In other words, the man whom, according to Colonel Isham, Boswell clung to as his philosopher and friend. And of course there are his writings.

Isham: His writings, yes. But I think that what Boswell has achieved in his *Life* is this: he has made a man live for us, he has made a great outline and filled it in with the little details that make for humanity. Like the genie in the fairy tale, from this book Johnson comes as from a bottle, and his strange shape fills the whole room.

Van Doren: Boswell, you remember, quotes Plutarch, who has the same theory of biography; I dare say it is the thing that makes Plutarch our first great biographer. Plutarch says it is the little things that count. On the other hand, no one should forget that little things are interesting only when they are told about a large man. If a man himself is truly little, then all the little facts you could collect about him wouldn't make him interesting.

Isham: But perhaps you might say about a curious man—not necessarily about a great man—that every little thing he did was interesting even if not great. Boswell was a collector of men in the main: not always great men, but always curious and interesting men.

Van Doren: One thing I admire Boswell for is his recognition of Johnson's great gift for what Boswell himself called imagery. Johnson, of course, was a wonderful talker, and many people make the mistake of supposing that he always talked in polysyllables, in abstractions. The conversation of Johnson as here reported is most of the time, as a matter of fact, made up of short words and fascinating words. He had a wonderful gift for summing up a thing he wanted to say in terms of things easily seen. There is the occasion, for instance, on which Boswell was asking him, as he often had before, why Johnson was so grudging in his praise of Robertson's history. Johnson said: The man wraps his gold in wool; most of the space in his box is taken up by the wool. Now I think that an incomparably brilliant way of saying what Johnson wanted to say. Wouldn't you agree that Johnson generally talks that way in this book?

Isham: Johnson probably spoke in a much more pedantic fashion than Boswell records. You'll find that in Scotland Boswell has to defend Johnson for his use of large words by saying that he was so long a school teacher—teaching Latin, so that it became second nature to use Latin words. I think he probably—in fact, we have evidence—tones the big words down and shortens them up a bit.

Van Doren: He was, of course, right in doing so.

Krutch: There is also evidence in the notebook, as I remember, that Boswell sometimes made Johnson talk better than Johnson did; that is to say, he edited the conversation. But to come back again to the question in what way Johnson was a great man. We've touched on one of the things that ought to be said. Carlyle talked about the hero as writer, the hero as soldier, and so on. You would have to call Johnson the hero as talker, because, though Johnson was a good writer, there is no doubt about the fact that the thing he did best was talk.

Van Doren: That is what Boswell himself says.

Krutch: Yes.

Isham: I think one thing must be said of Boswell—he was the greatest reporter of all time. He had a great sense of accuracy; he was a Scot; and also he was a lawyer—I'm speaking of the eighteenth century. He had doubly, therefore, a sense of truth and accuracy. And he also was the inventor of the interview, of personal journalism. Perhaps if he lived today he would have millions and be in danger of getting a peerage.

Van Doren: By the way, there's a certain irony there. I happen to remember a moment fairly late in Johnson's life when, after someone had heard him praise a certain lady whom he didn't know—I think an actress—he was asked why he didn't go to see her. He said: Sir, the reason I do not go to see her is that these days everything like that gets in the newspapers. And at that very moment, as you say, the inventor of the interview, the greatest reporter of all times, was preparing the greatest of all personal lives.

Isham: And never doubted his ability artistically to do it. Boswell often doubted his ability to stick at it long enough to complete it, but his artistic ability he never doubted for one minute.

Van Doren: Mr. Krutch, you were saying that Johnson's essential greatness lay in his power of conversation. Was there any special thing that he preferred to talk about, and do you have in mind any special thing that he said?

Krutch: There is no special subject that he talked about. Yet Johnson and Boswell, different as they were in temperament, were alike in one respect: both were interested primarily in men and manner. That is the reason Johnson liked London and didn't like scenery. The subject of conversation for Johnson, as for so much of the eighteenth century, was what human nature is like, how people behave.

Van Doren: Johnson wouldn't have traveled anywhere at all to see a mountain or a stream, and as a matter of fact he was too shortsighted to be able to see it anyway; nevertheless, he did love to travel, didn't he?

Krutch: He loved to travel. He told Boswell that he would no more live in Scotland for the sake of the scenery than he would live in Bologna for the sake of the sausage; but on another occasion he said that if he had no responsibility to man or God, he would spend his life driving very rapidly in a post-chaise with a beautiful woman; then he paused and added, "But she must be one capable of rational conversation."

Van Doren: He was more wise there than many persons are to-day who dream of living on a desert island with a movie star; they forget that they might be bored to death if she couldn't talk.

Isham: Johnson once said when some beautiful scenery was

being pointed out to him: "Sorry—a blade of grass is but a blade of grass. I am interested in mankind."

Van Doren: I remember, too, that he once said he couldn't tell the difference and didn't care about the difference between one green field and another.

Krutch: Johnson was a man who, of course, loved books. But I think he could have got along without books, whereas he couldn't have got along without conversation. It was *the* necessity of life as far as he was concerned.

Van Doren: Johnson hated to be alone, didn't he?

Krutch: Yes, his friends sometimes hesitated to go see him, because it was so hard to get away. He couldn't bear to be left at night.

Van Doren: And he had one of the most charming of traits—a thing that always makes us love our friends, and probably is the reason we choose those particular friends. When you went to call on him and to suggest that he go somewhere, for dinner or for a late supper or what-not, he was always willing to go. He would drop everything, and he was usually more frisky than the rest. Remember that occasion on which he bounded out of his lodgings with the remark: "I have a mind to frisk with you this evening, gentlemen."

Krutch: No one has mentioned the fact that Dr. Johnson was a pessimist who enjoyed life. Theoretically, he was a pessimist; practically, he was a man beset by fears, by illness, and by gloom. And yet few men ever lived who enjoyed life more thoroughly. He was a moralist without being an ascetic. Those pleasures—of society as well as of literature—which he could enjoy, he savored to the full.

Van Doren: Mr. Krutch, I seem to remember his saying—you could correct this quotation, or Colonel Isham could—that he felt life was something to be endured rather than enjoyed. That fits in, does it, with what you are saying?

Krutch: "There are more things in life to be endured than to be enjoyed." But he didn't say there is nothing in life to be enjoyed. On the contrary, he was a man who found a very large number of things to be enjoyed, and he enjoyed them very thoroughly.

Van Doren: His true greatness as a talker for me is that he was willing and able to talk about anything under the sun; no subject ever arose, no matter how little or how great, but what he immediately had a store of things to say about it.

Isham: He had a great store of knowledge, and I think he perhaps spoke well on a subject even if he had no knowledge of it. He would always speak with great authority.

Van Doren: With great authority. And even when he had no knowledge he had a kind of wisdom which told him what the limits of the subject were, what the bearing of that subject was on other subjects.

Isham: Great wisdom. And, of course, one of the great things of this book to me is that in it he reveals us to ourselves a bit. We are all subject to the same hopes, fears, doubts, and here we learn how a man gets through them, faces them, experiences them. That is valuable for us.

Van Doren: Wouldn't you say, Colonel Isham, that that was true of any good book?

Isham: Yes.

Van Doren: It tells us as much about ourselves as it does about the subject, or about its author.

Isham: The more it reviews ourselves, the better the book, I would say.

Van Doren: Mr. Krutch spoke of the gloom of Dr. Johnson, and the gloom of the man is famous. There were moments of great depression, I believe. People found him in these depressions as great men are likely to be found—Abraham Lincoln, for example.

Krutch: As great men and as wits are likely to be found.

Van Doren: It is notorious that wits are often deeply depressed. Even when they say things which amuse other persons, they have not found them amusing themselves. They do not say them in order to make people laugh. One of the things that Johnson seems to have been gloomy about was death. One of the things that he was chronically in fear of was his own dissolution.

Isham: And Boswell, too. Boswell lived in constant fear of death.

Van Doren: This is only the witness, isn't it, of the great love of life which both men had?

Isham: That is part of it. I think another aspect of it is that Johnson was a profoundly religious man who had the greatest difficulty in keeping himself from being a skeptic. Johnson feared death because he was orthodox enough to fear Hell, yet he was skeptic enough to doubt whether he had been good enough or whether he had faith enough to be saved. There is a continual struggle, I think, in his mind between what he himself calls his stubborn rationalism and his almost desperate reaffirmations of orthodox faith.

Van Doren: It is generally recognized, I believe, that those people are most religious for whom religion is most difficult.

Isham: It was difficult for Johnson. His insistence on orthodoxy, his insistence that the ordinary person must stay in the faith to which he was born, is evidence of the fact that he felt faith as something very easy to lose.

Van Doren: An interesting question always rises in my mind about Johnson, and it is this: Why is it that we respect him so much and think him so good a man and so right a man, in spite of the fact that we so often disagree with his opinions?

Isham: Because he was so fundamentally honest; because he was honest with his doubts. He wanted to believe; but when he couldn't, when he didn't, he disclosed it. He wants always to believe, as we all want to believe.

Van Doren: He is a great literary critic—I think he is one of the greatest of literary critics. But I say that in spite of the fact that, although I agree with him about Shakespeare, I disagree with him about Swift and Fielding, two of the great authors of his own century. I think he was outrageously unjust, both to Swift and to Fielding; and yet my faith in his literary criticism is not impaired, just as my faith in his virtue and his wisdom is not impaired by frequent remarks of his about conduct with which I do not agree. A certain paradox is there.

Krutch: One explanation is that Dr. Johnson was so continuously thinking. I know no great critic who is more often wrong, perhaps, but I also know no great critic who so perpetually has some point to make, something interesting to say.

Isham: As to Boswell's love of life and people, we find that he wrote to Dr. Hugh Blair for the date of a certain conversation he had with Johnson, and at the end of the letter—he is now working on the *Life,* in 1789—he says: "I am in the great lottery of life, in which, should I not get a considerable price, at least I have the agitation of present enjoyment." Very human.

Van Doren: Very characteristic. Colonel Isham, is there any paragraph from the *Life* which you think would sum it up better than any other?

Isham: I have one in mind, but I don't think it would sum it up. I think it would be what Boswell would call "characteristical."

Van Doren: All right.

Isham: It is where Johnson is speaking of being misunderstood.

"But, indeed, sir, I look upon myself to be a man very much misunderstood. I am not an uncandid, nor am I a severe man. I sometimes say more than I mean in jest, and people are apt to believe me serious. However, I am more candid than I was when I was younger. As I know more of mankind, I expect less of them, and am ready now to call a man a good man upon easier terms than I was formerly."

JOHN JAMES AUDUBON

American Scenery and Character

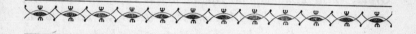

JOHN JAMES AUDUBON *is best known for his paintings of birds, but he was also a writer who had something unique to say. In his* Ornithological Biography, *which followed the great folio entitled* Birds of America, *he alternated descriptions of birds with descriptions of the country which they beautified; and it is these latter sketches, called by him* Delineations of American Scenery and Character, *that will survive along with his plates of the wild turkey and the swallow-tailed kite, the humming bird and the downy woodpecker. Audubon, coming in his youth from France to America, saw the New World in its golden age of maximum promise. The time was the early nineteenth century, when the country, feverish with expansion and ecstatic over its liberty, shone everywhere with confident hope in a limitless future. Audubon in fact saw this America more clearly than any of its natives did; for he brought with him the legends of a bright new world*

which Europe had been repeating for centuries, and which no experience with the reality had been permitted to tarnish. Many Americans at the moment were already tired and disillusioned, but Audubon never was. Traveling on foot and by horse or boat through the valley of the Ohio, through the then frontier, he saw everything in Homeric proportions, as if this were indeed the age of gold and these the progenitors of a perfect race to come. The result is his Delineations, *than which no more infectious description survives of America in her golden morning.*

John James Audubon is generally said to have been born in Haiti, the son of a wealthy Frenchman who had an estate, "Mill Grove," near Philadelphia. Audubon was educated in France, went to "Mill Grove" in 1804 and there devoted himself to observing birds and to making the first American bird-banding experiments. In 1808 he married Lucy Bakewell and lived chiefly in Kentucky, observing bird life and painting portraits. In 1826 he went to England with his Birds of America; *it was brought out, 1827-38, with engravings by Robert Havell, Jr., and with an accompanying text* Ornithological Biography (5 vols., 1831-39) *written with William MacGillivray. Returning to America, Audubon lived on the Hudson shore of northern Manhattan Island. There he prepared the smaller edition of his* Birds of America *and began, with John Bachman, the* Viviparous Quadrupeds of North America, *which was finished by his sons, J. J. and J. W. Audubon.*

DONALD CULROSS PEATTIE · ROBERT CUSHMAN MURPHY
MARK VAN DOREN

Van Doren: Audubon is a great man for many reasons. One is this book we are discussing today, although I am sure our discussion will go far beyond the *Delineations*. It is to me one of the most interesting of all books that describe America. It describes both the landscape and the people of America as of a century and a quarter ago, and it has a quality of admiration, love, energy, which has always endeared the author to me. But I am not an ornithologist, I am not a natural historian, and so I do not have the perspective which enables me to be confident that this is even an important aspect of Audubon. Mr. Murphy, is it so to you?

Murphy: There is no more important aspect of Audubon from the standpoint of American history, because of all the nature writers who pictured the country in its pristine days no one has left us the composite picture of Audubon. He saw America when it was still an Eden, the last garden of that sort remaining in the temperate world. He shows us by what he records that the destructive changes of the first two centuries matched in no way the damage that has been done since his time. There is no other such picture of the dawn of history in the United States.

Van Doren: Mr. Peattie, Mr. Murphy praises Audubon chiefly for his historical value, for being accurate—I dare say a little more than accurate—in his description of an America which once existed. I don't know whether I am quoting you properly or not, Mr. Murphy.

Murphy: Yes, that is quite correct.

Van Doren: Your emphasis was upon his accuracy with respect to a vanished America.

Murphy: Precisely.

Van Doren: Mr. Peattie, do you think that his description continues to have special interest or validity?

Peattie: It is still very true. I know that there are types of Americans which have vanished. We're not going to meet Daniel Boone anywhere, and we're not going to meet his exact like. But as you read in Audubon, in his *Delineations of American Character and Scenery,* you realize that though the scenery has changed somewhat, and sometimes for the worse, the American character is still there, and I am happy to say that the American character is no worse. In some respects it is better, but it is the same character.

Van Doren: Do you say so from personal observation—from having lived in certain places—or is it a faith that you have? I happen to agree with you, but I was wondering what your evidence is.

Peattie: It doesn't matter where you live or what experiences you have. Human character, American character, could be found just as well in a cross-section of modern America as in his time; you could find it in Brooklyn or you could find it in Oregon. If Audubon is telling a true story it should be the same, and our measure of whether he was telling a true story or not is our own observation—yours and mine. What is it like when you talk to a taxi-driver? Audubon never saw a taxi-driver, but just the same he is a human being, and Audubon was himself an intensely human person. He had all the human faults in excess, and he had the human virtues in excess. He was so human a being that he wore himself out at a comparatively early age and died without his full mental faculties. He burnt himself out in the some sixty-five years that he lived; he consumed himself in passionate living.

Van Doren: In these *Delineations* he obviously is very much in love with the people that he finds, as he is in love with the birds.

Peattie: He loved everybody.

Van Doren: In other words, he is inclined to give the benefit of every doubt to the individuals and the groups whom he meets.

Peattie: That is right. And at the same time if you read his original journals—the notes he kept from day to day—you find him often in a highly crotchety state of mind. He hasn't any money, his shoes are worn out, his feet are wet, he has no powder for his gun, the drawing he is making of a bird is spoiled—everything has gone wrong that day, and a great many people have insulted him. He was excessively sensitive to insult, being an artist.

Murphy: He says himself that no one could keep him down, that the only time in all his life when he was depressed for more than a few moments was when he lost his daughter and his daughter-in-law, or when the rats ate up his 120 or more drawings at Henderson, Kentucky. That, of course, was an advantage in the end, because he did them over much better than they were done the first time.

Van Doren: Nothing could ever discourage him.

Peattie: Well, not quite. Dr. Murphy and I were very interested to discover that in a Japanese book there was a description of Audubon and his experience with the rats.

Murphy: It was a translation of Samuel Smiles's old book, *Self Help.*

Peattie: That's right. And therefore it is a universal story; it appeals to all peoples at all times. When he had met with an adversity, he simply was made the stronger by overcoming it.

Van Doren: Mr. Peattie, you seem to refer to two stages of an account written by Audubon. You refer to his own journals, kept currently with his explorations, and to these *Delineations,* many of which seem clearly to have been written years afterwards.

Peattie: They were written years afterward, and the two accounts seem almost to contradict each other at times. Then you say: Which is the true one? And of course they're both true. The point is that when we have encounters on the street and someone is rude and we're out of money and jostled along, we are experiencing things that we wish we were out of at the moment, but at the same time we are living that experience. Say it is on Fifth Avenue. Years later, were you to describe Fifth Avenue, you wouldn't stress the fact that you had no money that day and that somebody was cross to you and you were jostled on the street. You would describe how the flags were lifted by the wind that is forever sweeping up it and how the crowds are forever surging backward and forward. Well, just so did Audubon, when describing American nature and American people, have the actual experiences of intimate contact; then, many years later, he recollected the scene and did what any good artist should do, he selected and composed. That is why we have two separate accounts. It wasn't until recently that most of the original journals, the ones that I might call the almost annoyed ones, came to life.

Van Doren: A man describing a people is always describing himself, isn't he?

Peattie: Oh, very distinctly. He is describing his own moods. But then so was Keats when he was listening to the nightingale. You wouldn't have the faintest idea how a nightingale sang, but you know a lot more about Keats. Well, Audubon was completely an artist by temperament. He became a scientist by training, and consequently he is forever describing himself.

Murphy: He took out what he put in.

Peattie: That's right.

Murphy: And he was a man of very rapid combustion, as you said before.

Peattie: But is that not true of all artists?

Murphy: It is true of all creative individuals.

Peattie: Sinclair Lewis describes the American scene, and his description is true; it is called "photographically accurate," and so it is. But it is also the most accurate photograph of Sinclair Lewis. That's why we read it. Let me point out, Mr. Van Doren, what I feel is very important here—that Audubon was an artist. I mean a graphic artist, a painter. Therefore, he was taught or he taught himself to observe with the most minute detail. Very few writers, myself included, know how to observe in that way. It so happens that he was also able to write. I don't mean that he was a great writer. He merely had a great subject. But it is just because he was taught to observe like a scientist and an artist, minutely, that he is a much better depicter of the American scene than most ordinary writers would be.

Van Doren: I should say, incidentally, challenging you, that your own books are very brilliant at description and they all seem to me accurate. But you refer to him as a great artist. We have not, so far, even mentioned the fact that most people know him for his *Birds of America,* which is a volume or a series of volumes containing pictures of birds. Would you say, Mr. Murphy, that he is a great artist in general or that he is merely a good painter of birds?

Murphy: I think he is a great artist whose work with birds has never been surpassed, and I believe that artists today, including those who belong even to the most modernist schools, have a constantly continuing appreciation of Audubon's work. Frank Benson, who is known the world over as a painter and etcher of birds among other subjects, a man with the finest academic training as an artist, says that Audubon as a painter of birds, by and large, has never been equaled; and Paul Manship, the sculptor, feels exactly the same way about him. He has many of his birds of prey on the walls of his own studio.

Van Doren: That judgment is a judgment of Audubon apart from his subject matter?

Murphy: As an artist. Precisely!

Peattie: Well, we can't forget that Audubon was a painter of mammals and of sporting scenes, of still life and of portraits.

Van Doren: What about his paintings of other subjects? Not that we want to get away from the birds; we shall come back to them. Have you seen very many such paintings?

Murphy: I've seen portraits and I've seen the mammals. There is a large oil, a deer, at the Brooklyn Museum, and there are many smaller paintings in the American Museum of Natural History, in several media.

Peattie: I know some of those, and I also know some of his portrait work. It is true that he never set up to be a great portraitist. He painted portraits merely in order to make enough money to be able to go on painting birds. But he loved painting the portraits just the same. Whether or not he loved the subject when he started out, he got excited about it; and he is a very vigorous portrait painter.

Van Doren: You mentioned once his having to do all sorts of painting, even on sidewalks, for a living or for money to go on with his explorations.

Peattie: I don't mean he painted on the sidewalks. I mean that he sat by the side of the road and would paint anybody who came by. Or he would ask some picturesque old codger around town to sit for him; that would attract a crowd, and then he would begin selling his pictures; that would give him enough to go on 100 miles and see more birds.

Van Doren: He would do anything in order to get on with his birds. I remember, I think from your *Life of Audubon,* the fact that even at the age of nine he was being beaten by his father, in France, because he insisted upon drawing birds rather than studying Latin or whatever it was that his father then wanted him to study. I suppose there are few examples in history of a man more completely given, almost from birth, to an idea.

Peattie: Very few, and particularly to that idea. Then it must be pointed out that he was a dual genius of art and science. There have been very few in the entire history of the world. Goethe was one and Leonardo da Vinci was another. But while each excelled Audubon in certain respects, I wouldn't say that they were more completely dual than he. He had those two great and almost incompatible gifts exquisitely balanced in him.

Van Doren: The gift of knowing a bird as a scientist would know it and of knowing a bird as an artist would know it. I wonder what the difference is? That interests me a great deal, because some time ago, when we were discussing the *Notebooks* of Leonardo here, we found it rather difficult to disentangle the kind of interest the scientist has in a natural fact from the kind of interest an artist has.

Peattie: And just after telling me it's so difficult, you ask me to venture upon the task.

Van Doren: Yes, I beg you to say what we couldn't say. Many

people would suppose it was a very easy distinction to state, because in most people's minds the scientist and the artist are very
far apart.

Peattie: I'm willing to try—and fall down on my nose in front
of everyone.

Van Doren: Go ahead.

Peattie: I would say that science knows its way toward reality,
and art feels its way toward reality. One is emotion and the other
is knowing.

Van Doren: Or could you put it this way: That both know,
perhaps, but the scientist knows the abstract, knows the general,
knows the laws involved—the classes and species involved—
whereas the artist is always concerned with the individual thing.

Murphy: No, it is not a matter of concern; it is a matter of the
impression with which you're to be left.

Van Doren: Yes, but Audubon, painting a particular turkey or
particular sandpiper or swallow-tailed kite, seems to have that
individual thing before him.

Peattie: That is right. He had a very, very strong sense of
exactly what species was to be described, and there must be no
other in his mind. I have heard a modernist artist say he didn't
care whether the object in his picture was taken for a cow or a
Chinaman, just so long as you were interested in the shape.

Van Doren: But I don't assume that it was enough for Audubon to have the species in mind. A scientist thinks in terms of
species; he wants his knowledge to be sound with respect to the
kind of thing being described or painted or what not. The artist
on the other hand is a man who can lose himself, so to speak, in
the individual before him. Isn't that true? For instance, take a
philosopher and a poet. It is perhaps the same sort of difference.
The philosopher is interested in truth everywhere; the artist, the
poet, is interested in the truth here and now; it is as if no other
man had ever existed before.

Peattie: Exactly, but now you bring us to the point of what
Audubon intended you to come away with when you'd seen one
of his pictures, and I'll show you why I think he was such a per-

fectly balanced dual genius. He painted the bird not as most artists would do, as an impression of that bird; he painted every single barb on every single pinion; you can count them if you want to, and they come out correctly. Every feather lies just where it should to please the most exacting ornithologist, and it lies as it looks on the living bird, not on a dusty museum specimen 150 years old. All right, so far it is scientific illustration; it is an illustration from which you could identify the bird at any time, and he will stop and give you in enlarged detail the finest details of the bill or the feet or some form even of the viscera of the animal. But when you have looked at the picture, even if you are not an ornithologist, you come away with a feeling that makes you think: I never saw a picture of an eagle that was more like an eagle in all my life—that is the most eaglish thing ever done. Or if it's a duck, it's the most ducklike; and if it is a small singing bird, everything is there but the sound. The bird is singing, the tree is flowering, the day is spring, the dew is on the landscape, and you feel as though it were the morning of all the world. That is where he is a great artist; he does both things at the same time. No other individual, either by combining science and painting or science and description or science and anything else, has ever more perfectly blended those two things.

Murphy: I agree entirely with that.

Van Doren: Your emphasis is still upon the certainty the spectator will have that he is face to face with a species. Would you go further and say that it is a particular day which seems to be rendered, Mr. Murphy? A particular day with dew on it, and a particular member of the species of sandpiper?

Murphy: Oh, decidedly. Everything is a factual experience. Audubon had seen the bird in his setting; in most cases, he had shot it himself.

Van Doren: Then it was one bird.

Murphy: It was one bird and one place and one time.

Peattie: So much so, Mr. Van Doren, that when he found a bird in a very peculiar attitude and he delightedly painted the bird going through that strange antic, fellow scientists, already enraged by his breaking all the holy taboos of science, said that he was a nature-faker and that no bird had ever been seen to do that before. But in actual experience every picture I know of that represents a peculiar attitude, or something else that might make you a little doubtful of its reality, has been substantiated later on. He was constantly doing individual scenes, individual days, and animals that were just those animals of all in the world. That is why he is a complete artist, at the same time that he is a complete scientist.

Murphy: It is a commonplace remark among taxidermists, who also know nature: "If I should ever mount a bird in that position, the Museum wouldn't put it on exhibition!" That's the sort of thing that Audubon illustrates and demonstrates.

Van Doren: But Audubon didn't worry.

Murphy: Not a bit. And he had of course a peculiar gift of observation. In his rambles near New Orleans in 1821, he heard a note and immediately pricked up his ears; he followed the bird until he obtained it, and he said: "I instantly recognized the note as one I had never heard before." He always knew that.

Van Doren: What was the bird, do you remember?

Murphy: I don't recall. It was a warbler, but I'm not sure what it was.

Van Doren: I suppose the birds he is most likely to render in fantastic postures are the long-legged ones and long-necked ones. It has always seemed to me that long-legged and long-necked birds can look sillier upon occasion than any other living thing.

Murphy: Well, he had to fit them into a plate. He chose a plate impression that would accommodate the whooping crane and the trumpeter swan and the turkey-cock, the largest species found in North America, and that meant that he had to use little tricks and conventions. In a few cases, the bill of the bird projects beyond the plate impression, or a bit of the tail makes an attractive artistic effect.

Van Doren: I have one rather naive question to ask both of you. I am sure you'll think it's naive. Why are birds so important? I'm convinced they are very important, and I assume that one of the reasons the world admires and loves Audubon so much is that he seemed to understand their indeed almost mystical importance. Can you say anything about this, or is it an embarrassing question?

Murphy: Dr. Chapman once said: "Birds are the most eloquent expression of nature's beauty, joy, and freedom." They've probably been the most observed members of the fauna of the world from the very earliest days, whether the observation was done in forecasting or whether for purely esthetic reasons, or for practical reasons other than augury.

Van Doren: It is in them that nature seems most alive.

Peattie: Mr. Van Doren, ask anybody on the street what he would rather be if not a man, and you'll get the answer why birds are important.

Van Doren: All right.

Peattie: They are important to our emotions.

Van Doren: And also, in a way, to our understanding of what everything is about. We can so easily believe that if we were birds we should have a power which would enable us to enjoy all the necessary, all the important experience.

Peattie: Dr. Murphy brought up a moment ago a point that would be interesting to pursue a little further, that is, the size of the plates. Audubon was making a uniform book. There were to be 500 plates, and every bird in North America was to be represented on it life-sized. It didn't matter if it was a titmouse or a great horned owl or a flamingo. They all had to be life-sized, so he had to take the largest possible size of paper he could get and fit his birds onto it, no matter how difficult that might seem at first flush. But what he accomplished is something that has never been surpassed in America, in science or in art, so far as I know. He did a book of 500 elephant-folio-sized plates. Now, that book sold for $1,000 when it came out, which was a staggering price. It would still be a staggering price.

Van Doren: I should think so.

Peattie: Yes, $1,000 for a book about birds. But do you realize that if you had one today you could sell it for $10,000?

Murphy: $15,000. Within a month, in New York City.

Peattie: But what happens to them is this: The plates are so valuable individually that as soon as one of these copies comes up for sale in an auction room, some one buys up the entire set, then breaks it up and sells it plate by plate.

Van Doren: By the way, does that seem horrible to you? Every now and then it appalls me to think of the book being broken up.

Peattie: No, it is not horrible, I'm sure, because as they are broken up they reach a larger number of people.

Murphy: Precisely.

Peattie: Were they all immediately bought up by brownstone-front institutions and put deep in a vault where you had to sign something before you were allowed to look at them, very few people would ever see them.

Murphy: It is the breaking up of the books that has created knowledge of Audubon and made him popular. There were probably 177 issued, or some number very close to that, and it is believed now that about 100 have been distributed.

Van Doren: And of course we can count upon all the plates that are taken out of them being preserved somewhere. Clearly people would want to preserve them.

Peattie: Correct. Now, if you want to buy an Audubon plate and you want to be sure of getting one of the originals and not one of the later reproductions, look in the lower right-hand corner. If it says "Lizars—Edinburgh" or "Havell—London," then you have one of the originals, and it is worth quite a good deal of money. If it says anything else, then it is not one of the original copper-plated, aquatinted plates; it is a modern or comparatively modern chromo-lithograph, and should sell for very much less.

Murphy: But well worth possessing.

Peattie: Well worth possessing nevertheless.

Van Doren: We are talking now of the book which most people associate with Audubon: *The Birds of America.* I should like to go back at the end to his *Delineations,* to a passage which I think is typical of that book for its tone, for its accent of one who is describing Paradise. He is describing the Ohio River by day and by night:

"The days were yet warm; the sun had assumed a rich and glowing hue, which at that season produces the singular phenomenon called there 'the Indian Summer.' The moon had rather passed the meridian at her grandeur. We glided down the river, meeting no other ripple of the water than that formed by the propulsion of our boat. Leisurely we moved along, gazing all day on the grandeur and beauty of the wild scenery around us. As night came, sinking in darkness the broader portions of the river, our minds became affected by strong emotions and wandered far beyond the present moment. The tinkling of bells told us that the cattle which bore them were gently roving from valley to valley in search of food or returning to their distant homes. The hooting of the great owl or the muffled noise of its wings, as it sailed smoothly over the stream, were matters of interest to us. So was the sound of the boatsman's horn as it came winding more and more softly from afar. When daylight returned, many songsters burst forth with echoing notes, more and more mellow to the listening ear. Here and there the lonely cabin of a squatter struck the eye, giving note of commencing civilization. The crossing of the stream by deer foretold how soon the hills would be covered with snow."

(1796-1859)

WILLIAM HICKLING PRESCOTT

The Conquest of Mexico

*T*HE CONQUEST OF MEXICO *is one of several heroic histories produced in America during the nineteenth century. The names of Parkman, Motley, and Prescott continue to be great names in an art of which Herodotus is traditionally called the father. The three men wrote as Herodotus wrote, with sweep and fire, and with a sense of the epic quality residing in their subjects. Their subjects involved vast areas and violent events and, as with Herodotus, the clash of alien cultures. This is particularly true of Parkman, whose imagination explored North America with the French, and of Prescott, who made himself a master of the Spanish-American South.* The Conquest of Mexico *remains standard for all who would read in English of Cortez and Montezuma, and of the civilizations which through them came into such disastrous conflict. Prescott, with fewer temptations than Herodotus to be partisan in his account, is equally with Herodotus the dis-*

[311]

tant, far-seeing, absorbed spectator: interested in every detail of Aztec life which he can recover from the available documents, and fascinated by every step in the swift catastrophe which overwhelmed the people of Montezuma. The landing of the Spaniards, their marches up the mountains of Mexico, their all but incredible feats of endurance and hardihood, and at last their appearance upon the dazzling scene which their fanaticism was to devastate—of such things is his moving spectacle made, and from such materials has he molded his heroic poem. For The Conquest of Mexico, *like any history which achieves a general fame in the world, always approaches poetry.*

William Hickling Prescott was born in Salem, Mass. He graduated from Harvard and entered his father's law office. After a serious eye injury, he abandoned law and resolved to devote himself to historical writing. He wrote numerous contributions for the North American Review *and in 1837 produced his first important work,* The History of the Reign of Ferdinand and Isabella. The Conquest of Mexico *(1843) was followed by* The Conquest of Peru *(1847). Prescott's eyesight had been failing constantly; it was practically gone when he started his monumental* History of Philip II *(Vols. I, II, 1855; Vol. III, 1858), which was unfinished at the time of his death.*

Prescott: The Conquest of Mexico

CARLETON BEALS · JACQUES BARZUN · MARK VAN DOREN

Van Doren: Prescott's *The Conquest of Mexico* is a book of great scope, a narrative crowded with most fascinating materials, and it might seem difficult to begin a discussion of it. It is clear to me today, however, that the most significant question to ask, a question which Prescott indeed keeps asking all the way through, has to do with the ethics of conquest. For this is the story, after all, of the destruction of one civilization by another. Mr. Barzun, does it strike you that that is in fact a leading question in Prescott's own mind?

Barzun: It seems to me so, for a number of reasons. For one thing, when Prescott was writing many people considered that conquest was the origin of most political rights; in the second place, there was a feeling that progress and civilization meant the replacing of one culture by a higher one, and Prescott tries to persuade himself that the Spaniards who invaded Mexico represented a higher culture than the Aztecs; yet again and again he is almost compelled by his materials to admit that the Aztec civilization had perhaps just as good a right to exist as the Spanish.

Van Doren: And that is why the thing remains a question in his mind. If it had been something other than a question, he would have been able to settle it very simply. Mr. Beals, does it seem to you that there is still a question as to which civilization was superior?

Beals: I think there is a very definite question as to which was superior. Certainly the Aztecs were using a calendar which was more accurate than the one we use in the United States today.

Van Doren: Was it their own invention, by the way?

Beals: It was not their own invention; they got it from the

Mayas, who had made greater progress in astronomy than the Aztecs had.

Barzun: Prescott is particularly upset by the fact that the Aztecs had human sacrifices and what he calls a superstitious religion, and he would like to persuade himself that that gave, as it were, a right to the Spaniards to introduce Christianity. But of course the way in which the Spaniards introduced it was so violent and destructive that it hardly seems an improvement on the native customs.

Beals: Of course Prescott does remark that they had a good precedent in the case of Mohammed who had spread his religion by the sword, and if it had worked for an obviously inferior religion, why shouldn't it be a doubly good method for a superior religion?

Barzun: There's always another difficulty about any conquest, and that is the difficulty of keeping the issue to the fore. I mean by that that people tend to fight first for a motive or a few motives, but pretty soon the necessities of military affairs make you fight just to fight, just to win. Cortez refers to the faith and the necessity of converting the natives very often as an afterthought. Doesn't he?

Beals: There's the old saying that the motives of the Spaniards were God, Glory, and Gold. It seems to me that those three motives were pretty much in their mind all of the time.

Van Doren: And if God was their motive, they expressed that motive as fanatically as the Aztecs sacrificed human victims on their altars. Prescott is always falling back on the word "barbarous" or "barbarian" when he wants to justify the conquest. The conquest is, incidentally—I suppose you both agree—in his own mind a very painful spectacle. He can't help admiring this relatively happy and relatively beautiful culture here on the great plateau of Mexico; it is painful to him to see it so brutally, so quickly, so amazingly destroyed.

Barzun: And for perfectly futile results, as far as that goes. It seems to me that the Spaniards got neither gold, nor glory, nor the gospel in any tangible and impressive form.

Van Doren: Yes, but whenever Prescott does want to feel better in his mind about this outrage, he falls back upon the word "barbarous" and "fanatical"—realizing, as he himself says, that he has to justify fanatical Spaniards too, because they came from the Spain of the Inquisition.

Beals: I have the feeling that while Prescott has some of the prejudices of his day, he is fairly objective in his treatment of the matter. He doesn't let these particular ethical considerations overrule his judgment very much in his relation of historical events.

Van Doren: And of course you remember that at the beginning of the book he points out that he will be, indeed has been, blamed by both sides in the question. The Spanish readers felt that he was too hard on the Spanish, and persons sensitive for the Mexican cause thought he was too indifferent to their disaster.

Barzun: But he has really, wouldn't you say, Mr. Beals, only one genuine object of admiration, and that is Cortez's ability. That is undoubted. Everything else has flaws, for certainly Cortez's followers were a mixed lot of adventurers and decayed noblemen and common plunderers, and there's very little to be said on their behalf.

Van Doren: How much is still to be said in horror concerning the ritual of human sacrifice among the Aztecs? That seems to be the thing that Prescott assumes he can always count upon—our taking it as horrible.

Beals: Well, the sacrifice of human beings in the Aztec Empire was a ceremonial and symbolic rite. I should say it was a far more civilized thing than lynching, for instance, or—maybe you might agree with me—the toll from automobile accidents in the United States, which we take for granted perhaps because people are insured.

Barzun: Insurance is the ceremonial.

Beals: With the Aztecs the ceremonial was part of the sacrifice.

Van Doren: Yes, we don't decide beforehand, we don't pick out 30,000—how many people do we kill annually with automobiles? About 30,000?

Barzun: Something like that.

Van Doren: We don't pick out the 30,000 beforehand and we don't dress them in a certain kind of costume so that all of the inhabitants of our land will know that they are going to die during the year. Nevertheless, when we read in the newspaper that 30,000 have died most of us Americans accept the number as somehow necessary. We say: Well, progress—

Barzun: Speed—

Van Doren: —speed, efficiency, and the mechanization of our life.

Beals: The Aztecs also accepted sacrifice as necessary. Most of their so-called victims were voluntary. Those elected were considered to represent the god himself, and for a whole year they were treated like gods; they were given the finest raiment and food and quarters; they were given beautiful music to listen to that year, any diversion they wanted; beautiful companions of the other sex were given to them.

Van Doren: That's a very nice way of putting it.

Beals: That's a very genteel way of putting it. And also I have since discovered that the Aztecs knew of anesthetics—perhaps the earliest use of anesthetics that we have record of—and that the victims were largely unconscious of the pain inflicted upon them when the hour came.

Barzun: There is an interesting consequence of this practice, however, and that is that since they extended the sacrifice to prisoners of war, they always tended to prefer to take their enemies alive. I should say that in fighting the Spaniards, again and again they lost great advantages through the desire to take possible sacrificial victims. That seems to me to show that our superstitions get in our way occasionally.

Van Doren: Most decidedly. We haven't mentioned another institution, which is more modern than Aztec culture and which Prescott is forced to admit is modern when he refers to the slavery imposed by the Aztecs upon the conquered laborers. He has to admit that slavery exists even in his own country, although he doesn't name the country where it exists.

Barzun: It was a rather mild slavery that the Aztecs exercised.

Beals: It was part of their collection of tribute.

Barzun: They seem to have had frequent manumission and perfectly easy social relations between slaves and masters.

Van Doren: What are we doing, gentlemen? Are we justifying human sacrifice?

Barzun: Plus cannibalism. Didn't they eat some of their victims?

Beals: That, too, was a ceremony.

Barzun: That's the utilitarian spirit, I suppose.

Van Doren: Well, will you answer my question now? Are we justifying human sacrifice? I'm just a little uncomfortable about that, I must confess.

Barzun: Can there be society without human sacrifice?

Van Doren: Perhaps that's the point. Perhaps it always happens and perhaps any society had better recognize that it is doing it.

Beals: Certainly I was not attempting to justify human sacrifice; I was merely pointing out the institutional aspect of it.

Van Doren: Yes, and pointing out that quite possibly a society is healthier when the sacrifice is recognized as sacrifice—which we deliberately refuse to do, I suppose, and which many militaristic nations of the modern world refuse to do in quite the same sense when they ask their citizens to die for the progress of the nation and to die cheerfully.

Barzun: There are other institutions than religious ones, and I wonder if we could come to some kind of conclusion about the government of the Aztecs—whether it was something inferior to what the Spaniards proposed to establish?

Beals: It had many aspects similar to that of Spanish civilization.

Barzun: You mean it was an empire?

Beals: It was an empire; it had feudal characteristics; as in old Spain, it had villages with common lands which were respected by the king and by the nobility; and this accounts for part of the success of the Spaniards in grafting their own civilization on to the native system; in fact, the Spaniards utilized the *Caciques* and married into the families of the native princes in order to cement their rule.

Barzun: Which in a sense recognizes the equality of the two civilizations.

Van Doren: Yes, and there was a hierarchy of priests in both cases, too, recognized as having great authority.

Barzun: Weren't you impressed though, Mr. Beals, by the incompetence of the home government in Spain in taking over this great area of conquest and making Cortez's life so difficult—standing in his way and being as inefficient as we always think most imperial governments are about outlying regions.

Beals: That is very true, although Spain did send over some great administrators to New Spain, or what is now known as Mexico.

Barzun: But long after the conquest.

Beals: No, fairly promptly.

Barzun: Well, Cortez after he had conquered Mexico for the second time simply hadn't a moment's peace; he was constantly being called in to be questioned; he was put on trial, he was exiled, and he died a poor and thoroughly unhappy man, as far as I can see.

Van Doren: What about Velasquez, whom he quarreled with in Cuba and from whom he had to escape so that he could reach Mexico? Was he a distinguished administrator, do you happen to know?

Beals: He was quite a distinguished administrator, yes.

Barzun: But Fonseca, the Bishop of Burgos, at home, was certainly a small mind who didn't understand what an empire was. Wouldn't you say that?

Beals: That's very true, yes. But the Council of the Indies itself passed some of the most enlightened legislation for the government of the colonies that has ever been put upon statute books by any nation.

Barzun: Could they enforce it?

Beals: No.

Van Doren: They would send a man over like Guzman, and he would act like that.

Beals: Communications were poor; it was difficult to enforce edicts, and in fact the home government almost precipitated a secession of the colonies as early as the sixteenth century by attempting to enforce this enlightened code.

Barzun: That suggests one question I wanted to ask you, Mr. Beals: Why didn't Cortez set up an independent kingdom with himself as the head? He was such an able administrator, governor, and military man; he had all the virtues of the leader; and yet he hesitated to do that.

Van Doren: You mean after Mexico fell?

Barzun: Yes, and after he saw that his enemies near by and his enemies at home wouldn't leave him a moment's peace to consolidate and really make a decent state out of the conquered territory.

Beals: The sense of disloyalty of Spaniard to Spaniard was very great, but his sense of loyalty to the Crown was tremendous, and it is quite possible that in spite of his conquest of Mexico Cortez was not sure that he could consolidate an empire without continued support from home.

Barzun: Of which he got very little because Charles V was much more interested in continental affairs than he was in transatlantic ones.

Van Doren: We now seem to be referring to that end portion of the book which is not exactly an epilogue, because Prescott includes it within the compass of the work, but which deals with the subsequent career of Cortez. This reminds me to say that Prescott earlier in the book remarks that it is more than a history he is writing; he seems to think that the historical portion of it proper deals only with the events involving the downfall of Mexico. There is this biographical portion at the end, and there is a portion at the beginning, the introduction, which he says is philosophical in the eighteenth-century sense of the term—descriptive of cultures. He seems to be aware of an analogy between his own book and Herodotus's *History*, does he not, because

Herodotus is biographical, is cultural, and is narrative in the same threefold way?

Barzun: Yes, their minds are very much alike, but I think that Prescott felt one thing that Herodotus did not feel, and that is the problem presented by the appearance of a man like Cortez upon the world scene. I think it is a problem that comes very close home to us. What would we do without Napoleons and Hitlers, without conquerors of the world?

Van Doren: I wonder, Mr. Barzun, if there isn't a closer analogy than you suggest. Xerxes tries to be such a man in Herodotus. He happens to have failed.

Barzun: But we don't see him there making his fate out of unlikely materials, as we do here.

Van Doren: Xerxes had illimitable man-power behind him, illimitable wealth.

Barzun: And he started from the throne.

Van Doren: Of course. Whereas this amazing man Cortez, starting with almost nothing and, indeed, leaving Cuba you remember that night with only half of the equipment that he needed and because he was afraid he would be held there—

Barzun. And ending with nothing, like Napoleon and other people of his class.

Van Doren: I think there must be few grander human spectacles than the life of Cortez, just as there is no more appalling and fascinating spectacle than the fall of Mexico itself. We've been perhaps giving too much the impression that Prescott is interested only in a moral question, the question of the ethics of conquest. He was also caught up in the great spectacle he was describing. His book is largely, I take it, narrative and descriptive. Does it seem to you, Mr. Barzun, as a historian, that the work takes high rank among historical classics?

Barzun: Oh, I think it does. Not only are the incidents in themselves picturesque and dramatic, but the proportion, the sweep, and the style which Prescott had at his command to convey them make the book one of the unforgettable books of history.

Beals: In fact, I would rate him somewhat higher than Herodotus. That may be heretical.

Van Doren: No, go ahead. You are perfectly free to do so.

Barzun: He had a more compact subject; a smaller canvas in a way, and that gives one a sense of unity and proportion that one doesn't get from Herodotus.

Van Doren: He has the same subject in a sense, too, the subject of a great war being fought between unequal forces. The smaller force in the case of Herodotus happens to triumph too, but it is a triumph in defense rather than in offense.

Barzun: And Prescott had one other advantage which any historian who wants to make a name for himself should be careful to select. He had a thoroughly improbable subject; it is almost unbelievable that this happened.

Van Doren: Time and time again at the end of a long paragraph recapitulating the monstrous facts, he says that they are utterly incredible and yet the literal truth. What is the most incredible thing, Mr. Beals, about the whole story?

Beals: Well, the thing which strikes one offhand is that a small group of Spaniards could overthrow a tremendous empire—

Barzun: He had sixteen horses.

Van Doren: He had sixteen horses; he never enumerates the cannon, I believe, does he? Or do you remember that he does?

Beals: No, I don't believe he does.

Van Doren: But probably just a handful. And the Spaniards were only a few hundred, were they not?

Beals: About 500, I should judge, from the statistics we have.

Van Doren: Oftentimes, of course, there were Indian allies.

Beals: You must remember that at times the Spaniards had thousands of Indian allies; I do not know how many thousands of Tlaxcalans went with them, and these were of course directed and organized by Cortez, who was a genius in tactics.

Van Doren: And yet these still relatively few men brought down an empire of—well, I wonder what the population or the military force of Montezuma was. I don't remember any figures if they were given.

Beals: It is impossible to get exact figures, although some historians put the population of the valley of Mexico around a million inhabitants; the size of Mexico City was probably at least a quarter of a million, a figure which it did not reach again, after its destruction by Cortez, until centuries later.

Van Doren: And of course Cortez does not conquer this amazing people by brutality alone, does he?

Beals: No, he couldn't have done it by such methods alone. He utilized existing fifth columns. The Aztec Empire had not really integrated itself; in other words, some of its conquests were very recent and the rancors against the Montezumas was very great among the Totonacos, the Tlaxcalans, and others.

Barzun: Still the Aztec Emperor Montezuma was able to exert absolutely undisputed sway, and the continued respect the various tribes had for him, after suffering many defeats from the Spaniards, is something which struck the Europeans with surprise. A monarch in Europe who had suffered so many reverses would not have stayed on the throne. So that Cortez really had tremendous odds against him, and he had the nerve to shut himself up with his 500 men in the very heart of this empire.

Van Doren: To shut himself up by burning his fleet at Vera Cruz, so that he could not retire.

Barzun: Yes, and by entering this valley guarded on all sides and by diplomacy and astuteness capturing Montezuma and making him dependent upon him.

Van Doren: That must have taken more than courage; it must have taken more than a willingness to be ruthless, because from time to time he is perfectly ruthless in the massacres he conducts; it must have taken a great deal more; it must have taken imagination.

Barzun: He had genius—that is, the capacity to see what he must do next, even though there was no precedent for doing just that in those circumstances.

Van Doren: The relatively small nations these days who are trying to conquer relatively huge nations or groups of nations—

would you say that any of them is led by a person equal in imagination to Cortez?

Barzun: No, I should say not. To be sure, their imagination is active and we suffer from it precisely for the same reason that the Aztecs suffered from Cortez. They have a certain originality which their enemies—ourselves—haven't got. But they are also much more limited in their tactics; they repeat the same thing over and over again, whereas Cortez was always inventing new devices, new schemes.

Beals: I think there is one lesson we might get from all this, if we're looking for lessons in our own case. However much strategy or force Cortez used or whatever other things he used, he was always on the alert, no matter if he was in the most friendly territory; he never relaxed his vigilance for one second, day or night.

Barzun: Yes, in fact, to read Prescott is to think that Cortez didn't sleep for three years.

Van Doren: He really had genius. And meanwhile the hundreds of thousands, possibly millions of persons he was going to bring down seem to have gone on day after day thinking that nothing really could happen to them because there were so many of them, because they were so rich, because they had such an empire.

Barzun: And even if they didn't consciously think these things, they lost simply by continuing their habits, their normal habits. But I'm struck by one discrepant element in Cortez's character; I mean his irrationalism, his sudden desire, time and again, to try to convert the natives by violence when it would have completely ruined his prospects. He was stopped only by the interference of Father Olmedo, the priest.

Beals: I have the feeling that he either intuitively or consciously was aware that until he struck at one of the main sources of Aztec ruling power, he could do nothing; that it was necessary to destroy the power of the priesthood in order to set up a new allegiance.

Van Doren: Well, Mr. Beals, he ended by destroying the whole works. I wonder if you would be willing to read the final paragraph in which Prescott introduces a further reason why that was possible.

Beals: "The Indian empire was in a manner conquered by Indians. The first terrible encounter of the Spaniards with the Tlaxcalans, which had nearly proved their ruin, did in fact ensure their success. It secured to them a strong native support, on which to retreat in the hour of trouble, and around which they could rally the kindred races of the land for one great and overwhelming assault. The Aztec monarchy fell by the hands of its own subjects, under the direction of European sagacity and science. Had it been united, it might have bidden defiance to the invaders. As it was, the capital was dissevered from the rest of the country, and the bolt which might have passed off comparatively harmless, had the empire been cemented by a common principle of loyalty and patriotism, now found its way into every crack and crevice of the ill-compacted fabric, and buried it in its own ruins. Its fate may serve as a striking proof that a government which does not rest on the sympathies of its subjects cannot long abide; that human institutions, when not connected with human prosperity and progress, must fall—if not before the increasing light of civilization, by the hand of violence, by violence from within, if not from without."

(1822-1885)

ULYSSES SIMPSON GRANT

Memoirs

Wʀɪᴛᴛᴇɴ *in the last year of its author's life, when he knew he was dying, the* Memoirs *of General Grant had a success of which he was never to be aware. The success of this book at the moment might have been what it was had its intrinsic merits been less than they were. For two unfortunate terms as President of the United States had not destroyed Grant's popularity, and the war he had won twenty years before was still the outstanding event in America's memory. Furthermore, his literary champion and promoter was Mark Twain, who not only saw that the book was written but brought it about that its circulation was immediately immense. But as time has gone on the* Memoirs *has taken its place among the permanently valuable military autobiographies, as well as among the sincerest known documents of self-revelation. Not that Grant in writing it seems to have thought about himself; his only expressed desire was to render a clear account of his*

career in the Mexican and Civil Wars, and to avoid any conceivable injustice to others who, with him or against him, were also involved in those wars. It is in fact this feeling for justice, along with a disposition not to think unduly of himself, that reveals him to a degree which Rousseau, standing at the opposite extreme of autobiography, never quite achieves. Grant's book, composed without any discoverable style beyond that of the best military report, becomes nevertheless an impressive and appealing personal record; and it has stood as history. This or that judgment may be challenged, but the author's integrity has never been called in question; nor his modesty, nor his sense of the tragedy in which he had played a part, nor his magnanimity to his foes, nor his perfect clarity of tone.

Ulysses Simpson Grant was born at Point Pleasant, Ohio, and reared on the family farm. After graduating from West Point (1843), he served in the Mexican War and in 1854 resigned to enter a succession of small businesses. In 1861 he enlisted in the Civil War and began his brilliant service to the Union Army, of which he became chief commander. He was elected president as the Republican candidate in 1868 and again in 1872, and after retiring from the White House made a two-year tour of the world. The banking firm in which his funds were invested collapsed; fatally ill of cancer of the throat, Grant undertook his Memoirs to rehabilitate his fortunes.

ALLEN TATE · JACQUES BARZUN · MARK VAN DOREN

Van Doren: I suppose the first question we ought to try to answer is the question whether Grant's *Memoirs* is simply another book by a soldier about a war in which he happened to take part, and therefore a book that takes its place among thousands of others, or whether it is a classic—a neglected classic, because I am not under the impression that it is widely read—a classic, that is to say, of military autobiography which has the power to suggest Caesar's Commentaries on the Gallic Wars or the Civil Wars. Mr. Barzun, have you an opinion upon this point?

Barzun: I would agree with you that it is a neglected classic.

Van Doren: By the way, I didn't say it was. I said we should ask whether it was.

Barzun: Well, I agree with you about the asking of the question. I never read anything but excerpts from these *Memoirs* before reading them for this morning's discussion, and I confess the book was a revelation to me. I don't know that I would agree that it is necessarily a classic of military autobiography, but it is of autobiography in general.

Van Doren: So you don't think it is necessary, if it is to be established as a classic (not that we have the vanity to assume that we could so establish it in half an hour), that it be discussed purely in military terms?

Barzun: No. I'm trying to take precautions against Mr. Tate here, who knows so much more than I do about the Civil War and its memoirs. I'm basing myself simply on the merits of the book as the portrayal of a man by himself.

Tate: Mr. Barzun, I don't know whether I can agree with you or not. Grant's self-portrayal certainly leaves us the image of a very sympathetic character, and he is, of course, trying to make himself appear sympathetic. He's perfectly ingenuous about it, and perfectly honest and sincere, but I can't feel that his range of awareness, either regarding himself or the world in which he lived, was large enough to justify the high praise that you are giving the book. I think it does have a very considerable merit. I can't see that it is a great autobiography from any point of view. I think it is a great historical document, and I find it extremely interesting from that angle.

Barzun: Well, do we start on the common ground, Mr. Tate, that Grant himself was a great man?

Tate: No, we don't.

Barzun: I see!

Tate: I think he was a great general.

Barzun: I fail to see the distinction, because man is man before being general; it's a two-way connection. If he is a great general he must be a great man.

Tate: But it seems to me that a general doesn't have to be a great man. Generals must have pre-eminently the instrumental intelligence, and it's a highly specialized talent. I think there is a moral which we might draw from this book, and that is: It is very dangerous to let a great military man get outside his sphere. I think Grant's two terms as President ought to prove the point. He was wholly inadequate. He was an honest man who wanted to do right, but he was imposed upon by nearly every scoundrel in the United States at that time.

Van Doren: Well, Mr. Tate, I wonder if we have the right to put the book to that particular test. No one, I think, makes any claims for Grant as President, but I wonder how pertinent that is to the book?

Tate: Mr. Van Doren, doesn't a great man, as a rule, have an instinct for those situations in which his character will be able to function at its best? I think he will avoid those situations which don't suit his character. Just contrast him with Lincoln in that respect. Grant just doesn't have a chance.

Barzun: I think you're confusing two points, Mr. Tate. Because a man gets put into a situation where his abilities do not serve him right does not mean that in other capacities he isn't great—great as a functioning human being and as a man. Lincoln tried strategy, too, and failed.

Tate: Yes, Lincoln was a poor soldier. But Lincoln's whole job included much more than strategy. In the long run we'll have to give Lincoln part of the credit, at least, for Grant's strategy, because he had the supreme authority and he let Grant carry it out.

Barzun: Yes, but you see, you rule out Nelson and Wellington. I can think of those two on the spur of the moment as great characters and great heroes like Grant—if you limit Grant to generalship.

Tate: I certainly wouldn't rule Nelson and Wellington out as heroes, nor would I rule Grant out as a hero, although it is only in recent years that I have been able to see him in that light at all. A hero is something quite different from a great man.

Barzun: I see! Well, we disagree in definition there, and we haven't time to go into it, but would you admit this—that from his own portrayal, which is what we are discussing, we see a man starting from very modest beginnings, modest both from the sense that he doesn't think he is of great importance and that his position is slight, and meeting every succeeding emergency with increasing power and coming out at the head of the field in one of the most difficult, tangled, complex, and soul-testing situations? If that isn't the definition of greatness then I withdraw the adjective altogether.

Tate: I think your definition of greatness is a very good one. My objection would be that Grant doesn't meet it.

Barzun: We've read two different books, I see.

Van Doren: You ask a very interesting question when you ask whether a man can be a hero without being a great man.

Tate: Yes, I think he can. We have men who do heroic things, perform special tasks—

Barzun: You mean, stop run-away horses and the like?

Tate: Oh, I don't mean that! Like Lt. Pearson Hobson, you see, when he ran past the torpedoes in the Spanish-American War. He was a hero.

Van Doren: But Mr. Barzun surely didn't mean heroes in that sense. Grant was not a hero by accident, or even by a series of accidents. As I read the book, even though I am not competent to judge military affairs or military genius, I find its author convincing me that he has some kind of power of being right, some kind of power of judging men upon whom he is going to depend, some kind of power of seeing the elements of a situation simply and clearly. It does not seem to me to be a matter of accident at all.

Tate: Oh, no, it's not accident!

Van Doren: I couldn't help thinking of another American military hero, Washington, who, like Grant, is of course never brilliant. He is curiously unconscious of his powers, but the final sign that he possesses them is that somehow he doesn't lose.

Tate: Precisely! I think that the parallel between Washington and Grant as soldiers is a very just one, and it's a more just parallel than that between Grant and Lee or Washington and Lee.

Barzun: That's true.

Tate: Lee was a much more complex character than either of them, much more sophisticated, and—well, let me make the contrast this way. I don't expect to get much agreement here, but I think of Grant as a good man, a man with a special talent, who was brought up to high place by a great crisis in the country, and it seems that as soon as that crisis was over his usefulness was over, too. Then he merely functioned again as a good man. Can you possibly make out a case for Grant as a great man, either before the Civil War or after it? There are lots of good men like Grant who have financial adversity, and they have good instincts; they're honest and gentle.

Barzun: He was very sensitive.

Tate: Yes, and after the war I'm sure he remained that way, but the war used a certain special talent that he had, and when the war was over that talent was put aside.

Barzun: But you forget, I think, by a kind of prejudgment, the one thing that does answer your question. After the Civil War, after the Presidency, he wrote these *Memoirs,* and they are, I think, the work of a great writer as well as the recollections of a great general.

Tate: No discussion of that is possible, then, because I can't see the *Memoirs* as the work of a great writer.

Van Doren: If we take writing for a moment in possibly its very smallest and most technical aspect, the *Memoirs* seem to me to be the work of a very good writer, and Mr. Barzun's word "sensitive" is pertinent there. Now I find this book to be the work of a man extremely sensitive to the power of words—so sensitive to the power of words that he is almost afraid of them. That produces a curious effect of understatement when he is speaking of the most dreadful or the most important things; but his understatement itself reveals the power in him. His letter, for instance, to the Adjutant General of the United States in 1861, when the war had just started, offering his services in any way that the Adjutant General would desire, but suggesting at the end that he thought he had the right to consider himself capable of commanding a regiment—that letter, it seems to me, was a masterpiece, although it would be extremely difficult to offer any reasons why it was to anyone who didn't think so. The simplicity of the letter, the absence of false modesty in it, the fact that Grant is willing to announce his capacity as colonel although he has never been a colonel to date, and, indeed, the whole tone of the letter seems to me nothing more or less than right.

Barzun: There is even brilliancy, I should say, Mr. Van Doren, in this understatement, because it isn't the result of a formula. I think of this kind of remark—he is explaining toward the end of the book that somehow the Southern cavalry captured a Northern gunboat—and he says: "That is something very hard to account for." On another occasion he is speaking about the interference of Secretary of War Stanton in the grand strategy, and particularly about his preventing troops from leaving the neighborhood of Washington, and Grant says: "The enemy would not have been in danger if Mr. Stanton had been in the field." There's a perception there, and a simplicity, which amounts to wit—wit that isn't sought after, and I should say that the comparison with Washington in just this matter of ability to convey the man's own impressions is in favor of Grant. He is a better writer than Washington, a more varied mind, more alive to all sorts of nuances of character.

Van Doren: I think we should ask Mr. Tate, Mr. Barzun, about the rightness of some of Grant's judgments of his contemporaries, most of whom, incidentally, whether they were Southern or Northern generals, had been friends of his at West Point.

Tate: I think his judgment was very good, but I don't think that we can claim it as a special insight for Grant. Now, I'm sorry to seem so unco-operative about this.

Barzun: Well, we're not.

Tate: But at the same time I've read a great many Civil War memoirs, and it's absolutely true that the best generals on both sides knew who the other best generals were. They all did; there's no doubt about it. Grant knew, Lee knew, Sherman knew, Longstreet knew, both in their own armies and on the other side. Now, I think Grant's real insight came in judging his subordinate men.

Barzun: And judging them ahead of time.

Tate: Precisely! That is where Grant's talent comes in. He knew what men to promote, what man to give high command. Of course I don't know whether we can express that in terms of percentage or not, but it is at least 50 per cent of military talent.

Barzun: But, Mr. Tate, his judgment was not always, I should say, a technical, military judgment.

Tate: No, no, a human judgment.

Barzun: Which seems to me very important.

Van Doren: The quiet sentence destroying Stanton, and many a sentence or many a paragraph about Johnston or Sherman or Sheridan and, of course, finally Lee—all of them seem to me to be the work of a man with a singularly clear and selfless view of other men.

Tate: Quite true!

Van Doren: His own self somehow did not get in the way of his seeing the other men. That is a talent absolutely necessary to a great soldier.

Tate: Absolutely!

Barzun: And that appears in a larger way, too, in the impressions one gains of the war itself and of his view of the war. This is not a general writing about his triumphs and his mistakes. This is a man, simply a man, who has no illusions about war, about soldiering, about his own career when he had small commands at first in the Mexican War, and that seems to me to be the earmark of a great military man writing about war. You find it in Nelson, you find it in Wellington. Other generals think of themselves as generals in full uniform on a horse, and you never think of Grant as that.

Van Doren: For some reason you remind me, Mr. Barzun, of the very rich paragraph where he contrasts General Scott and Zachary Taylor. Do you remember that?

Barzun: Yes.

Van Doren: It is very amusing, really, this contrast between two generals both of whom he admired, but one of whom, as he very quietly says, he would rather have served with than under. He was proud to serve under both, but he would have preferred always to serve with Taylor, since Scott was a man with a great sense of parade, a man who made all his decisions as if they were historical, and who saw things through the eyes of his staff rather than through the eyes God had given him.

Tate: There is a very good example of that, and I think a much more brilliant one, actually, in Grant's first major campaign, the campaign at Fort Donelson. He knew perfectly well the three Confederate officers there, General Pillow, whom he had known in the Mexican War, General Buckner, and General Floyd. Floyd was a politician who was promoted to high rank in the Confederate Army, and he knew that Pillow was in command. He was afraid that Buckner might be in command—that would be bad, because Buckner was a good soldier. He knew all their characters with great accuracy, and he knew that Pillow would give up without a fight, which is exactly what happened. I'm not detracting from Grant's great reputation when I make this point—it's a very interesting point in terms of the Civil War as a whole and the rise of a great many generals—it was nothing less than luck that Grant was opposed both at Donelson and at Vicksburg by incompetent Confederate generals. If he had been opposed by a man like Lee from the beginning he might have gone the way the others did, but he got his chance by first opposing generals of the second order, and then he got the confidence of Lincoln, and after that he was permitted to show his great powers.

Barzun: Yes, but your point is the common denominator of all wars.

Tate: Precisely!

Barzun: Which is simply this—that there is only one good general on each side, usually.

Tate: Yes. And it's largely chance whether that good general will rise to the top.

Barzun: Yes. One of the things we get from this book is the sense of the confusion and chaos that war is. Other generals of lesser order try to give it a perfection and efficiency which war cannot in the nature of things exhibit.

Van Doren: Mr. Tate, would you mind if I were autobiographical for a minute?

Tate: Not at all.

Van Doren: Two of the most interesting moments in my life were moments when I was with you, once at Fort Donelson, when you showed me the gun emplacements—

Tate: I remember that. I enjoyed it.

Van Doren: —and how they commanded the river, and another when in New England, of all places, one summer day on a blackboard you showed me with chalk the layout of the field of Gettysburg. All of that is preliminary to my asking you what your judgment is of Grant's rightness in his description of the campaigns: Shiloh, Vicksburg, the Wilderness, any or all of the campaigns. Do you find that he jibes sufficiently well with other accounts, and with accounts that you can believe?

Tate: I think that his accounts in most cases tend to be adequate, but he didn't have sufficient knowledge, for even a general directing an army doesn't know enough to write about it without getting access to information which is very difficult to get soon after a war.

Van Doren: A very curious thing, isn't it?

Tate: Yes. They never know enough, so they have to do as much research as a scholar does in order to function properly. I would think on the whole that Grant is pretty accurate except in his account of Shiloh and except for his account of certain phases of the campaign of '64. It is not so much that he was inaccurate in his account of 1864 as that he leaves out too many things. He doesn't touch on very important matters. For example, he is constantly overestimating the power of the Confederate Army against him. Well, that's a tendency of all generals. They always think that when they win a battle they've overcome tremendous odds. But I shouldn't think that Grant's military narrative here is intrinsically important in itself without a great deal of study elsewhere. It is one document that certainly must have great authority in the total picture we build up.

Barzun: I agree with you there. I don't think it's important as a military history of the Civil War or even as a part of it, but I think it is important as a military history at large, and I know of no other account, except perhaps the fictional one of Tolstoi, in *War and Peace,* that represents war as it is with the political considerations involved with the human difficulties. The trouble that Grant had getting his orders executed is a revelation.

Tate: Yes.

Barzun: Other generals are slow, are conceited, are absolutely embarrassed by simple matters—such as strategic ideas of their own—but Grant presents these difficulties without any animus, without any complaint. He is always saying that such and such a general had good qualities, but with such and such a defect "which he could not control," and this curious attitude of Grant's —that people are made as they are and you've got to work with them as they are, that you cannot ask the tardy to be quick—is a very interesting thing, which I have found in no other book.

Tate: I would say, going back to Mr. Van Doren's point of a moment ago, that Grant has a very impartial point of view. I'd like to bring up one incident in which he doesn't show his best self, because I think the fact that it is the only one in the entire book serves to throw into bold relief his real virtues. At the battle of Cold Harbor he launched several very foolish attacks and in twenty minutes, in one attack, he lost eight thousand men. He was baffled and disappointed and suffered terribly over it. He said later that he regretted it. The wounded men were lying between the lines and ten-to-one they were Union men, because the Confederates hadn't come out of their trenches. Grant wouldn't admit defeat, and he wouldn't ask for a truce. He wanted to shift the responsibility to Lee for the sufferings of the wounded. As far as I can tell, that's the only ungenerous thing he did, and he did it in a time of great stress.

Van Doren: The correspondence between him and Lee consumed forty-eight hours of time, during which all but two of the men died.

Tate: Yes. Now, it is significant that even though Grant didn't behave at his best, in the *Memoirs* he gives all the correspondence, he is objective to that extent. He gives Lee's letters and his own letters, so that the reader can form a judgment of his own— although not a full judgment without knowing certain other things.

Barzun: And it wasn't a quirk of character that made him do that. It was perhaps the evil effect of the stubbornness which, in the end, won the war.

Tate: Yes. I think it was the defect of his qualities. He couldn't believe that after three great battles, hammering an army smaller than his own, he could be thrown back. It is like the four attempts to get Vicksburg, trying, and trying, and trying again.

Van Doren: One moment you remind me of was during the negotiations over the surrender at Donelson. The Confederate commander answers Grant's first overtures for surrender with the remark that these overtures are unchivalrous. Is that the word?

Tate: Yes, he used two.

Van Doren: Unchivalrous is the one I remember. Now, I

looked in the text immediately following that letter for some remark by Grant about the word, but he ignores it altogether, as if willing to accept it if need be, but he just was not going to argue over the merits of a term. One quality of this book that we haven't discussed—I don't know whether you would agree—is that Grant, without ever knowing he is doing this, is very frequently giving us a place, an atmosphere. In the early chapters he creates the back-country America of the Ohio River valley, I think, without knowing that he did so. He was so much a member of that society, he was so much a back-country man himself, that I suppose he didn't realize he was one. So oftentimes in the descriptions of battles, not only when he is talking about himself, as when he is in the rain under the tree at Shiloh or when he is walking on crutches, but also when he is not in the picture at all, he has a great power of vividness.

Tate: I agree with you. I think that is quite true.

Van Doren: He never seems to describe anything and yet the scene is there before us; his account of Lee, which seems to me one of the richest accounts on record, is not an account that he seems to know he's giving.

Barzun: No, his awareness was immediate and not the awareness of the self-conscious. It wasn't a full-dress presentation of Lee. It was casual, and given in the course of his ordinary narrative.

Tate: Grant's account of the surrender at Appomattox is certainly one of the most moving that we have. We couldn't expect of one of the two great participants there a full and objective account. He is just giving us his impressions. I would think that General Horace Porter's account of it is the best one. It includes a great many things that Grant couldn't observe. One of the most moving things is Grant's remark that he got so interested in talking to General Lee that he forgot the object of the occasion. It is extremely moving. I'd like to read that passage.

Barzun: Please do.

Tate: "We soon fell into a conversation about old army times. He remarked that he remembered me very well in the old army and I told him that as a matter of course I remembered him perfectly, but from the difference in rank and years (there being about sixteen years difference in our ages) I had thought it very likely that I had not attracted his attention sufficiently to be remembered by him after such a long interval. Our conversation grew so pleasant that I almost forgot the object of our meeting. After the conversation had run on in this style for some time, General Lee called my attention to the object of our meeting and said that he had asked for this interview for the purpose of getting from me the terms I proposed to give his army. I said that I meant merely that his army should lay down their arms, not to take them up again during the continuance of the war unless duly and properly exchanged. He said that he had so understood my letter."

POLITICS AND SOCIETY

Speeches

DEMOSTHENES *(384?-322 B.C.)*

DEMOSTHENES *was the last great Greek of the democratic era, and the fame of his speeches, not to say their character, derives from this fact. For now in the fourth century,* B.C., *a military autocracy, that of Philip the Macedonian, threatened the Greek states from the north; and the entire effort of Demosthenes was an effort to unite the democracies of the peninsula—particularly Athens and Thebes—against this threat. He succeeded only to the extent of delaying the catastrophe. For Philip made good his threat; and those who had been confident that the Macedonian power would dwindle with his death were forced to see a still more ruthless soldier, Alexander the Great, succeed him in conquest. The glory of Demosthenes is then a glory which the darkest sort of background throws into relief. Accused in his own day of leading a battle which could not be won, and convicted by some historians since that day of no greater virtue than obstinacy, he* *yet continues to be honored for the strength of mind with which he went on speaking as if the ancient ideals of Greece not only were worth saving but could be saved. His* Philippics *against the northern dictator, and later on his oration called* The Crown—*a defense of his right to public honors in spite of the defeat which his policy had so disastrously met with—reveal him in the full brilliance of his powers as a rhetorician. The art of public speech has had no more admirable technician; nor has it ever been put to more valiant use than that to which Demosthenes the die-hard put it.*

Demosthenes, the greatest Greek orator, was a pupil of Isaeus. His political career was marked by an undying hatred of Philip of Macedon as the prime enemy of Athenian liberty. Against Philip he directed the three Philippics *and the* Olynthiacs. *His oration* On the Peace *(346 B.C.) advocated the treaty ending the Phocian War;* On the False Legation *(343 B.C.) was an unsuccessful attack on Aeschines.* On Alexander's death in 323 B.C., *Demosthenes tried to raise a general revolt but was forced to flee and killed himself with poison.*

ABRAHAM LINCOLN *(1809-1865)*

THE ORATORY of Abraham Lincoln is so effective that some suppose it not to be oratory at all. But this is to be ignorant of the great tradition in public speech. The great orators have always been more than "mere" orators. Like Demosthenes they have first of all had something to say, and then they have proceeded to say it with the utmost possible economy and clarity. It is the presence of those two cardinal virtues in speech which guarantees the sincerity of the speaker's thought; nor can they ever be present in high degree unless powerful feelings are also there. Lincoln's instinct, which took him directly to the center of any subject he considered, took him at once to the center of the oratorical art. From the first he dispensed with those ornaments which his contemporaries employed because they could penetrate to nothing deeper. He penetrated to the place where nothing but clarity counts; and he learned there how to achieve his rhetorical end with the fewest words. The brevity of his speech at Gettysburg is the first noticeable thing about it; though there are other things to notice, among them being that we know what he thought and felt as he spoke, and that we cannot forget what he said. So his open letter to Horace Greeley in 1862 made one point clear and one point only; but that made all the difference in a complex national situation of great gravity. Lincoln's longer speeches, and particularly the one he delivered at Cooper Union in New York in 1860, had more points to make. The method, however, is the same; and the success of these speeches calls for no new explanation. Lincoln was in the great tradition.

Abraham Lincoln, the sixteenth President of the United States, was born in a log cabin in the backwoods of Kentucky, the son of a shiftless, migratory carpenter and farmer. He grew up in Indiana and schooled himself by reading and rereading a small stock of books. In 1831 young Abe settled in New Salem, Ill., working at odd jobs, and failing wretchedly as a storekeeper. Later he became a lawyer in Springfield, entered politics, and as opponent to Stephen A. Douglas as candidate for the Senate, engaged in the most famous series of debates in American history. Elected President in 1860, he guided the country through the four tragic years of the Civil War. Re-elected in 1864, at the outset of his new term he was assassinated at Ford's Theater in Washington by the actor John Wilkes Booth.

CARL VAN DOREN · JACQUES BARZUN · MARK VAN DOREN

Mark Van Doren: I wonder whether the particular relation between Demosthenes and Lincoln that is most interesting today is a relation of resemblance or one of difference. Mr. Barzun—but I think I shall call you Jacques, since I shall have to call my brother by his first name, too—which does it seem to you that the relation is?

Barzun: Well, it is a little of both. There is a difference in that Demosthenes is trying to get a war started and that Lincoln did his best to prevent a war from being started. At the same time, the underlying resemblance seems 'to me to be this—they are both concerned with the issue of union and whether it is worth paying a price for. Lincoln wanted to maintain a union and, in a sense, Demosthenes was trying to prevent it.

Mark Van Doren: Carl, Jacques said "yes and no." Are you willing to say "yes" *or* "no"?

Carl Van Doren: I'd like to make one point which concerns chiefly their methods. They are very much alike in the fact that neither appears to be an orator in the traditional sense of the word. Each of them is intensely anxious to convince people by the straightforward presentation of ideas which seem to him too important to be merely adorned or blown up in the ordinary way of orators. Lincoln almost ended in the United States what is known as the "spread-eagle" type because of his insistence that ideas themselves were the best arguments and so the best oratory. And this is equally true of Demosthenes. I think they are both the same kind of man.

Mark Van Doren: You mean the same kind of artist?

Carl Van Doren: The same kind of artist, yes.

Mark Van Doren: Neither, certainly, was an ordinary orator. I suppose the very fact of their eminence means that they rise above that vulgar level to which you refer. Perhaps when any orator is good we have the sense that he is referring to facts, referring to situations; that the truth of a situation, at any rate as he sees it, is not something, as you say, to be dressed or created in words, but something that already exists.

Barzun: The vulgar orator with his hokum no longer interests us when the effect is past, because we are more interested in the reality of the issue than in any sophistry that may be made out of it.

Mark Van Doren: Of course. And your use of the word "reality" is very interesting. I suppose that is the excuse for pointing out today some of the many startling parallels between the situation which Demosthenes was treating, the situation which Lincoln was treating, and our own situation at the moment.

Barzun: You mean that in both cases it was their view of the reality that swung events away from one line and into another?

Mark Van Doren: I mean rather that history as it is writing itself today makes especially alive the history of Demosthenes' time and the history of Lincoln's time. Isn't that true? Don't you see parallels between the situation which either of those two men is referring to and our own situation?

Barzun: Yes, Demosthenes was trying to awaken the Athenians to the danger of a dictator who was trying to unite Greece, the dictator being Philip of Macedon—who makes us think, as we talk about him, of Mr. Hitler.

Mark Van Doren: And the question is not merely whether he resembles Hitler, for he does, but whether Demosthenes was right to stand out against what so many people then, and a good many now, consider an inevitable future.

Carl Van Doren: That makes the parallel, I suppose, more exact for our present. Philip was what might be called the wave of the Greek future, but Demosthenes didn't believe that such a future was inevitable. It was something that the present might determine. He turns out to have been wrong, because Philip did triumph. You can't compare Demosthenes with Pitt, for example, fighting against Napoleon. Napoleon lost, and Pitt turned out to be on the victorious side. At the same time, it is interesting to realize that the things Demosthenes insisted upon, the old virtues liberty and justice, are the things which we remember about the Athenian democracy which was overthrown. We remember Philip of Macedon as the ruler who overthrew a freedom which is of immortal value.

Barzun: Yes, but I am struck a little unfavorably with your use of the word "wrong" as applied to Demosthenes. What test are we going to apply—merely the fact that Demosthenes, or rather his ideas, were vanquished temporarily by Philip? Or do we apply a wider standard than that, one which will cover more historical instances than any one defeat or failure?

Carl Van Doren: Of course the word "wrong" was used only in reference to a fulfillment or non-fulfillment of a hope. That is, Demosthenes thought the Athenians might defeat Philip, or protect themselves against Philip, if only they and the rest of the Greeks would unite. The Greeks wouldn't unite, and he later on said that he was not to be blamed for his counsels. His people had failed to give him support. And also, it was not the will of the gods that they should unite and win.

Barzun: I asked the question because of a rather interesting effect of contemporary feelings upon the reputation of Demosthenes. In the middle of the last century, after Germany had begun to achieve her unity, German scholars turned away from Demosthenes; they wrote books against him which showed him as a man who had delayed a very necessary process. Of course, nowadays we come back to Demosthenes because he seems to voice our particular aspirations and fears.

Mark Van Doren: The terms "right" and "wrong" are obviously ambiguous. Demosthenes was right in his prophecy that certain things would happen if Athens didn't behave in a certain way. Athens did not behave in that way and the things did happen.

Barzun: We can ask the same thing about Lincoln, can't we, Mark?

Mark Van Doren: How is that?

Barzun: We can ask whether he was right in thinking that the union was more important than anything else and that a war must be waged to preserve it in its outward form.

Mark Van Doren: You mean, do I agree with him?

Barzun: I mean to put "right" in quotation marks, just the way we used "wrong" in quotation marks before.

Mark Van Doren: Is this the point of your question? Are you asking what we should now be saying if the Civil War had gone throughout the four years as it went during the first two years or even in the first three years, that is to say, against the North?

Barzun: But you could take the question even a little farther back and ask whether a continued series of compromises would not have extinguished slavery without a war. There is a group which believes that.

Carl Van Doren: Lincoln himself believed, and kept insisting, that if the issue was slavery, all the North had to do was to compensate the South for their slaves and clear up the whole business. It would cost far less to buy the slaves and satisfy their owners than it would to wage a war. That was his own policy, persisted in as long as possible.

Barzun: He said that all the slaves in Maryland could be compensated for at the cost of one day's fighting.

Carl Van Doren: Of course. We come back to a general point, which is that history is written by the survivors. We have always to remember that it's very difficult for the survivors not to write history so as to interpret what happened by whether or not past events pointed to present circumstances. There were, in Demosthenes' time, some Greeks who favored the Macedonian new order—let us call it—as better than any casual league of the separate Greek democracies. These Greeks desired a union of themselves under some such rule as Philip's. They felt that Demosthenes was wrong in opposing it, and that the outcome proved this. To cite another parallel, John C. Calhoun before the Civil War might have argued very strongly against what he might have called a Northern aim to play Philip of Macedon to the South. And Southerners did often identify themselves with the Greeks.

Mark Van Doren: Yes, because it seemed to Calhoun that the North, as finally personified by Lincoln, was rolling over the South.

Carl Van Doren: It was!

Mark Van Doren: Lincoln and industry and finance were the wave of the future.

Barzun: Still, the survivors, it seems to me, divide very soon into two or three or four parties that take very different views of what has happened and what should have happened. Perhaps an even more puzzling question, historically and for our own conduct these days, is this—what shall the statesman decide on, the issue of expediency and compromise, or principle at all costs? It seems to me that that issue is raised by both these men.

Mark Van Doren: Yet both of these men are terribly earnest, and I think that is what makes them good orators—granted, of course, in addition to that, genius in speech, and that is granting a great deal. They are terribly in earnest and therefore terribly simple. It seems to each one of them that there is a truth about the contemporary situation which only he can see. In the case of Demosthenes we have more arrogance; Lincoln always had a certain humility and, indeed, a certain humor, too, which prevented him from being arrogant. Demosthenes must have seemed, at any rate to his listeners, most arrogant. He is always castigating his contemporaries because they cannot see as absolutely and simply true what he can see. Lincoln on the other hand, at the same time with his humility, also has a very insistent note in his voice as he states over and over and over again a truth about the situation which he does not want obscured.

Barzun: There's the complication, too, in Lincoln's case that he really wanted to address the South rather than the North, and he knew the South wouldn't listen to him. His proper audience, so to speak, is as far away and as deaf to him as Demosthenes's audience, right at his feet, was far away and deaf to him.

Carl Van Doren: That was true because Lincoln, after all, had been born in Kentucky, and a great many of his closest friends sympathized with the movement of secession. I've been struck by the fact that in each of these orators—Demosthenes and Lincoln—there is a particular devotion to history, as furnishing what seems to him examples for his present argument. I have recently been reading Lincoln's works, closely and minutely. It's obvious that something happened to Lincoln, when he was about forty or so and still fumbling around for a career which he hadn't made up his mind to. That amounted to falling in love, if you can use that expression, with the Declaration of Independence. He discovered it, as somebody might discover what he thought the will of God or a great fundamental idea. From that time on Lincoln kept on talking about the Declaration as a kind of gospel for Americans and freedom. In his great Cooper Institute speech, you perhaps remember, he is primarily concerned with what seems to him the historical truth about the attitude of the fathers of the Republic toward slavery. Now, in a sense, Demosthenes is just as much interested in the famous history of Greece, the old freedoms, the old tolerations, the old intelligences. He is always finding in history—a persuasive and powerful argument—the reasons why the Athenians had first become what they are now and why they should continue to be that. All he couldn't find was union. Lincoln thought there had been a union, which was to be maintained at all odds.

Mark Van Doren: The union which Demosthenes wanted was a union which had never existed, as Carl says. He wanted the Greek states to unite as indeed they had never been united; whereas Lincoln could refer to an active union in the past among the American states and to a document establishing that union, the Declaration of Independence.

Barzun: Yes, but isn't there a complexity about the Greek situation which did not exist in the American one? So far as I can see, Demosthenes wanted to keep up the old system of alliances and balance of power which, from a certain point of view, can be considered backward because it led to endless wars and quarrels. Philip of Macedon wanted to steam-roller that into a complete unity and uniformity. Lincoln's steam-roller was much less apparent since the union had already existed, and I think that that indicates a difference between the two men. Demosthenes is always talking in terms of expediency and Lincoln, most of the time, in terms of principle—not without expediency, but with expediency subordinate to principle.

Mark Van Doren: And in terms of law, too.

Barzun: Well, they were both lawyers.

Mark Van Doren: And in terms of history. It is very interesting how history can be used. Lincoln was very conscious of history. Remember the conclusion of his address to Congress, July 4th, 1861, where he says: "We cannot escape history. We are now making history and we must be conscious of that fact." History was something which he never seemed able or willing to escape.

Barzun: Well, of course, history is a quarry we can all use for any building we want to put up.

Mark Van Doren: Southerners can and undoubtedly do deny that the union to which Lincoln is referring in the past was a union in anything like the sense in which he interpreted it.

Barzun: Yes, most Southerners say that the doctrine of the union, with a capital U, is something that Lincoln and a few others invented around 1859 and '60.

Mark Van Doren: And that still has never come to pass!

Barzun: But to go back a moment to this question of history, which interests me very much, couldn't it be said that only people with a sense of history know what is going on in front of their eyes?

Mark Van Doren: That is quite true. It is only when you know how to use history that you have a civilization at all.

Carl Van Doren: Certainly, you can interpret events only by drawing a line between what has been in the past and what has more recently come about. But that line has no absolute power over the future, because you can so often leave out of account future elements that we don't know about or understand.

Barzun: And I suppose you can't have prophecy unless you have history, can you?

Mark Van Doren: No.

Barzun: It is remarkable, the extent to which good historians have prophesied truly. They can't prophesy in detail but they can prophesy tendencies, estimate the force or significance of events, much better than people who come to them with fresh, naive eyes.

Mark Van Doren: Well, what has Lincoln been able to prophesy? Do you have in mind parallels that exist between certain situations in the past and certain situations now?

Barzun: Not only parallels.

Mark Van Doren: Those are dangerous, aren't they?

Barzun: If they're not checked by a sense of what I might call repetition. A single parallel five hundred years ago proves nothing, but if between the point five hundred years ago and today something has happened again and again, one can assert that tradition is alive or a party is powerful, or some such thing.

Carl Van Doren: The advantage which the person who knows some history has over persons who don't is that the latter are always convinced that any current event is unprecedented, catastrophic, and final. But if you know a little history, you may realize that that sort of thing has happened again and again and again and men have survived it.

Barzun: Many people today feel and are under the impression that the things they don't like are happening particularly to plague them and have never bothered mankind before.

Mark Van Doren: The news is somehow bad because it makes them feel bad. That is all it can mean to them.

Barzun: Demosthenes apparently notes the same thing in his contemporaries. Do you remember where he taunts the Athenians with going about in the market place and saying: "Is there any news today? Is Philip dead?" And the answer is: "No. Philip is only ill."

Carl Van Doren: There's an interesting point, it seems to me. When Philip steam-rollered, as you say, the older democracies, of Greece, he helped bring about such a spread of Hellenistic ideas as they probably would never have achieved by themselves. The Hellenistic Empire, covering the Near East and reaching rather feebly as far as India, was the creation of Philip. That long period in which the Near East used Greek as its language and in which Greek ideas got among the Arabs is in a sense due to Philip. You might even say that Demosthenes was resisting a development by which the splendors of Greece were to reach the rest of the world. It brings up a nice point. We may even wonder whether Demosthenes was right, if you like, or justified in fighting something that was going to assist in the dissemination of Greek ideas.

Mark Van Doren: Well, Carl, I think the extent to which he was right might be measured by the difference between the word "Hellenistic" and the word "Hellenic." That is to say, the spread of culture which followed upon the great military success of Philip and Alexander was after all only a spread. Apparently the culture itself did not continue to be vital and new.

Barzun: I think that's the point. What Philip and Alexander spread would be the culture they had destroyed.

Carl Van Doren: That is, the original culture, the great achievements of the Greeks, were ended by the method which took them out of reality and put them into libraries and museums.

Mark Van Doren: That's right. You've got great libraries instead of great authors.

Barzun: I suppose there isn't enough energy to do both things unless the amount of energy is enormous. But you said, Carl, that Philip swamped the democracies under a uniform empire. We have to remember a very important political fact there. Some of the so-called democracies were already tyrannies; Demosthenes was pretending, as we do today, that certain allied states were free, but their citizens had frequently been tyrannized and treated very much as Philip was going to treat them.

Mark Van Doren: Can we say anything true, do you think,

about the two men as artists in oratory? Can you say whether one is better than the other, and can we say in what respect they are different? I hinted earlier in the hour that Lincoln has certain qualities which Demosthenes does not have. I do not find in Demosthenes the humor or the irony of Lincoln. I mean the delicate and free irony of Lincoln. Demosthenes is a heavy hitter, but he is a master of scorn and sarcasm, I should say, rather than of irony.

Barzun: Already in his own day people said that his orations smelled too much of the lamp—that they were worked up as literary exercises.

Carl Van Doren: It seems clear to me that Demosthenes was not so elevated and certainly not so humorous as Lincoln. For instance, there are certain things Lincoln said that are completely beyond the reach of Demosthenes. There is Lincoln's story of a man who was so insolent that, having murdered his father and mother, when he came before the court he asked for mercy on the ground that he was an orphan. Or there is that sort of vaudeville story Lincoln told to apply to the two parties in the United States that were claiming to have interchangeable ideas. They reminded him, he said, of two drunken men he once saw fighting in their overcoats. They were so drunk they didn't put up much of a fight, except that each of them fought his way out of his own coat into the other man's.

Barzun: Of course, the relation of the orator to his audience is different in the two cases. There was a kind of familiarity between the orator and the audience in Greece which does not exist in the case of Lincoln.

Carl Van Doren: I don't quite think that. Of course an Athenian orator might perhaps be acquainted with a good many of his hearers who were also his fellow-citizens. But Lincoln often talked to an audience of farmers to whom he was, as a matter of fact, very close. You notice that when he debated with Douglas he was not altogether the same in his methods as in his Cooper Institute speech. Then he had come from the prairies to New York, where he was to speak to a critical audience. On that occasion he adjusted himself to this different audience and was somewhat more formal and more learned than he had usually been in Illinois.

Barzun: That's true. The world "familiarity" was wrong. I meant to say that almost every one in Demosthenes's audience was an orator also. They were all equals in talking politics as in a kind of caucus, whereas Lincoln was talking to people who were not politicians.

Mark Van Doren: I suppose we could never find passages from the two orators which could be compared, but I wonder, Jacques, if you have something from Demosthenes.

Barzun: Yes. This is the end of the first Philippic—and by the way, it might be good to remind ourselves that the word "Philippic" is generally misapplied. Demosthenes had a great respect for Philip's ability and was not attacking him in vulgar fashion. He's speaking here, however, to the men of Athens.

"You too, men of Athens, if you are willing to adopt this principle, now if never before, if each citizen is ready to throw off his diffidence and serve the state as he ought and as he best may, the rich man paying, the strong man fighting, if, briefly and plainly, you will consent to become your own masters, and if each man will cease to expect that, while he does nothing himself, his neighbor will do everything for him, then, God willing, you will recover your own, you will restore what has been frittered away, and you will turn the tables upon Philip. Do not believe that his present power is fixed and unchangeable like that of a god. No, men of Athens; he is a mark for the hatred and fear and envy even of those who now seem devoted to him. One must assume that even his adherents are subject to the same passions as any other men. At present, however, all these feelings are repressed and have no outlet, thanks to your indolence and apathy, which I urge you to throw off at once. For observe, Athenians, the height to which the fellow's insolence has soared: he leaves you no choice for action or inaction; he blusters and talks big, according to all accounts; he cannot rest content with what he has conquered; he is always taking in more, everywhere casting his net around us, while we sit idle and do nothing. When,

Athenians, will you take the necessary action? What are you waiting for? Until you are compelled, I presume. But what are we to think of what is happening now? For my own part I think that for a free people there can be no greater compulsion than shame for their position."

Mark Van Doren: And, Carl, have you a passage from Lincoln?

Carl Van Doren: I have a passage, but not from one of his orations. It is a "Meditation on the Divine Will" which he wrote out for himself in the fall of 1862.

"The will of God prevails. In great contests each party claims to act in accordance with the will of God. Both may be, and one must be, wrong. God cannot be for and against the same thing at the same time. In the present Civil War it is quite possible that God's purpose is something different from the purpose of either party; and yet the human instrumentalities, working just as they do, are the best adaptation to effect His purpose. I am almost ready to say that this is probably true; that God wills this contest and wills that it shall not end yet. By His mere great power on the minds of our contestants, He could either have saved or destroyed the Union without a human contest. Yet the contest began. And, having begun, He could give the final victory to either side any day. Yet the contest proceeds."

(1689-1755)

MONTESQUIEU

The Spirit of Laws

I**N THE** *eighteenth-century France for which he wrote Montes-quieu was always under fire from extremists. Extreme conserva-tives found him too rational in his investigation of established things; extreme critics of society were disappointed because his reason did not carry him further into denunciation and wrath. He was in truth an eminently reasonable man whose view was his-torical rather than doctrinaire, and whose only desire was to see the world, past and present, in the sanest possible light. His book on the decline of Rome, which preceded* The Spirit of Laws, *can be said almost in itself to have created the now familiar thing called philosophical history. And* The Spirit of Laws, *whatever its shortcomings, did more than any book in that age to promote the comparative study of human laws and institutions which now is taken for granted as the chief discipline of historians. Montes-quieu's subtitle ran:* The relation which Laws should bear to the

Constitution of each Government, to Customs, to Climate, to Religion, to Commerce, etc. *The validity of any law was for Montesquieu a relative matter about which decision could not be reached until everything was known concerning the people for whom it was written. Human society was for him a whole thing, and nothing that served it was more than a servant. The view is now so commonplace that the originality of Montesquieu is easy to underestimate, particularly when it is remembered that scholarship has rejected many of his facts. But it is a real originality, as his book—measured, modest, and humane—is a genuine classic.*

Charles Louis de Secondat, Baron de la Brède et de Montesquieu, French jurist and political philosopher, served the parliament of Bordeaux as councilor (1714) and as president (1716-28). Except for travels in Europe, he lived in retirement in his feudal castle near Bordeaux. His Persian Letters *(1721) brought him immediate notoriety; in them he satirized and criticized French institutions under the guise of light, colorful studies of the Orient. In 1734 he produced a scientific historical study of the rise and fall of Rome, and in 1748 completed his greatest work,* The Spirit of Laws.

JAMES T. SHOTWELL · JACQUES BARZUN · MARK VAN DOREN

Van Doren: The first question to ask is what *The Spirit of Laws* is about. We are all familiar with the fact that a philosophical work published in France in the eighteenth century, particularly if it had a political subject, was not necessarily concerned with its ostensible subject. I am not at all sure that Montesquieu's main interest is not after all represented by his title. And yet in reading the book this week I found it possible to wonder whether he had in mind either a more specific or a more general subject than law. Mr. Shotwell, have you an answer to that question?

Shotwell: I think it quite clear that he had an ulterior purpose, as practically all the philosophic writers of the eighteenth century had. They were reformers in a disguised kind of way, and certainly Montesquieu's *The Spirit of Laws* was not an abstract disquisition on the growth of the law. Throughout it had an application to the modern world.

Van Doren: He seems to want to give the impression that his view is disinterested, distant, and utopian, and he refers from time to time to a method which he might have called scientific. Mr. Barzun, does it seem to you that he is disinterested, or has he a special thing to communicate?

Barzun: I think he is disinterested in the sense that he isn't going to distort history for the purpose of proving something immediate and narrow, but he does have a very general purpose, which is to establish his own philosophy of society. Today we would call him a sociologist, and both the words of his title, it seems to me, are intended to convey this very subtly to the reader. Spirit signifies general meaning, and laws in his use of the word mean everything from the laws of nature, with which he starts, to customs, religions, educational habits, virtues, and indeed everything under the sun. There is hardly a subject that one can think of which isn't referred to somewhere in this book.

Van Doren: You say laws of nature. I've always been puzzled by the term. Mr. Shotwell, does he go as far with that subject, does he make it as meaningful, as other philosophers of the time did, or those before him?

Shotwell: No, I should say that the opening book in which he deals with the laws of nature is a very sketchy performance. He seems almost in a hurry to get away to positive law, leaving the laws of nature for other more metaphysical minds. I should on that point, perhaps, comment on Mr. Barzun's statement that he was a sociologist. I imagine the sociologist would have developed Book I a good deal more than did Montesquieu, who was a French jurist with the training of the *noblesse de la robe.*

Barzun: Mr. Shotwell, I think I have an explanation for that Book I and for your objection about his sociology. Montesquieu throughout is playing on the word law and on the word nature. He tries to make things derive from the nature of things, and he uses history as an indication of what the nature of things human is, but at the same time he is constantly suggesting that a good many things that are in France or in Europe of his own day oughtn't to be, and in order to reconcile both these notions he's got to say that the nature of things is this, but somehow it has got perverted. It has departed from its true nature. What else can you do if you're going to suggest reform by means of history?

Van Doren: Is a sociologist chiefly concerned with the nature of society? Most sociologists of my acquaintance seem to be referring to a nature in society which has been lost or ignored. They usually proceed, I think, on the assumption that that nature has still to be realized. But they do assume that there is such a thing.

Barzun: That is true. The modern scientific fallacy about the study of nature is that we can find out what it is. But since mankind can do a great many things with what is, can easily twist it about, the point of view of the eighteenth-century philosopher seems to be sounder: You use nature as a kind of hypothetical fiction in order to suggest what changes you want.

Shotwell: Well, you don't get really very far toward a sound method by starting with an unsound hypothesis. When you begin with the Golden Age, as you have it in Plato and in much of classical literature, you can turn out such neat aphorisms as that of Rousseau's *Social Contract:* "Men are born free and are everywhere in chains—and now let's see what it is all about." It would seem to me that here is where we go back to what you spoke of, the purpose which underlies that concept. Let me say a revolutionary consequence—that we are to get rid of the chains, to get back to a golden age. Surely that is contrary to the whole development of civilization as we know it now.

Barzun: That is probably true if taken literally, but if you take the other alternative you are left with the fact that whatever is, is right, since nature and history produce it together—and then you have no right to complain.

Van Doren: Isn't Montesquieu being apparently very disinterested when he tells us that in any given kind of society, under any given kind of government, despotic, monarchical, aristocratic or democratic, there is a certain spirit which if observed will make the people who live under it happy and at peace? He even is willing to grant that under despotism—though surely he likes that form of government least—under despotism a certain spirit, if observed, will bring order; and that in an aristocracy, a certain understanding of what such a society should be, on the part of everyone, will make that society function well.

Barzun: Yes, and these classifications, which are extremely useful, could be attacked as unreal also, since every government differs from every other, and in another way all governments are alike. So these classifications are just such hypotheses, it seems to me, as nature is.

Van Doren: They are traditional, aren't they? He reminds you at once of Aristotle's classification?

Barzun: But no one pushed the classifications so far in a constructive sense and gave so many deductions from the general statement of what a monarchy or a republic was.

Van Doren: Is it clear to you, Mr. Shotwell, that although he has the air of saying that any particular kind of government has its form, and if that form is recognized by all the parties concerned then order will exist—does it seem to you nevertheless that his prejudice is distinctly in favor of democracy, of the republic?

Shotwell: Perhaps, we might say, of the democracy as we have it here, or of some moderate form; that's quite true. But if I may for a moment revert to what Mr. Barzun has said, I'd like to make allowance for a theory of development rather than a hit-and-miss theory of hypotheses. Now that's a little unfair, I know; but let me just say in connection with the contrast between Montesquieu's view of world history and that which has resulted from the scientific work of today in its analysis of the various states of society: His book is fundamentally based, not on a conception of possible progress, but on pessimism. Professor Chinard, for instance, is fully justified in entitling his recent essay *The Historical Pessimism of Montesquieu.*

Barzun: But it seems to me, Mr. Shotwell, that the historical work of, let's say, the early nineteenth century was made possible by people like Montesquieu and Rousseau—who are incidentally much closer together than people generally think—because the very thing for which Montesquieu is noted, his theory of climate as conditioning human institutions, is already the germ of a development hypothesis, the notion that we start with a physical base and then produce moral, spiritual and other institutions; that culture is rooted in physical fact. That is the presupposition of a history based on evolution, isn't it?

Shotwell: That is the realism in Montesquieu which gives him his value, certainly. You would almost think you were reading Buckle on the influence of geography and environment upon social life, except that his realism did not give him a philosophy which enabled him to clarify some of the fundamentals in the history of government. He never, for instance, understood the

English. Perhaps we can come again to that at a later time. I have the feeling, when reading him, of a magnificent figure in the tradition of the French *noblesse de la robe,* the lawyer class of France, which was the outstanding exponent of political ideas, in a country where there was no representative government. And I can't help but feel that that limited the sweep of vision of the man. It doesn't seem to me that he has more than a cautionary philosophy, with safeguards. In fact, it was as if in his own mind, if I may say so, Mr. Barzun, there were checks and balances which enabled him to produce a moderate and systematic scheme of political philosophy, but not a living, vital thing such as you could get from the philosophy, we'll say, of the late nineteenth century.

Van Doren: I gather, Mr. Shotwell, that you were not satisfied with the unusually long chapter in which English government is described. That chapter reminded me, incidentally, of Voltaire's account of English freedom and of the English government in his *Philosophical Letters on the English Nation.* Is it that he misses certain details of that government, or does it seem to you that he misses the whole spirit of it?

Barzun: Mr. Van Doren, I'd like to plunge in and interrupt you here, because I think Mr. Shotwell is having things too much his own way.

Van Doren: All right.

Barzun: Professor Shotwell has said that Montesquieu didn't understand the English. I think Montesquieu takes care of that by saying, after he has described something which we know wasn't quite there, that he is not bound to describe how the British Constitution works. He merely is bound to describe what its spirit and provisions, ideally, are.

Van Doren: And it seems to you that he finds those?

Barzun: He does find them, and whether he was right or wrong I think we must give him credit for having had a tremendous influence on the future history of English-speaking peoples, for between the middle of the eighteenth century and its end Montesquieu was the most quoted author in the press of this country.

Most of the men who made the state constitutions and the Federal Constitution—

Van Doren: And who wrote the *Federalist Papers*—

Barzun:—and who wrote the *Federalist Papers,* believed in and applied his doctrines.

Shotwell: Of course I'm a little concerned by your phrase "whether he was right or wrong," because that is one of the things we should consider—whether he ever understood the English system on which he spent so much time. He was two years in England and he knew the leaders of English thought. But when he came to apply his categories of government, the three-fold divisions which we have taken from him, the executive, the legislative, and the judicial, he didn't find in England a judiciary of sufficient dignity and strength to be given the title of a separate and distinct organ of government. I can't get away from a feeling, as I read his account of England, that he never fully appreciated the work of a man like Coke in the development of English common law, nor have I ever discovered one trained in the tradition of the Roman law who did fully understand the tradition of the common law and what it meant in England.

Van Doren: You mean to say there was more law in England, more judicial procedure and judicial genius, than he was able to recognize?

Shotwell: Not only that, but the common law was a check upon sovereignty. Take the twofold aspects of Coke's work. On the one hand, later on, he linked up with Pym and Hampden in a Parliamentary opposition to the King, but his chief opposition was to a king who was trained in the Roman law, James I. Coke practically remade Magna Charta and gave the English a sense of the way in which a document, or a modus operandi like Habeas Corpus, could become the very antithesis of the kind of government that led to the Bastille. I don't think Montesquieu ever saw where the safeguards of English freedom really lay.

Barzun: That might even be granted you, Mr. Shotwell, without completely throwing out the value of Montesquieu's description, because I feel very strongly that Montesquieu is writing a practical book, directed largely at French readers and to a lesser extent at British leaders of a certain liberal cast of mind. For them it seems to me that the insistence upon the necessary division between executive and legislative is the important thing, and of course we've embodied it in our own Constitution in this country.

Shotwell: Through the Bill of Rights, which has received a great deal of attention recently, and the Fourteenth Amendment and the use by the Supreme Court of that great document, we have certainly brought our safeguards of liberty under the Constitution over into the judicial sphere. So we have here not only the distinction between executive and legislative but the strongest kind of safeguard of the whole function of the judiciary; and that is in line with Montesquieu's philosophy as understood by Madison and the rest.

Barzun: Oh, yes, we have the three powers, even though England doesn't show, to his mind, a very strong third power.

Shotwell: I don't want to force this issue. But I do feel that had Montesquieu understood the English better we might have had a clearer public understanding here of the character of these three elements in the Constitution of England, as well as of the debt we owe to the common law.

Van Doren: But isn't there significance in the willingness of so many political thinkers in France and England and America in the eighteenth century to accept his description?

Barzun: If I may change the subject for a moment, we oughtn't to forget the very strong negative work that Montesquieu puts in against despotism.

Van Doren: That is what I am most interested in—finding out to what extent the book could at the time have seemed for any intelligent person loaded against despotism. Would you say that it was loaded against anything else? I myself was greatly impressed by a certain moral force in the book. Remember, he says that whereas the spring of action and of order in a despotism is fear, in an aristocracy or a monarchy it is honor, and in a republic it is virtue—meaning by virtue merely the love that everyone must have for the whole of his society. I should think, Mr. Shot-well, that he was describing the English when he talked about virtue, a thing that was notably lacking in his own society but which he admired, just as Voltaire admired it, across the Channel.

Shotwell: There I'm in hearty agreement—the emphasis on virtue; which I like to translate into our current term of "the public interest," or the sense that each citizen has, in the democracies, both in England and here and in any other live democracy, of his responsibility for making things go even if the Constitution may be rickety or whatnot.

Van Doren: And he is realistic, it seems to me, when he points out how difficult it is to maintain virtue, how arduous a task it is for each citizen to maintain his own virtue.

Shotwell: The phrase I was wanting to find was "public spirit." That, I think, is fundamental in his conception of the interplay of the private citizen with the intelligent, responsible government.

Van Doren: Even though a despotism might work with fear as the spring, even though a monarchy or an aristocracy might work with honor as the spring, he seems to prefer, does he not, the picture of a republic succeeding through virtue?

Barzun: He does. In the end he calls that honor which operates in monarchies false. That is, it is a false idea which everyone has of himself in order to hold himself up to a standard of behavior.

Van Doren: Yes. Every kind of government other than the democratic has to depend somehow or other on falsity or on fiction. He seems to say that a democracy thrives upon truth.

Barzun: We should remember, though, Mr. Van Doren, that when he speaks of democracies he speaks really of small geographical units where people make their own laws, and what he calls an aristocracy might very well correspond to what we call a republic today—that is, he would call the government of this country or of England a representative aristocracy, in which the leaders, the governors, are elected by the people; of course it is a federated one too.

Shotwell: There is one aspect, Mr. Van Doren, of his thinking and of the sources of his thought which we haven't mentioned, and that is his deep study of the processes of the Roman Republic, where the powers were divided in the course of time; this not only safeguarded the liberty of the citizen but made for efficiency as well, up to the point where war cut in with the development of the "Imperator" with his universal scope of power. Now, it would seem to me of some interest to bring out in the study of Montesquieu that same thing which Machiavelli studied as well in the *Discourses on Livy.* There were two Machiavellis. One was very similar in his conclusions to Montesquieu in his analysis of the Roman Republic as a thing worthwhile. Then, when Machiavelli had to write a practical manual for a prince, he wrote it as for a despot. Here is where I come to pay my respects to Montesquieu. Living under a French monarchy of a fairly despotic character, he nevertheless did not make himself the instrument of apology for that form of government. The Roman Republic remained for him the practical scheme that seemed most worthwhile in the history of government.

Barzun: That is where the limitation that you formerly criticized, his belonging to the nobility of the robe, came in very handy, because it was the tradition of the *parlements*—of one of which Montesquieu was President—to oppose the King at every turn. So that we can't have the good without the bad, can we?

Shotwell: I agree. But you know, Mr. Barzun, it does seem to me an interesting thing that his work has the flavor of a Frenchman writing from the background of the *parlements,* which were of course law courts holding a kind of a veto power over the King's decrees. Now, John Locke in his *Treatises on Government* enjoyed an advantage in that he had in view a Parliament in the representative sense and could give the world a picture which we copied as much as we did Montesquieu's, although not externally. Locke's was a picture of self-government with representative bodies in it; and this brings me to another point: that he dealt with a particular phase of society where capital and the capitalist class come to the fore.

Barzun: But somehow Locke was a good deal less a man of practical business and legal affairs than Montesquieu, though there is one point on which they agree and that is the great importance in democratic or representative governments of education. They both wrote about education, didn't they, Mr. Shotwell?

Shotwell: Oh, yes. Both were interested in that. As a matter of fact, in *The Spirit of Laws* Montesquieu brings education right to the fore, next to his consideration of the forms of government. It is the first of his considerations of detail. May I read a section from the Fifth Chapter of Book IV?

"It is in a republican government that the whole power of education is required. The fear of despotic governments naturally arises of itself amidst threats and punishments; the honor of monarchies is favored by the passions, and favors them in its turn. But virtue is a self-renunciation, which is ever arduous and painful.

"This virtue may be defined as the love of the laws and of our country. As such love requires a constant preference of public to private interest, it is the source of all private virtues; for they are nothing more than this very preference itself.

"This love is peculiar to democracies. In these alone the government is entrusted to private citizens. Now, a government is like everything else: to preserve it we must love it. Has it ever been known that kings were not fond of monarchy, or that despotic princes hated arbitrary power?

"Everything therefore depends on establishing this love in a republic; and to inspire it ought to be the principal business of education."

Reflections on the

Revolution in France

and

The Rights of Man

EDMUND BURKE *(1729-1797)*

*E*DMUND BURKE, *the great philosopher-statesman who had so far sympathized with revolution in the American colonies as to urge upon the British government a policy of conciliation toward those colonies, could not sympathize with revolution when it happened nearer home, and in an intenser, more terrible form, in France. His* Reflections *are the agonized outpourings of a spirit dedicated to political change but aghast at the direction which change had suddenly, and to him arbitrarily, determined to take. It was not that he was reluctant to see human conditions improve; it was rather that all his training, and all his knowledge of the gradual way in which British institutions had for centuries been moving toward a possible perfection, rendered him unable to stomach the spectacle of violent and bloody deeds done in the name of liberty. For him no future could be better than the present unless it built securely and legally upon the past. He was in*

*love with constitutions but he saw them as composed of prece-
dents which had been proved in the slow fires of history. In his
view no society could begin again with any other result than the
wreck of much that was precious and irreplaceable. So he proceeded to bemoan the things which were dying in France, and
to doubt the life that would succeed them as long as fanatics remained in power. The extent to which history has justified him is
a question which two types of mind must still debate. Meanwhile his book stands as the classic expression of conservatism in
its noblest phase; and as one of the most musical and gloomy
works of English prose.*

*Edmund Burke was born in Dublin. He graduated at Trinity
College, Dublin, and entered the Middle Temple in London, but
abandoned the law to write and, later, to enter politics. His*
Vindication of Natural Society *and his* Philosophical Inquiry into
the Origin of Our Ideas of the Sublime and Beautiful *were published in 1756. He entered parliament (1765) as a Whig for the
"rotten borough" of Dendover and gained, by his character and
eloquence, a foremost place. Burke protested the coercion of the
American colonies, but his speeches on American taxation (1774)
and conciliation (1775) failed to avert the inevitable result.
His denunciation of the British administrator in India, Warren
Hastings, is one of the masterpieces of English oratory.*

THOMAS PAINE *(1737-1809)*

*THOMAS PAINE, or Tom Paine, as his affectionate worshippers
continue to call him, was one of the most effective pamphleteers
ever to seize the pen as if it were a sword. Coming from England
to America on the eve of the Revolution, he threw himself with
all of his swift, hard energy into the colonial cause and produced*

in Common Sense *and* The American Crisis *a series of pamphlets which contributed as much as a fresh army could have contributed to the success of that cause. Paine was simply and frankly a doctrinaire, committed to eighteenth-century revolutionary principles in their starkest form and admitting no compromise with prejudices from the past or with sentiment based on love for an order which the accidents of history had established. The colonies free, he returned to England. Franklin had said: "Where liberty is, there is my country." Paine said: "Where is not liberty, there is mine." And now in England he read the* Reflections *of Burke. No two men could be more different; everything in Paine revolted against what he read. "He pities the plumage," he cried, "but forgets the dying bird."* The Rights of Man, *which was his answer to Burke, was like all his works hard-hitting and brilliant. He still has no peer in epigram, in the flashing sentence where alliteration and antithesis assist the arts of anger. But* The Rights of Man *is a classic for better reasons; it is the standard statement of the doctrinaire position with respect to social change, and consequently it is the standard complement to Burke.*

Thomas Paine was the son of a Quaker farmer and stay maker of Thetford, England. Before coming to America in 1774, he had been an excise officer, twice dismissed, and an agent of the excisemen to agitate for higher salaries. In America he was soon deeply interested in the outbreak of trouble between the colonies and the mother country; his Common Sense *(January, 1776) had a tremendous effect in helping to bring about the Declaration of Independence, and his series of pamphlets called* The American Crisis, *or simply* The Crisis, *continued to appear throughout the Revolution, with excellent moral effect. However, for the attack on the Bible and defense of deism in his* Age of Reason *(1793) he was practically ostracized in the United States.*

LYMAN BRYSON · JACQUES BARZUN · MARK VAN DOREN

Van Doren: Burke's *Reflections on the Revolution in France* and Paine's *Rights of Man* are both concerned with the theme of liberty and both written by men who loved liberty. But the difference between the two men is more interesting today, I assume, than the resemblance. We have the very interesting phenomenon of two men who had in one degree or another sympathized with the American revolution some years before, now differing with respect to the Revolution in France. Burke's book is an attack upon most of what had been done under that name, and Paine's book is a defense of what had been done. Mr. Barzun, does it strike you, as a historian, that it is possible or easy to explain the split that here appears between Burke and Paine?

Barzun: I don't know whether it's easy, but perhaps it is possible. It is perfectly clear that Burke had felt at the time of the American Revolution that here was a constitutional quarrel among Englishmen about particular points of policy—of expediency, in fact—and he was wholly sympathetic then to the idea of greater liberty and a more just distribution of rights and duties. But when he came to examine the French Revolution he felt that it was a complete overturn, that nothing of the past remained to be reformed or worked with in the present, and he was wholeheartedly against any such starting afresh and making all things new.

Van Doren: Mr. Bryson, does it seem to you that that is a statement of what happened?

Bryson: Insofar as one can guess at what Burke was thinking about, I suppose it is. I wouldn't be at all inclined to disagree with it. Probably Burke himself would have hesitated to apply the term revolution to what was happening in America. There was no overturn, that is, no great overturn of the people actually in power in America. The leaders of American life more or less held their own, and he didn't feel that the institutions were being destroyed. He felt, as he said, that Americans were fighting for the liberty of Englishmen. They were Englishmen and they were fighting for that, as Mr. Barzun says. There may have been something, of course, in the passage of time too. It may be that by the time the French Revolution broke forth he was not quite so sure that the American Revolution had been a success from the standpoint of an Englishman. He doesn't say so anywhere, but I think you can perhaps imagine that that took place in his mind, although it isn't enough to explain what he did.

Barzun: But isn't the underlying point that political change is something that Burke is entirely willing to consider on its merits? It is the mode of change that these two men are arguing about in the year 1790, about a year and a half after the events that we call the beginning of the French Revolution.

Bryson: Oh, I think so. The difference between them is almost entirely the one that you stated. Burke doesn't want change by violence.

Van Doren: He was very fond of the image of paternity, of fatherhood. You may remember he is always referring to the state, or rather to society, as the father of living men, and he comes again and again to a contrast between that way of reforming one's father which consists of killing him, and therefore renovating him, and that form which consists of respecting him first of all and merely endeavoring to bring his affairs into order.

Barzun: That's where he engrafts his idea of inheritance; he points out that mankind is continuous and doesn't break off at stated points at the end of each generation. Therefore there must be a continuity in the government too, and therefore the government must proceed by inheritance of the crown, of estates, of power, of responsibilities.

Bryson: Isn't one of the things that make Burke so interesting, that make reading Burke fun even today, the fact that with that theory of change by expediency, change by respecting one's father rather than assassinating him, as you say, goes this extraordinary poetic imagination, this exuberance, all this rhetoric, all this profusion of beautiful images and words about what is after all rather a dull and stodgy doctrine. Did any Irishman ever waste so much eloquence on an essentially British idea, before or since in history? I don't know of any.

Van Doren: I wonder if there isn't something of an affinity between Burke and Swift at this point?

Bryson: In reverse?

Van Doren: Well, no. Swift was set down in his time as a conservative. Swift thought of himself as a conservative, a man whose glance was always backward. Swift distrusted theory, as Burke does.

Bryson: As most satirists do.

Van Doren: Yes. Swift could be positively infuriated by theory. The mere look of abstraction on someone's face could make him froth at the mouth.

Barzun: The extraordinary thing is that though Burke seems to be looking backward, his power of prophecy is much greater than Paine's. He predicts on very slender evidence that this French Revolution will be extraordinarily powerful as an agent of future revolutions in the nineteenth century, and he is completely aghast at things that most people, most of his friends in England, thought were simple and admirable reforms.

Bryson: Because they hadn't yet run their full course.

Barzun: No, there had been no massacres, no terror, nothing except a very small degree of emigration.

Bryson: But isn't Paine, in thinking that the revolution is going to continue in the more placid phases of its beginning, a typical revolutionary? Don't nearly all revolutionaries suppose when they get the world started into a crisis that it's going to stop at just the right point? And aren't they usually surprised?

Van Doren: I'm still interested, Mr. Bryson, in your remark that Burke might not have called the American Revolution a revolution. I think that is not the most important point that we can consider today. We must return eventually to the general theory of political change. But you are aware of course that a number of historians are becoming more and more reluctant to use the word "revolution" in this case. They call it the "first American civil war."

Bryson: It was a war of secession.

Van Doren: And the first gun fired was a document: the Declaration of Independence.

Barzun: And very much in the spirit of Paine, that document.

Van Doren: Its authors were considered at the time to be doctrinaires, were they not? Jefferson always had about him something of the doctrinaire, and as a matter of fact he appreciated Paine more than Washington or Hamilton or Madison, for instance, could ever have done. It is said that Jefferson actually urged upon Washington once, and indeed only after the composition of the *Rights of Man*, that Paine be made a member of Washington's Cabinet.

Barzun: But wasn't Burke right in considering that in France there was a revolution in spirit, no matter how many precedents there had been for a declaration of the Rights of Man? I was struck by the fact that he constantly recurs to the idea of honor. Now honor, according to Montesquieu is the mainspring of a monarchy and it had disappeared under the mechanical and geometrical—those are the words Burke uses—ideas of Paine and his friends. Abandoning honor means a change in the mood of individuals and nations.

Bryson: Yes, but at the same time, Mr. Barzun, Burke is constantly insisting upon the career open to talents. His idea is not a government of expediency which shall rest entirely upon the inheritance of title and the inheritance of money and the inheritance of political power. He himself, after all, was a commoner who had gained great power by his eloquence and his brains; and doesn't he always insist that the kind of government he wants is a government in which there shall always be the rising to power of the intelligent and talented commoner? He is not merely an aristocrat.

Barzun: Oh, no, I didn't mean to imply that, but rather that he places a great value on the intangibles and imponderables and on self-restraint. He speaks somewhere of Nature, meaning not the natural rights of Paine, but the right instincts, the proper feelings that people have without knowing what the grounds of those feelings are.

Van Doren: And of course his use of the word "right"—this may be relevant today in view of our renewed interest in the Bill of Rights—is obviously so much broader and richer than Paine's. Most persons think of the rights of man purely in negative terms. Men have the rights not to have certain things done to them: cruel and unusual punishments, and so on. Burke is by contrast positive. Burke says that we have a right to inherit the past; we have a right to continue to enjoy the structure of society as it is; and curiously enough he says we have a right to be restrained. Government is a contrivance of human wisdom, he says, to provide for human wants. Men have a right that these wants should be provided for by this wisdom. Among those wants is to be reckoned the want of civil society, of a sufficient restraint upon persons. Society requires not only that the passions of individuals should be subjected, but that those of the mass should too; the inclinations of men should frequently be thwarted, their will controlled, and their passions brought into subjection.

Bryson: And how typical it is of Burke to use the word wisdom as he does. Wisdom is a word that, if Paine used it, he would use with much less unction.

Barzun: He would probably use the word "knowledge," wouldn't he?

Bryson: Yes, because he is thinking of the abstract, the purely intellectual, rather than any understanding that comes from use and familiarity.

Van Doren: His assumption would be that among all possible theories one theory was the best.

Bryson: That's right.

Van Doren: And that would be wisdom for him. But Burke of course is mortally afraid when he hears such language being used, because wisdom for him is something both larger and vaguer than what is suggested by the word "knowledge."

Barzun: And wisdom isn't always trying to uncover its own roots to see whether it is growing properly. Both men deal with this question—which is basic in all political theory—of original conquest, that is, of might. Does it generate a right? Burke says yes, because a right is simply the making reasonable and acceptable of an initial act of violence. Paine really wants to go back and have a conquest over the conqueror, some ten centuries later, and ground *his* rights on a basis of established knowledge, which Burke says is quite impossible.

Bryson: And which of course obviously is impossible. The kind of abstract reasoning which Paine is such a great exemplar of would wreck us, wouldn't it, if we followed it?

Barzun: If we all started thinking about it at once it would.

Van Doren: Burke is afraid that revolution will finally give him no government to reform, no society to reform.

Bryson: Whereas Paine is perfectly sure that you can sit down in a vacuum, as we say today, and think out the perfect government and make it start working right from the beginning.

Van Doren: And he has a faith—you may remember he expresses his faith on two or three pages running—that somehow or other government is not really necessary, that society knows how to take care of itself, that society suddenly deprived of the thing we call government would as suddenly begin to function in a political fashion. A notion which would horrify, which did horrify Burke, because for him the slow and very patient skills that have to be built up over a long history in political experiment were something he couldn't bear to see scrapped.

Bryson: But there is another side of it, Mr. Van Doren, besides this literary and political one, and that is what you might call the scientific one. It strikes me that Burke is very much more in accord with modern political science or philosophy of government than Paine is. The modern person who approaches government from a study of anthropological evidence, the study of the way society is put together, is very much more likely to follow the general line of Burke, that societies grow and that men take on ways of doing things, rather than the idea that they are based upon abstract principles.

Barzun: Well, his basic notion of what men are like is sounder. He was a politician after all and Paine was only a writer. Paine's assumption that when you state something in words you have the thing itself is what made Burke so angry, so scornful.

Van Doren: You say Paine was not a politician, Mr. Barzun. Did he even have any political sense about his own career?

Barzun: No, he was the most impolitic of men; he alienated almost everyone he came in contact with.

Bryson: Of course that is what makes one want to reverse oneself, Mr. Van Doren, and say that, after all, Paine was a very admirable old boy. He was always getting himself into trouble, but it was because of things that he thought were right. He was perfectly willing to ask for trouble if in doing so he could make one of these abstract notions of his get somewhere nearer fruition. That's heroism.

Van Doren: I agree with you, Mr. Bryson, and I hope very sincerely that before we are through today we shall be just to both men. I admire Paine very much. One reason I admire him, for example, is that he would have detected the danger latent in a phrase of Montesquieu whom Mr. Barzun quoted a minute ago. Montesquieu you may remember said once: Liberty does not consist in doing what one pleases; liberty can only consist in being able to do what one ought to do. Now that is very fine and I think in some ideal world true and safe.

Bryson: But a great text for a tyrant.

Van Doren. Of course. Paine is one of those men who understand how easily tyrants can decide what it is that we ought to do.

Bryson: Another famous remark of Paine's about liberty which you may not remember just occurred to me. When Benjamin Franklin said that where liberty is there was his home, Paine replied, where liberty is not, there is mine.

Van Doren: Isn't it pretty clear that you can't get along without either type of man?

Barzun: You certainly can't. With Burkes everything could endlessly be justified in its present state, and under Paines you would have no government.

Van Doren: That is the difference.

Barzun: You would have a constant discussion of what the next government ought to be.

Van Doren: Jefferson, who was something of a Paine as we were saying, and much disliked by many Americans for that reason, said, you may remember: That government is best which governs least.

Barzun: And he wanted a revolution every twenty years.

Van Doren: Yes.

Barzun: Not specifying quite what he meant by revolution.

Bryson: And I think this is true, isn't it, Mr. Barzun—I don't think it ought to be overlooked—that the American Revolution, whose exact nature we were talking about a while ago, was not under Jefferson's control in any critical phase. It was managed by people like Washington and Hamilton and Madison. Jefferson didn't actually get his hands on the American government until the revolutionary phase was pretty well over.

Barzun: That's true. And those others whom you mentioned were more like Burke than they were like Paine.

Bryson: They believed in expediency.

Van Doren: And the authors of the *Federalist Papers* were, on the whole, Burke men rather than Paine men.

Barzun: What is extraordinary to me is that this conflict between the two types of men—if we can raise it to that status—hasn't ceased yet. In France, for example, the Revolution is still being fought out, and the failure to fight it out intellectually has a great deal to do, it seems to me, with the recent collapse of the Republic. And in many other contexts one finds the political theorists of the Paine type battling endlessly with the Burke type without ever arriving at a common ground. Do you think, Mr. Van Doren, that a common ground is impossible?

Van Doren: I hope not at any rate, because I see very little future for the race if some common ground is not found. Wouldn't you say, Mr. Barzun, that in France not only did men of the Paine type argue with men of the Burke type, but they argued with one another? Perhaps that is a sufficient account of the collapse of the French Republic.

Barzun: You mean—

Van Doren: Too many parties, too many theories, too many pure theories, the government falling to pieces meanwhile.

Barzun: I think that is rather an exaggerated view of French politics because the parties do solidify into two halves—the conservative, royalist, right and the radical and progressive left.

Van Doren: Well, they can be said to solidify into those two halves. I wonder, however, if a difference isn't made nevertheless by there being actually a considerable number of them, with the division not as sharp as it might be if there were two parties by name and by constitution?

Barzun: Of course there are as many factions and subfactions in the two English parties, but perhaps you mean that the passion for making things explicit in France makes political action more difficult.

Bryson: Wait a minute, Mr. Barzun. I'm shocked by Mr. Van Doren's saying that he thinks the human race will be destroyed unless we finally get some kind of compromise—or did you say common ground—between the theorist and the practical man. Isn't the constant struggle between those two and the oscillation of power between the two exactly what makes the world keep on going?

Van Doren: Yes, but this oscillation and this argument of which you speak implies common ground. Can two men argue without a common ground?

Bryson: You don't mean a compromise in the sense that they would stop their differences, but that they would find common principles upon which to argue?

Barzun: Oh, definitely. It is only the possession of common principles which makes arguments continue.

Bryson: I see what you mean.

Barzun: For example, in these two books, both men say perfectly outrageous things which they're saying only for argument's sake, and those are the things that party resentments form around, it seems to me.

Bryson: And they tend to last forever, Mr. Barzun. I have an edition here of Tom Paine's *Rights of Man* which is dated 1919, and which contains a most outrageous slander on the private character of Burke. It has nothing whatever to do with the argument or with Tom Paine, but they're still fighting it out on those terms.

Barzun: It is interesting to note that after Burke had published his book many of his friends said that they couldn't possibly understand why he objected to the French Revolution merely because insults had been offered to the Queen. Now that passage in which he speaks of the insult to the Queen is just a fragment of a two-hundred-and-fifty-page book. And yet that's the kind of thing that strikes people and makes them belong to one group or another.

Bryson: Of course it's also the penalty you pay for being a poet like Mr. Van Doren, Mr. Barzun—if you write too well you attract attention to what you say even if it isn't important.

Van Doren: Both men write wonderfully, wouldn't you agree?

Bryson: Yes, certainly.

Van Doren: With very different styles. Paine's style is brisk and brittle and full of epigram, full of alliteration, full of perhaps obvious arts yet brilliantly practiced ones, while Burke is slower and richer and more seemly. Indeed the difference always appears to me as the difference between richness and brightness.

Barzun: Yet I detect in Burke's book a superiority which may characterize even his political thinking. Burke's book is not divided into sections or chapters or anything else, and he seems to be wandering all over the lot, and yet it has a real form, whereas Paine's book is divided into chapters which have subjects at the head, and the book has no form whatsoever. It is purely a mechanical collection of items and arguments.

Bryson: But don't you agree, Mr. Barzun, that just as we need both styles, both richness and brightness, we also need both kinds of men?

Barzun: Yes, I think we need both kinds of men. We have to have people who appeal to natural rights, to hypothetical ideas.

Bryson: Who argue about principles.

Barzun: Who argue about principles, and principles which have no roots as yet in the structure of things. For instance, it is no doubt shocking to many persons to have principles attacked as Burke attacks them. Now Burke was an excellent man, in my opinion one of the best of men, and yet in this book he is attacking the procedure, the political procedure, based upon principles. I think there are many respects in which he is sound in doing so; on the other hand, we must continue to respect principles or we have no guide to action. That is why we have to have both kinds of men forever, and that is all that I had in mind, Mr. Bryson, when I said that I hoped the common ground would always exist on which they could argue.

Bryson: And of course if you have both kinds of men they will be quarreling with each other as well as among themselves. You said a while ago that the doctrinaires of the Paine type quarreled among themselves. Well, so do the men of expediency, but they quarrel about something different. They quarrel about how you're going to do the thing. Not the basic principle that justifies your doing it.

Barzun: Of course Mr. Bryson's point that the friction between the two keeps the world going around is seemingly justified by history. Both men described the events of the latter half of 1789, and they give of them a very different description—the tone and feeling and emotions aroused in the spectator are entirely different; but if you look at the events themselves, the taking of the Bastille, for example—here was an act which hadn't any of the symbolic character it has since acquired when it first took place. It was merely the desire on the part of the mob to get some firearms which were supposed to be hidden there, and the massacre, the murder, the destruction of the prison, all those things which have come to mean something else, were based on a kind of mis-apprehension. History is just a succession of those things.

Bryson: The myth-making power is always at work, isn't it?

Barzun: Yes, perhaps through the inability of a man like Paine and a man like Burke to know what the other is really talking about.

Van Doren: And of course one may perceive every now and then both men being—well, not exactly crooked in their argument, but very imperious and quite willing to misquote each other in order to slip something over.

Barzun: It is only once in a while that each of them really expresses fully and clearly and without overstatement what he means. I think that this passage from Burke is very characteristic of his best thought. He says:

"The nature of man is intricate, the objects of society are of the greatest possible complexity, and therefore no simple disposition or direction of power can be suitable either to man's nature or to the quality of his affairs. When I hear the simplicity of contrivance aimed at and boasted of in any new political constitution, I am at no loss to decide that the artificers are grossly ignorant of their trade or totally negligent of their duty. The simple governments are fundamentally defective, to say no worse of them. If you were to contemplate society in but one point of view, all these simple moves of polity are infinitely captivating. In effect, each would answer its single end much more perfectly than the more complex is able to attain its complex purposes. But it is better that the whole should be imperfectly and anomalously answered than that while some parts are provided for with great exactness, others might be totally neglected, or perhaps materially injured by the overcare of a favorite member. The pretended rights of these theorists are all extremes, and in proportion as they are metaphysically true, they are morally and politically false."

Bryson: Now, Mr. Barzun, against that I would put a paragraph of Paine's in which he opposes his abstract theory to Burke's ideas of expediency, and it is interesting too to see that in this paragraph, which is from *The Rights of Man,* he calls his own revolution a counter revolution. I suspect that most people do that. They try to give a moral superiority to the revolution that they're supporting by saying the other fellow started it, so to speak. Paine says:

"The revolutions which formerly took place in the world had nothing in them that interested the bulk of mankind. They extended only to a change of persons and measures, but not of principles, and rose or fell among the common transactions of the moment. What we now behold may not improperly be called a counter revolution. Conquest and tyranny have at some earlier period dispossessed man of his rights and he is now recovering them. And as the tide of all human affairs has its ebb and flow and directions contrary to each other, so also is it in this. Government founded on a moral theory, on a system of universal peace, on the indefeasible hereditary rights of man, is now revolving from west to east, by a stronger impulse than the government of the sword revolved from east to west. It interests not particular individuals but nations in its progress, and promises a new era to the human race."

(1712-1778)

JEAN JACQUES ROUSSEAU

The Social Contract

JEAN JACQUES ROUSSEAU is famous for many attitudes which he took and for many books which he wrote. In education, in psychology, in morals he has been a pervasive influence since his death; and like most men of such influence he has been damned as often as he has been praised. He was an unstable genius with a superb literary talent, so that anything he published was from the first successful if only because of the intensity with which he expressed himself. In the domain of political thought his best-known work is still The Social Contract, *an essay in which he enlisted both history and reason in the service of a theory he had and an emotion he felt concerning government. It is misleading to say of him, as many do, that he almost alone brought on the French Revolution at the end of his century. Many men did that, and many conditions. Nor do political speculations bulk large among his writings; nor, probably, would he have liked the*

Revolution if he had lived to see it. But his Social Contract *reenforced other thinking done in the century; and at any rate it remains, despite the flaws of logic and fact that are so easily found in it, one of the basic essays on the relation between government and the governed. The doctrine of consent, even if Rousseau arrived at it through guesses about "the state of nature" which nobody now can share, is one which political philosophy has never lost sight of.* The Social Contract *is solidly intrenched as a republican classic.*

Jean Jacques Rousseau, French philosopher and exponent of democracy and romanticism, was born in Geneva of Huguenot parents. From an early age he led a wandering and irregular life, settling in Paris, where he lived in a garret (copying music for a livelihood) and formed an enduring liaison with an illiterate servant. He made literary acquaintances there and began to write. After a quarrel with Mme d'Epinay, who loaned him a cottage, "The Hermitage," he moved to Montmorency near by and entered on the productive period of his life. In the next few years he wrote his great works: La Nouvelle Héloise *(1761),* Le Contrat Social *(1762),* Emile *(1762). Among his other writings were a dictionary of music (he also composed fluently) and articles on music for the* Encyclopedia, *as well as two posthumous autobiographical works, his* Confessions *and* Reveries of a Solitary.

JOSEPH HERGESHEIMER · JACQUES BARZUN · MARK VAN DOREN

Van Doren: Mr. Barzun, I might begin by asking you a question. Not that I want to exclude Mr. Hergesheimer, but we discussed Tom Paine's *Rights of Man* and Edmund Burke's *Reflections on the Revolution in France.* My question is, whether *The Social Contract* strikes you offhand as being more like Paine or more like Burke?

Barzun: It strikes me very definitely as being more like Burke, contrary to what one might at first think; Burke attacks Rousseau, and Paine and Rousseau are frequently linked together as makers of the French Revolution—at least intellectually—but in grasp of concrete things and in political wisdom I would definitely place Rousseau and Burke together, as against the more superficial and abstract Paine.

Van Doren: That was the conclusion I reached also, very much to my own surprise. It is years since I first read *The Social Contract,* and during that time I had tended, as I believe most persons do, to simplify it in my mind, to think of it as something doctrinaire, like Paine, something over-simplified. I find it to be far from a piece of over-simplification. Mr. Hergesheimer, are we telling the truth, or are we talking about a book you don't know?

Hergesheimer: Oh, yes, Mr. Van Doren, I think it's the truth. As a matter of fact, although I've talked about *The Social Contract* and Rousseau for years, I think the past week is the first time I have read it carefully. I was very glad to do that, because it answers a question I had considered for a long while—whether the books that are read as philosophy have to do with reality or are works of the imagination. It is quite clear to me as a result of reading Rousseau that they are works of art rather than of reality.

Van Doren: Do you make so hard and fast a distinction between art and reality? I should think that good art at any rate had much to do with reality.

Hergesheimer: In such a short time as we have to make our distinctions, it is harder perhaps and faster than it should be. What I really mean is that in dealing with a theory of government, in dealing with the realities that I am obliged for the moment to call politics, such books seem to defy the law of perspective, to follow each other into infinity along tracks that never meet. What I have seen actually in the political works of man has no relation whatever to these handsome theories that I suspect exist more as literature. I am quite serious about that. More as literature than as fact.

Barzun: In other words, Mr. Hergesheimer, you are denying the possibility of political theory in the sense in which we have mathematical theory or physical theory. Is that what you're doing?

Hergesheimer: I'm denying its usefulness in application to such experience as I've had with political arrangements of countries, men, or governments. Theory is a charming occupation, and of great value possibly, but I cannot find that it has any bearing on what men do, or on their motives.

Barzun: A thing that is both charming and valuable, as you say this is, strikes me as justified by those very terms.

Hergesheimer: That is why I spoke of it as a work of art.

Van Doren: Mr. Hergesheimer, you are talking about something that touched me very deeply as I read. I must confess that for a number of years I have been undervaluing this book. Perhaps I overvalue it now, but it seems to me, again very much to my surprise, one of the wisest books about politics and society that I know, and precisely because it is good theory, precisely because Rousseau has the courage to keep on being theoretical when of course that is what he should be if he can. It seems to me that politics has never ceased to need theory.

Barzun: Or explanation. The problem he takes up is this: How it is that everywhere we find man he is bound down by rules and regulations which limit his freedom? Rousseau says that his object in the book is to discover how that happens and why it is legitimate. This is the very opposite of most people's notion of Rousseau as a man desirous of breaking down all rules; he is trying here to discover their rationale. That strikes me as extremely important if we have a government that rests on the consent of the governed. Presumably consent comes from understanding, from explanation.

Van Doren: His famous first sentence, "Man is born free; and everywhere he is in chains," is surely misunderstood by most persons; it is quoted as meaning something that Rousseau does not think it means. He is not complaining about the chains, is he?

Barzun: No, he is going to justify them. Which he does.

Van Doren: He is going to justify the chains on the ground that if man is not to be an animal—to be sure, if man wishes to remain an animal he may be as free as he pleases—he will have to recognize and indeed desire chains.

Hergesheimer: Yes, but, Mr. Van Doren, one of my difficulties—you have discovered it before this—is the difficulty of definition, of knowing in a workable and actual way what people mean. Now here is a statement of Rousseau that brings up the point. He says: "Every man has naturally a right to everything he needs. A man must occupy only the amount he needs for his subsistence." That is not two contradictory phrases; it is one phrase which is impossible of definition or limitation. Who can decide, human nature and biology being what they are, who can decide for another man what he needs? You may need a blonde, you may need a steamboat, you may need liberty; or if you're a sensible man you don't want liberty—it's a nuisance and very dangerous. How can we define for other people what they need and put a law on it?

Barzun: Mr. Hergesheimer, you've overlooked the very important initial point contained in the word "naturally," which implies a purely hypothetical state in Rousseau's words. We don't

[388]

know what man "naturally" is, but we cannot think of him except as deprived of all the things that society gives him.

Hergesheimer: That's quite true, but natural law, man's natural right, is just as English in its philosophy as it is French. You're quite right, but we must needs establish then, if that's the way we feel, that we're perfectly safe in asserting that there was always a natural law regulating what men should have, since if it hadn't existed always, it couldn't have come into being. Is there a natural law? Have we a right to breathe? Who gave us the right to breathe? Can it be defined politically? I'm not sure. I don't know. I'm afraid of natural laws.

Barzun: I don't see how you can be afraid of natural laws when they're used instrumentally; it's like the atom which we don't see and handle, or the perfectly frictionless body which physicists deal with and which doesn't exist. It can't be found at the ten-cent store. Now, natural man is just such a creature, and we have to understand his essence as natural man before we can see whether a particular political state is just.

Hergesheimer: That's quite true. But on the other hand, there is no necessity to look for an atom in the ten-cent store, whereas I couldn't tell you where to look for a natural law. We can find an atom in a laboratory, but the natural law that gives me certain rights, except by agreement with other people, except as a sum total of natural rights, each one not too strongly in collision with the others—that, it seems to me, isn't a natural law, a law like gravity. But we can let the ten-cent store drop. We can go to the laboratory for the atom, we can see neutrons; but where are we going to see a natural law? I don't know.

Van Doren: I'm a little bewildered by all this discussion about natural law, since it seems to me that Rousseau is chiefly concerned here with human law—with the law of art, if you please. In spite of his reputation as being a man who thought most of the time about nature, here it seems to me he is thinking about the very thing that you have named, namely, art; society is an art for him, and of course a highly difficult one. Any good art is difficult. He finds it most difficult to say where it is that political wisdom and social wisdom, if they exist, come from.

Barzun: It seems to me that Mr. Hergesheimer's position amounts to saying that whatever is is right. If one says the opposite of that—that there may be something to be changed or to be reformed in accordance with reason or human desires— then one has only two grounds of appeal. One is history: the theory that in the past we, whoever "we" may be, had rights which are now disregarded. That leads generally to the falsification of history. Now Rousseau neglects such an appeal on purpose. He says: Let us appeal to nature, which is a hypothesis, something that never existed, something non-historical, a concept; and he promises that it will be tested, like all good concepts, by its consequences. It seems to me that there is simply no getting out of this simple choice.

Hergesheimer: That's perfectly true, but when you said "history" what you actually meant was pre-history, since that's the history that Rousseau must go back to for the natural man. We've got no history, as such, of natural men, I think.

Barzun: No, I think that's your misconception. "Nature" is not pre-history; it never existed in time or space.

Van Doren: And Rousseau doesn't think for a moment that it did.

Barzun: No, he doesn't.

Van Doren: As a matter of fact, I find Rousseau in this book— elsewhere he seems to me quite frequently detestable and foolish —to be very wise, to be wise in the way in which the greatest social and political philosophers have been wise, because he begins by recognizing the heart of the problem, which might be put this way: How is it that man is going to know what he should do as man? It is relatively easy for man to know what he should do as animal. He has appetites which are all too obvious.

Hergesheimer: Fortunately.

Van Doren: Yes, and they are constantly clamoring for satisfaction. But he knows very soon that human life is something more than a circus in which the appetites may be either frustrated or satisfied. All men are possessed by the question what it is to be men. We are the only animals who are possessed by that question, the only animals who have to ask the question; horses and elephants don't seem to have much difficulty being horses and elephants respectively.

Barzun: Rousseau has another problem at the other end, it seems to me. Men generally know what they have to do as institutional creatures, as bishops or marquises or peasants, but if society ever gets into a state where change seems necessary, then you have to ask what on the one hand man must do, as you point out, and what on the other hand he must no longer do as an institutional creature.

Van Doren: That's right. There is of course an area of freedom for him, just as there is an area of necessity.

Barzun: Yes, he needn't wear powder in his hair, or a wig, or silk knee breeches. He can do something else.

Van Doren: It seems to me that Rousseau has a very sensitive, delicate, and profound feeling for the difficulty of the problem.

Hergesheimer: Then, Mr. Van Doren, if we must leave reality for theory, I must go back to the troubles that Rousseau has created for me by another quotation. I take it that we are dealing with great books in the terms of our own times, that if they are great they are pertinent today; they are of use to us. They stay alive. Rousseau says in *The Social Contract:* "Lands where the surplus of product over labor is only middling are suitable for free peoples. Those in which the soil gives a great product for a little labor call for monarchial government." That is to me a question. That has its effect on me as a statement.

Barzun: Yes, but can you take a statement like that out of its context?

Hergesheimer: It isn't out of its context; it's perfectly fairly quoted. Now here is another thing that makes trouble for me. "The horse, the calf, the bull, and even the ass are generally of greater stature and always more robust and have more vigor, strength, and courage when they run wild in the forest than when bred in the stall." That is completely, utterly, and entirely erroneous, as the history of the racehorse will show you. It simply is not fact.

Van Doren: Well, Mr. Hergesheimer, what about this sentence: "The moment a people allows itself to be represented, it is no longer free. It no longer exists." That seems to me a very startling statement, and one which even if untrue has got to be considered; and I see, with the context of the whole work in mind, that it may contain a great truth. Do you see what he might mean by saying that the moment a people allows itself to be represented, it is no longer free?

Hergesheimer: Yes, Mr. Van Doren, and there is a second quotation that comes very, shall we say, liltingly after that: "Whoever refuses to obey the general will shall be compelled to do so by the whole body." Now it's this sentence again that lands me on the littoral. This means nothing less than that he will be forced to be free.

Van Doren: I think that is one of the profoundest things said by Rousseau.

Hergesheimer: Well, Mr. Van Doren, let's admit its profundity very quickly.

Van Doren: No, it is what I want to talk about. I think it is very important that we should find the profound things in this book.

Barzun: Yes, we now have an assortment of quotations which are all very interesting.

Hergesheimer: But they do bear generally, I think, on what we're talking about—that is, his right to address us on the universal subject must depend on the correlation of his knowledge, his deductions, and his feeling. So I don't think they are scattered; they bear on the man's essential being and authority.

Barzun: Well, I entirely agree with you about definition, but it seems to me that an error of fact about wild horses doesn't quite come within our purview if we are discussing . . .

Hergesheimer: No, that's right, but I'll tell you exactly and how it does, and I must do so very quickly. It seems to be the essence of philosophers to discuss great and universal problems.

They discuss problems that can have no human limitation, and at the same they are hooped by the limitations of knowledge which are current with their own lives. So they express themselves currently; but things change—as we speak of atoms instead of astrology—and that's what I mean by being born as thoughts but dying as literature.

Barzun: Well, that's what *I* meant. The historical information that is available in a particular century necessarily conditions thought. But thought can transcend—

Hergesheimer: Can it really?

Barzun: —errors of information.

Hergesheimer: You see again, these very words are slipping beyond my complete grasp. I'm afraid one of them is truth.

Van Doren: Mr. Hergesheimer, you used the word "limitations." I don't know any political philosopher more aware than Rousseau is of the limitations of human wisdom, and of his own wisdom.

Hergesheimer: That is true, Mr. Van Doren.

Van Doren: I think it's very important that it is true. When he says, for instance, that the perfect legislator for a people will be if possible a person who has no stake in the government of that people, if possible an outsider, either a person called in for the job or a mysterious stranger who happens along and out of his wisdom pronounces laws; when he goes on indeed to say that quite possibly the only true source of the laws of a nation, expressing its general will and exercising its sovereignty, is the gods, he is paying tribute to human limitations such as I should say few political philosophers have ever paid.

Barzun: And every one of his statements on these key points, it seems to me, has to be interpreted in the light of his own use of language. I'd like to go back to the question you raised, Mr. Van Doren, about a represented people not being free, because that has given many readers the impression that he considers representative government tyrannical. On the contrary, he says that the best government is what he calls an elective aristocracy, namely, what we have in this country or in any country where there is a parliament. What he means of course by representative government not leaving the people free is the simple fact that while they're represented they're in the hands of somebody else, and that the perfect government would be one in which everyone participated, everyone took his equal share in the decisions. He points out why this is almost impossible.

Van Doren: Isn't his stress put not so much upon the possible tyranny of the representatives as upon the willingness, the perverse willingness, of the people to elect representatives and then forget them. That is when a nation dies: when it elects its representatives and then out of contempt, out of indifference, or out of shortsightedness, forgets them.

Barzun: Yes, and there can be corrupt methods by which they are elected. Another statement that made Mr. Hergesheimer feel uncomfortable was the one about the general will compelling a member of society to be free. It is simply a statement of fact that majorities obtained in one way or another rule minorities, and must do so if we are to have government.

Van Doren: The great majority of human beings, I suppose, do not have the courage to desire to be free. Freedom is a burden and a responsibility, as Mr. Hergesheimer himself suggested. Rousseau once has a very amusing phrase: "the yoke of the public happiness." Public happiness is a burden which we must all severally and collectively bear.

Hergesheimer: And pay for.

Barzun: Yes, it's a bilateral thing; most people want only the privilege and not the duty.

Van Doren: Rousseau says as eloquently as anyone I know that when we forget the duty we are, as a society, dead. Our duty is a willingness to be forced to be free.

Barzun: The most brilliant instance is his explanation of why the criminal who is about to be executed is fulfilling his own will in being executed. That is superb, and very likely the only justification of punishment.

Hergesheimer: Which seems to me to neglect a certain sociological and biological fact. Whether in the pursuit of your inescapable biological entity you have any choice to be executed or not is to me fantastic.

Van Doren: Why, Mr. Hergesheimer, what theoretical, hypothetical, and philosophical words you're using—"entity," "biological," "sociological"!

Hergesheimer: "Entity" and "biological" as having to do with the functions of the body. Entity is the entire person himself.

Van Doren: I thought you were interested in reality.

Hergesheimer: I'm interested in why man commits crimes; he commits them from perfectly discoverable and even scientific reasons.

Van Doren: Are you sure?

Hergesheimer: I am assured by men who know more about such things than I do that that's a fact. We're all, as we say, bound in time, so all that we can do is to lean on the best opinions of the best men we know.

Barzun: Your determinism is impossible to rear any theory of government upon. You have to believe that men have free choice whether they have it or not.

Van Doren: My own conviction is that Rousseau does not lean upon the opinions of experts. I am very grateful to him for trying to cut through into the heart of his question, using nothing but his own intuition, nothing but his own wisdom.

Hergesheimer: You see, Mr. Van Doren . . .

Van Doren: I don't care what an expert tells me is an entity.

Hergesheimer: My definition of an expert is a man who knows more than I do about a given subject. I care about the opinion of such a man.

Van Doren: My definition of an expert is a man who is wiser than I—in the present case, Rousseau.

Hergesheimer: Expertness doesn't mean wisdom. I think it might mean knowledge, but I doubt if expertness and wisdom are a happy marriage.

Van Doren: Which is the more important thing, knowledge or wisdom?

Hergesheimer: I should say that knowledge was the fact and wisdom the ability to use and penetrate and control the fact. One is the equipment and the other is the result.

Van Doren: So then I should say that if Rousseau is wise—now of course he may not be, I am merely saying that he seems to me to be wise—that is a much more important fact than that he knows or does not know this or that thing.

Hergesheimer: May I spill into this another irrelevant pearl of his wisdom?

Van Doren: Right.

Hergesheimer: "Space, art, sciences and law were wisely invented by men as a plague to prevent too great multiplication of mankind, lest the world should be too small for its inhabitants."

Barzun: That's good Malthus, isn't it?

Hergesheimer: Yes, it's splendid Malthus, but again I can only go back and say I don't know. Boys, I don't know. My opinion must be Rousseau's opinions as a whole, because it seems to me that although these things may be a little detached, they are beginning to form for me the picture of man who has to do, as I said at the beginning, with art and literature but not with sound or practicable reality.

Barzun: When he applied his ideas to the government of Poland, which is a perfectly practical job, he did in the opinion of all experts who should know, Mr. Hergesheimer, a splendid job not so much of compromising as of adapting his ideas to the concrete and hopeless state of Poland in the eighteenth century; so that if the test of an idea is its application, we agree both on the test and on the mark that Rousseau gets.

Hergesheimer: In other words, when he was concerned with politics he was a splendid fellow, but when he began to write books the same thing happened as happens to all of us when we begin to write books—we get elaborate and fancy.

Barzun: No, I don't think that follows at all.

Van Doren: Mr. Hergesheimer, I want to throw another sentence at you, or rather, two sentences. This it seems to me is written by a man who could be called nothing except wise: "Much trouble, we are told, is taken to teach young princes the art of reigning, but their education seems to do them no good. It would be better to begin by teaching them the art of obeying." I see no answer to that at all.

Hergesheimer: It's completely sound.

Van Doren: Well.

Barzun: We've spoken as if the book were a collection of maxims.

Hergesheimer: No, it's a philosophy of life.

Barzun: A course of very tightly knit arguments. It is one of the best-reasoned books ever written, contrary to the general opinion that Rousseau was impulsive and a heedless fellow. There's hardly an implication, there's hardly a difficulty, that he doesn't see and meet or postpone or say that he can't meet. So that our form of treatment strikes me in some sense as being poor criticism.

Van Doren: It is, decidedly.

Hergesheimer: I think it isn't intended as criticism. I think it's intended as a discussion of a book and of what it does to each of us, separately and together.

Barzun: I am not trying to stop the discussion; only to indicate that something else might be accomplished than objections to particular wise or unwise statements.

Hergesheimer: That's quite true, but the only method I have of argument is to proceed from the particular to the general and never from the general to the particular; and proceeding in this case from the particular, the particulars as I said have troubled me.

Barzun: Yes, but there aren't that many particulars in *The Social Contract*. He is assuming a knowledge of Greek and Roman history, of which he was full, like all of his contemporaries; he is assuming a knowledge of all the political theorists from the Middle Ages right down to his day; the book is written as much looking backward as looking forward. We always forget that. This whole notion of nature, for example, is not something invented; it is something he had to cope with because it was there. Perhaps if I read a short passage which bears on the civil state, we might get something of his theoretical power. He says:

"The passage from the state of nature to the civil state produces a very remarkable change in man, by substituting justice for instinct in his conduct, and giving his actions the morality they have formerly lacked. Then only, when the voice of duty takes the place of physical impulses and right of appetite, does man, who so far had considered only himself, find that he is forced to act on different principles, and to consult his reason before listening to his inclinations. Although in this state he deprives himself of some advantages which he got from nature, he gains in return others so great, his faculties are so stimulated and developed, his ideas so extended, his feelings so ennobled and his whole soul so uplifted, that, did not the abuses of this new condition often degrade him below that which he left, he would be bound to bless continually the happy moment which took him from it forever, and, instead of a stupid and unimaginative animal, made him an intelligent being and a man."

THOMAS ROBERT MALTHUS

Essay on Population

THE RATE *at which the population of the earth increases or decreases might be dismissed as a purely biological phenomenon. And so it was until the "dismal science" of society which was born in the eighteenth century reached out to take it in. Then it became a social and economic problem, or at any rate the determining aspect of one; and ever since it has been so treated. The dismal scientist who reached out to take it in was Thomas Robert Malthus, who in 1798 startled England and Europe with his* Essay on the Principle of Population as it Affects the Future Improvement of Society. *For Malthus there was in fact but one principle: population, unless unchecked, increases in a geometrical ratio, while the supply of food necessary to sustain human life increases in an arithmetical ratio. Thus in time the number of living people tends to exceed the amount of food available to keep them alive, unless of course accident and necessity conspire to reduce the*

number. The accidents which do indeed bring about this reduction are war, disease, famine, and misery. But necessity will more and more need to operate: conscious control, that is, of the earth's population. In succeeding editions of the Essay, *which extended its length until it became a treatise, Malthus developed his formula in opposition to an indignant and incessant criticism ranging all the way from complaint that he seemed to condone war and famine as providential calamities to disgust that he should consider the subject of human birth at all. The controversy has gone on, and Malthus has been corrected where correction was necessary. His essay stands, however, as the classic it was and is.*

Thomas Robert Malthus, English economist, received his B.A. at Jesus College, Cambridge, and from 1793 to 1804 was a fellow there. He took holy orders in 1797 and in the following year produced his famous Essay on Population. *He went abroad for further study in 1799 and 1802, and in 1805 became professor of history and political economy at the East India Company's college at Haileybury. His later studies were* Observations on the Effects of the Corn Laws *(1814);* Inquiry into the Nature and Progress of Rent *(1815);* Principles of Political Economy *(1820); and* Definitions in Political Economy *(1827).*

HENRY PRATT FAIRCHILD · JULIAN HUXLEY · MARK VAN DOREN

Van Doren: As you know, gentlemen, this is a program which discusses classics. But we have today, in the *Essay on Population,* a classic with a difference. It is not a classic, I assume, in quite the same way that *Hamlet* or the trilogy of Aeschylus, or *Tom Jones,* or *Crime and Punishment* is. It is a classic in a science. Insofar as sociology is a science, here is a classic in that science. I am wondering if you can assist me in distinguishing between what the word "classic" means in literary art and what it means in the realm of science. Mr. Huxley, have you an answer offhand?

Huxley: I could perhaps begin by quoting a remark that my grandfather once made. He said: "Books are the money of literature, but the counters of science." It's inevitable, of course, that in science, which is a progressive growth of many minds, that you should find your classics becoming out of date, however good. Darwin's *The Origin of Species* is out of date in a certain sense. On the other hand, *The Origin of Species* is a classic. It will bear rereading by the specialist and by the general reader, because it started people off thinking along certain lines. It marked a stage in man's thought, and it is important that we should know about it. It created a new way of looking at the problem. The same is true of Malthus' *Essay on Population.*

Fairchild: May I interrupt you just a moment there, Mr. Huxley? Your reference to ideas as money is very interesting, because one of the friends of Mr. Malthus himself said that the ideas of a great man are like the money of a great potentate—they circulate on the authority of him who issues them, and the more they circulate the more they become worn and defaced until they completely lose their original significance. I think that has happened to a very considerable extent with Malthus' ideas.

Van Doren: Anyone seems to take for granted these days that much of Malthus is outworn. Yet the book is in print, is read, and is still paid homage to as a classic. I heard someone say the other day that the best book in any science is the last one. You wouldn't agree with that, Mr. Fairchild?

Fairchild: I certainly would not agree with that! This very same author said that the trouble with a great scholar is that as soon as he becomes an authority everybody quotes him and nobody reads him. Exactly that has happened in the case of Malthus.

Van Doren: As an expert in population, then, you say that any student of population would do well to read this earliest book on the subject?

Fairchild: I think he certainly *must* read this book—and read it in the original, not in the commentaries, because the commentaries are likely to go very far astray from the original.

Van Doren: In other words, the quality that Malthus had must have been a quality of the imagination. It was a quality which permitted him to see a problem where no one else had seen one and to understand it in a way which continues to seem necessary.

Fairchild: I am interested to see that you rank imagination as an intellectual quality. Many people think that the scientist mustn't have imagination.

Van Doren: Oh, that's what he has above all else.

Fairchild: There actually is a man here who can speak for science.

Van Doren: What do you think, Mr. Huxley?

Huxley: Obviously, I take it for granted. But wouldn't you put it this way: science tries to discover uniformity, and is always postulating continuity? When it is trying to get at something new, it is likely to flounder in many ways. Malthus thought out to its logical conclusion the notion that population was bound to increase more rapidly than food, and therefore that population, here and now, must always be pressing on the means of subsistence. He then drew certain other conclusions, which we shall deal with later, that are now out of date because the organization of society is different now from what it was then. But the general conclusion still holds; so we may say that while Malthusianism in the narrow sense is out of date, Malthusianism in the broad sense is always with us.

Van Doren: In other words, he used the word "principle" in his title and he had a right to use it, because his principle is still with us.

Huxley: I should like to hear Dr. Fairchild speak about that, because he really is a great authority.

Fairchild: Thank you very much! I agree entirely that the essence of true science is permanent. Truth itself does not change. Once a thing is established in the realm of nature, you understand, as absolute and positive, then that does not change. But the manifestations of our interpretation of science change all the time, because we keep learning more and more. In the social sciences, obviously, where we attempt to interpret the relationships of human beings to each other, those relationships are continually changing and what the scientist tries to get at is the underlying fundamental forces—or principles, as you say, Mr. Van Doren—which are permanent. In that respect I think Malthus was absolutely sound. He started, as both of you remember, by saying that all he asked was that you grant him two postulates, and on the basis of those two postulates he could prove that a perfected state of human society was impossible. Of course, he started this whole business from arguments with his father about the perfectability of human society.

Van Doren: And he had been reading Godwin.

Fairchild: Yes, and Condorcet, and the whole school that believed that the ills of human society were due to faulty political systems, so that if you could just doctor up the political systems then all the evils of unemployment, poverty, vice, and so forth would fade away.

Van Doren: That sounds very modern!

Fairchild: Yes, very modern!

Van Doren: You remember the very interesting paragraph in

which he says that perhaps the greatest ills of society are brought about by those who think that government is the only operating influence in society and that a mere change in government will somehow make everybody happy.

Fairchild: Exactly! Those people might be the champions of the New Deal.

Van Doren: Or of any "ism" at all.

Fairchild: Exactly!

Van Doren: Whereas he is trying to be a sort of physicist or chemist of society, is he not? He seems to see forces working there which no government could modify, and which no government could have produced in the first place.

Fairchild: Well, of course, it is very hard to identify Malthus as a particular brand of scholar. What he had to say was so important that it covers many fields. For instance, I was quite interested this morning to hear the announcer speak of Malthus as an economist. Eventually he came to be thought of as an economist because he, along with Ricardo and John Stuart Mill, was very influential in formulating what they called the "classical system of economics." But we mustn't forget that fundamentally, or, at least in the beginning, Malthus was a clergyman.

Huxley: And then a sociologist.

Fairchild: And then a sociologist. And afterward, in his way, a very elementary biologist. Too bad he didn't know more biology, but there wasn't much biology to be known at the time.

Van Doren: He was called with rather heavy irony in his time, I believe, Parson Malthus.

Fairchild: Yes, the "gloomy parson," because of the implications of his system.

Van Doren: He had done what no parson ought to do. He had meddled with problems.

Huxley: Dr. Fairchild was saying there were two fundamental principles outlined by Malthus.

Fairchild: The first one was that the passion between the sexes, as he called it, is permanent. He originally called it the instinct for marriage, but then he realized that there was no such thing as an instinct for marriage, so he called it the passion between the sexes and said it was permanent. The second postulate was that food is necessary. Now, he made an assumption there which, of course, today we would challenge.

Van Doren: Which one?

Fairchild: The assumption was a *third* postulate, really. Namely, that the passion between the sexes must necessarily result in offspring. Now that is where Malthus, I think, was influenced by his clerical connections. We have every reason to believe that Malthus knew more about artificial interference with propagation than he wanted to admit, but he did not give any place to that in his system. So, as I say, he *assumed* that the passion between the sexes was a means of expressing the great reproductive principle which holds good in all animal and plant life and, on that basis, he said that population tends to increase at a geometrical ratio. Now there, I think we can agree, is a scientific population principle that has not changed, that is universal. The human being is like other animals in this one respect. We know that the natural relationship between the sexes results in a tendency toward a geometrical increase. But no species, either of plant or of animal, ever realizes in nature that geometrical increase. It is impossible. A geometrical ratio leads to infinity.

Van Doren: If it did, the earth would soon be covered by nothing except one species.

Fairchild: Absolutely! *Any* species could cover the earth in a very few generations if its geometrical increase were not checked by another tendency, or by its own restraint.

Huxley: Exactly.

Van Doren: We've all been scared, haven't we, by scientists who said that if nothing interfered the earth would be six feet deep with grasshoppers?

Fairchild: That's it. Or seventeen-year locusts.

Huxley: The other point he is said to have made is that food tends to increase at an arithmetical ratio, isn't it?

Fairchild: He didn't actually say that.

Huxley: You're perfectly right.

Fairchild: That is one of the prevailing misconceptions of the Malthusian theory, and it is in fact the principle point of attack on Malthus. Now, Malthus wanted to suggest the upper limit of this restraining influence on population increase which he called food, or, more often, subsistency. He said, we've got to get an idea as to the possibilities of food increase; then we will have some sort of idea of the possibilities of human increase, because one limits the other. So he said: let us make a supposition which, without pretending to accuracy, is more favorable to the increase of food than we have any reason to believe possible; let's assume that food cannot increase faster than at an arithmetical ratio— which, you see, is a very different thing from saying that food increases or tends to increase at an arithmetical ratio. Now then, he said, there are these two things—a tendency toward infinity, and a restraint on the other side. Now I submit, Mr. Van Doren and Mr. Huxley, that that's a completely up-to-date proposition, that those fundamentals are just as true today as they ever were.

Van Doren: You mean to say, population is still pressing upon subsistence?

Huxley: Ah, not necessarily! Because a geometrical ratio may be either negative or positive. That is to say, if population is multiplying itself by two every generation, that is a positive ratio, resulting in geometrical increase; but if it is halving itself in each generation that is still a geometrical ratio, but it is negative and leads to progressive decrease. That is the whole difference today. It is possible, for the first time in history, to have progressively decreasing populations.

Fairchild: Yes, Mr. Huxley, but don't forget we are talking about the *inherent* biological tendency of the human animal to increase.

Huxley: But there is no such necessary tendency! You are seeing it today; all the advanced populations are tending not to increase but to decrease.

Fairchild: But do you think that's a biological proposition?

Huxley: Well, sure. Isn't that very definitely human biology?

Fairchild: I know it, but you wouldn't claim for a moment that there has been any diminution in the basic sex impulses of man as a result—because of civilization, shall we say?

Van Doren: How did it happen in France, for instance?

Huxley: I don't think there's been any diminution in the basic sex impulse. But we are talking of the tendency of population to increase or decrease. Malthus, as you said, equated the passion between the sexes, the reproductive instinct, with a tendency to geometric increase. I was merely saying that this is no longer true. Now that we have birth control—which started the really spectacular part of its career somewhere about fifty or sixty years ago—we have then the possibility, and in some cases the actuality, of a decreasing geometrical ratio, which is the reverse of Malthus' increasing ratio.

Fairchild: Yes, but now here we're getting mixed up in words again. You are talking about the tendency of population to increase as an actual sociological phenomenon. I'm trying to talk about something back of that, which I think Malthus was talking about—the inherent biological tendency which is the manifestation of a certain complex of emotions and desires with a physiological set-up.

Huxley: No, no, I'm sorry, but after all we're talking of human biology. Malthus said himself that there were checks on this fundamental tendency to increase. There were the positive checks in the shape of war and famine, disease, pestilence and—

Fairchild: And vice.

Huxley: Vice, and so forth; and there were also the preventive checks, among which the most important in his view was restraint in the sense of delaying marriage.

Fairchild: Or giving it up entirely!

Huxley: Well, already you've got facts of a human thing interfering with your fundamental biological tendency. He maintained that in spite of all these checks there was still a tendency not merely toward a geometrical ratio but toward a geometrical increase. What I'm saying is that now the possibility of geometrical decrease is open; but he did not even envisage that.

Fairchild: Perfectly! Certainly not! As I understand the tendency to geometrical increase, it is something which will happen, or would happen, if something didn't stop it. Now, the tendency of all material objects is to fall to the center of the earth. I hold this pencil over the table here. The tendency of this pencil is to fall clear down to the center of the earth. That's what it would do if it weren't stopped, but here's the table to stop it, and if it weren't for the table the floor would stop it, and so on. Now Malthus was trying to say that if nothing stopped the increase of human beings they would go on in this geometrical ratio. I'm sure we're in agreement, Mr. Huxley.

Huxley: The difference is that I was introducing a quantitative aspect, which I think is important and which he hadn't thought of.

Fairchild: The really important question, I think, in this whole realm of inquiry and knowledge is: What are the checks? That is really important.

Van Doren: There was one check that he was always putting forward in the later editions of his work: the check which he called moral restraint and by which he seems to have meant nothing more than delayed marriage. Mr. Huxley referred to it.

Fairchild: That has been a very much debated subject. The phrase "moral restraint" leaves much doubt as to exactly what he did mean.

Van Doren: As a newcomer to the book, I can say that I got the impression very clearly that he meant by it chiefly the willingness of human beings to wait.

Fairchild: Chiefly, yes.

Van Doren: The willingness of human beings to delay the happiness of marriage until it was certain that the two parties to the marriage would be able to feed and clothe their children and keep them from being miserable.

Fairchild: But we know, of course, that one of the earliest exponents of what came to be called neo-Malthusianism was Francis Place, who had been very happily married and was the last person in the world to deny the good effects and the pleasures of marriage, but who also was very conscious of the drawbacks because he had fifteen children. So he was one of the first ones, as you know, to try to find some way out of this prospect of misery that caused Malthus to be called the "gloomy parson" and the arch-pessimist of all times. Place tried to find out whether there weren't some ways whereby the real benefits of happy married life and so forth could be harmonized with a moderate increase of population. Malthus, of course, whatever we may think about the meaning of moral restraint, made no place in his system for what today we call contraception, or birth control. He repudiated that whole thing. He knew about it, but he wouldn't give it any place in his system.

Van Doren: Has it occurred to you that we haven't covered the whole case of society today? Although we can think of certain areas of human society where the rate of population increase is not rising, we can easily think of areas, can we not, where population is pressing upon subsistence at a rate—well, sufficiently great, for instance, to cause wars?

Fairchild: Oh, absolutely! Whatever we may say academically, as to whether Malthus is out of date in the United States or in what we call the Western world, I suspect that the scholars of Japan and China and India would not be so inclined to think that Malthus was out of date, because the very conditions upon which he based his theory are rampant in those Far Eastern, overcrowded countries.

Van Doren: He has a very interesting passage in which he promises to a humanity which will take his word about population a cessation of war, because the absence of over-population would make offensive war unnecessary—no nation would go out to annihilate another nation to take its room—and the nations which were living reasonably, that is to say, with a proper population, would be perfect at defense. They could never be conquered; they would be impregnable because they would have their happiness to defend.

Huxley: There is also the point, isn't there, that just as the Nazis and Fascists in general have rationalized completely false pseudo-scientific theories of race to justify their ideas of world domination, so they have rationalized completely false theories of population to justify their lust for power. They say, "We are overpopulated and we therefore need living space." And at the same time they encourage further population growths by anti-contraception laws, bonuses for children, and so on.

Van Doren: And, yes, look at the countries they overrun. Germany overruns one of the most populous countries, namely France. Not that its population has been increasing, but it is full of people. Germany overruns France; Japan overruns China and Java.

Fairchild: There is a very interesting concrete illustration of that, Mr. Van Doren. A man by the name of Nitti, an Italian who wrote one of the leading books on the anti-Malthusian point of view, claimed that there was no such thing as over-population, that whenever the Lord sent mouths into the world he sent food to feed them. He made a great point of that until he came to be himself the Premier of Italy; then he made a very quick flop and said that Italy needed to send out every year three hundred thousand of her people in order to keep some sort of balance.

Huxley: Could I make an approach from a rather different angle to this contrast between Malthus, when he wrote, and Malthusianism today? I'd like to take it from the point of view of the biologist, because I think it ought to be remembered that Malthus has another claim to fame, quite apart from his own work. It was reading Malthus which gave Charles Darwin the idea of Natural Selection and, therefore, gave the world its belief in evolution.

Fairchild: In just what way, Mr. Huxley? What would the connection be?

Huxley: Well, Malthus' idea that there was always this pressure of population upon subsistence, which meant a struggle. Darwin generalized this as the idea of a struggle for existence. In this struggle for survival, those which were better equipped would survive; that is Natural Selection.

Fairchild: Could we say then, in a sense, that the same struggle for existence in human society now manifests itself in war?

Huxley: I wouldn't like to go into that. It's much too complicated a question, and would be taking us right away from our subject.

Fairchild: Well, go ahead. That interests me very much.

Huxley: I was going to say that there are two types of struggle; one of the recent concepts of biology is that when your struggle is mainly within the species and not of the species against its enemies or against external nature, the struggle may have bad results for the species itself; in other words, that natural selection and the struggle for existence are not always a good thing. But that is by the way.

Fairchild: Yes.

Huxley: To go back to Malthus: his effect on Darwin was a very important event; and you can generalize Malthus' idea in that way. But evolution proceeds in general by the perfectly blind, wasteful, and often cruel forces of over-multiplication and of failure or success in life's race. However, as a final result of this blind force, human beings were evolved. They became the dominant species owing to their conscious reason; and then through their conscious reason they began modifying the way selection acts. One of the most interesting ways in which they have modified natural selection is by discovering how to control reproduction; and through that the whole Malthusian theory has been transformed. Some of the conclusions that Malthus, quite legitimately, drew from his theory sound absolutely appalling to us today. He talks, for instance, of the "inevitable and desirable disgrace of dependent poverty." He talks of what a good thing it is that landowners don't build more and better cottages, as otherwise they would encourage early marriage. All social services, all unemployment benefit, anything like that, are for Malthus merely means of encouraging population growth and therefore greater misery. Today we have a totally different problem. We have to think of the possibility of population decreasing; but the Malthusian principle still remains, namely, that any change tends to exaggerate itself because it tends to occur in a geometrical ratio. Accordingly we have now got to think of balancing the results of birth control, which is the tendency that may diminish population, against those which make for population increase, such as family allowances and so on, in order that the rate of change of population shall not be too rapid. Instead of thinking all the time of over-population and its disastrous results, we've got to think of a balanced and gradual rate of change, whether upward or downward. Would you agree to that?

Fairchild: I agree with you absolutely, and I'm very much pleased to see that you do not interpret modern methods and ideas about voluntarily controlled population as a refutation of the Malthusian theory but, rather, as an amendment of it, a bringing of it up to date.

Van Doren: It has always seemed to me so, incidentally. I have never felt that there was an absolute difference between neo-Malthusianism and Malthusianism.

Fairchild: I'm glad you said that, Mr. Van Doren, because today it seems to me vitally important that we realize that the fundamentals of Malthus, or, rather, the fundamentals of his system, are still at work in the world. There are great areas which years ago were indicated as danger spots in world population because of the certainty that if population kept on increasing, as it was increasing in those areas, there was bound to be an upheaval, an explosion of some kind. Japan and Italy were two of those areas.

Van Doren: In other words, this is a classic.

Fairchild: Very much so!

Huxley: Indeed!

Van Doren: And a classic is a book which remains indispensable. Malthus himself in his conclusion makes it very clear how eager he is for something like a science to exist within his field. "To the laws of property and marriage," he says, "and to the apparently narrow principle of self-interest, which prompts the individual to exert himself in bettering his condition, we are indebted for all the noblest exertions of human genius, for everything that distinguishes the civilized from the savage state. A strict inquiry into the principle of population obliges us to conclude that we shall never be able to throw down the ladder by which we have risen to this eminence; but it by no means proves that we may not rise higher by the same means. The structure of society, in its great features, will probably always remain unchanged. . . . It would indeed be a melancholy reflection that, while the views of physical science are daily enlarging, so as scarcely to be bounded by the most distant horizon, the science of moral and political philosophy should be confined within such narrow limits, or at best be so feeble in its influence, as to be unable to counter-act the obstacles to human happiness arising from a single cause. But however formidable these obstacles may have appeared in some parts of this work, it is hoped that the general result of the inquiry is such as not to make us give up the improvement of human society in despair. The partial good which seems to be attainable is worthy of all our exertions, is sufficient to direct our efforts, and animate our prospects. And although we cannot expect that the virtue and happiness of mankind will keep pace with the brilliant career of physical discovery; yet, if we are not wanting to ourselves, we may confidently indulge the hope that, to no unimportant extent, they will be influenced by its progress and will partake in its success."

(1850-1898)

EDWARD BELLAMY

Looking Backward

*L*OOKING BACKWARD *is a romance of the year 2000. Edward Bellamy wrote other romances, and some of them were likened in their age to those of another New Englander, Nathaniel Hawthorne. This one differed from its fellows not only in its temporal setting; it distinguished itself by its theme, which was neither love nor time but the organization of human society. And the immense, continuing success of* Looking Backward *is explained by the presence in it of that theme; as well, of course, as by the peculiarly appealing manner of its presentation. Another writer might have invented, as Bellamy did, a citizen of the year 1887 who suddenly found himself living a little more than a hundred years later. Indeed it was and is a common device, just as it is conventional for such writers to proceed then with a sketch of the future which throws into relief the miseries or the follies of the present. Bellamy did all that, but with a difference.*

The spirit with which he describes the cooperative common-wealth to come, wherein all men benefit freely and equally from the fruits of an industry which all combine freely and equally to support, is a spirit the purity and disinterestedness of which no reader can be cynical enough to deny. A given reader may conclude that people will never consent to behave as reasonably as this, but he will not doubt the motives with which Bellamy employed his own reason, and in addition to that his own fancy. If the book, circulating as it has in all countries, remains a parable for thousands who dream of a juster and more peaceful society than any yet known, the cause is Bellamy's character, which everywhere simplifies and beautifies his vision.

Edward Bellamy was born in Chicopee Falls, Mass. He worked on the New York Evening Post *and later edited the Springfield (Mass.)* Union. *In 1881 he helped to found the Springfield* Daily News *and in 1891 founded in Boston the* New Nation, *which for a time he edited. His first ventures in fiction were short stories of genuine charm, collected, after his death, as* The Blind Man's World and Other Stories *(1898). His novels,* Dr. Heidenhoff's Process *(1880) and* Mrs. Ludington's Sister *(1884) were overshadowed by his masterpiece,* Looking Backward, *as was its sequel,* Equality.

MAX EASTMAN · JACQUES BARZUN · MARK VAN DOREN

Van Doren: Looking Backward, you will remember, was written in 1887 and looks forward to the year 2000 when society shall have become universally happy, prosperous, comfortable and well ordered. A little more than half that time has now passed, that is to say, we are now almost fifty-five years on the way. Mr. Eastman, does it occur to you that that fact alone—the history, I mean, of the past fifty-five years, and the history of this moment, for that matter—throws any special light upon the validity of Bellamy's vision?

Eastman: Yes, very decidedly. I noticed that the new society which he described was supposed to have come into being about fifty years before the year 2000, which would bring it just about now. And in light of what is happening today, particularly in Russia and somewhat also in Germany and Italy, I think the prophecy becomes rather pathetic. It is such a naive and Sunday-schoolish anticipation of the lovely and rather bland delights of humanity under a collectivized economy.

Barzun: And, Mr. Eastman, perhaps also prophetic. I was struck by the fact that Bellamy kept comparing the working of the new society to the working of an army and that he propagated his views in lectures, after writing his book, under the name of Nationalism, which are two pretty startling anticipations of things we are seeing now.

Van Doren: Mr. Barzun, were you struck also by the fact that Bellamy assumes that the transformation of the world which took place about now—let us say about the year 1940—took place not through the exercise of any individual's will or any group's will, but took place, so to speak, automatically?

Barzun: Yes. He may have seen more truly than he realized when he saw that society would be completely regimented, that people would have no individual motives and that happiness would be of a very animal kind.

Van Doren: Well, we have a world today which is groaning with change, possibly one which is bleeding to death in an attempt to change itself. Bellamy doesn't seem to have foreseen such a period of struggle, does he?

Barzun: No, he made the mistake of thinking that the change would come by means of reason because he thought that the product itself was reasonable. But the product was not so much reasonable as efficient, which is a very different thing, it seems to me. Efficiency may be unreasonable in many situations in life.

Eastman: I think he had a false idea of human nature; that was really the basis of his mistake. If human nature were as benign and good and sweet as he thought, this new society could come into being in that automatic and easy fashion. His constantly talking about soldiers in an army struck me too. But he thought that the soldiers didn't have to have a belligerent and fighting motive to keep them behaving this way. He thought they could behave like soldiers and yet *be* Sunday-school teachers.

Barzun: That is perfectly true. No one in this book has any motive for doing anything, or, as far as I can see, for living, except the contemplation of perfect order.

Van Doren: They all tend in this wonderful Boston of the year 2000 to spend their time congratulating one another upon living in the perfect state, upon living in a perfect time when things, so to speak, are done for them. I also have the notion that each citizen of that time thinks of the world about him as running itself. It isn't the result of anything that he himself brings to it.

Barzun: And to get any pleasure out of the world they have to look backward constantly and see how dreadful it was in the year 1887—as of course it was.

Van Doren: You remember, once we are treated to a sermon which was preached over a sort of broadcasting system, and the only thing that the preacher can find to discuss is the difference between our time and that time. And so with a novel which is described as being written in that period of such great intellectual and literary power. We learn about this novel what is not in it rather than what is in it.

Barzun: Would you say, Mr. Van Doren, that the underlying fallacy of the book is the notion that happiness can be striven for directly instead of coming as a by-product?

Van Doren: The question states itself for me rather more bluntly than that. Is not the limitation of this book—if it has a limitation, and we all three are talking as if it had a very serious limitation—that which is found in all utopian books? For this book surely does belong in that class, does it not? We can think of Plato, we can think of Samuel Butler, of Sir Thomas More, of Francis Bacon, and of many other men. There might be two questions here: One, whether this book merely participates in the failure of all such books to be finally convincing, because I take it that all such books in a way do fail, and two: Whether this book fails to be all that it could be within its type?

Barzun: It certainly seems to me that Plato's *Republic* has a quality of toughness and veracity that this book lacks. If this book is a classic—which in many ways it is, since it continues to be read and talked about—it is because it expresses the unveracious, the soft utopia which I suppose resides in many people's minds.

Eastman: Plato had what I should call radical common sense; he had a sense of what human nature really is. This man I think hasn't. I don't agree with you that happiness shouldn't be striven for. I think our failure to strive for it is one of the chief reasons why we get into such insane and neurotic troubles. But it ought to be a different kind of happiness than this rather namby-pamby one that Bellamy outlines for us. These people, aside from not having anything to do, apparently are so mollycoddle. They spend so much time congratulating themselves that they don't have any prize fights. I kept wanting to introduce a character like Ernest Hemingway into this society. I think if you did that, and got a humorist like J. P. McEvoy to write the scenario for it, it would make a wonderful movie.

Barzun: I think you're a little hard on Bellamy. He has repeated moments of insight, as when he sees that there was a kind of nobility about the struggle for being generous and fair and decent in the year 1887, and he seems to ask himself unconsciously: Why is there no such motive, no such struggle now? The answer is that there's no necessity, when you're comfortable, to strive.

Van Doren: Yes, there is an appalling silence and blankness everywhere in this world, a sort of hospital cleanliness; there's an antiseptic quality about the Boston of the year 2000. That is why citizens of that age are forced always to return in their imaginations to our own time, that is to say to 1887. "Ah, my friends, believe me," says one of them, "it is not now in this happy age that humanity is proving the divinity within it; it was rather in those evil days, when not even the fight for life with one another, the struggle for mere existence in which mercy was folly, could wholly banish generosity and kindness from the earth." In other words, nobility, divinity, generosity, kindness are qualities which are assumed to have been possible only in our own miserable time.

Barzun: They exist by contrast. You have to have a chiaroscuro; if everything is light, you don't see any object.

Van Doren: But, Mr. Barzun, mustn't you say something like that after reading any utopian work whatever?

Barzun: I don't know. A utopia might very well be regarded as a difficult task. In Plato, the guardians are not having a good time being the governors of the state; they govern with great self-sacrifice.

Van Doren: But isn't that one reason why the commonwealth of Plato is unthinkable? As a matter of fact Socrates himself abandons it—before the end of the *Republic*.

Eastman: The basic trouble with all utopian books is that they never locate the source of power. Now the dictator in this book, as also in Plato's *Republic,* is the author of the book. You notice, for instance, they have these wonderful printing presses, and they are government printing presses, but they don't exercise any censorship. They must print whatever is offered to them, he says. But where does that "must" come from? It comes from Edward Bellamy.

Van Doren: Edward Bellamy sees to it that the reader does not form the notion somehow or other that anyone did anything against his will, that anyone was unhappy.

Eastman: That's right. He has society entirely regimented, as you say. But then he asserts that it is free, that individuals are free as never before. That is why I think it is a pathetic book.

Barzun: It is an excess, of course, of regimentation. Bellamy must have seen very clearly that a little more order would make the nineteenth century go better, and the order was coming. It was an industrial order; it was the coming regulation of traffic, so to speak. But the idea that system must be extended to every minute of one's waking time is the absurdity, really, of this type of utopia.

Van Doren: All these people must constantly be conscious of living in Bellamy's world. It isn't their world at all, as you say, it isn't even the world of the President of the United States then; it is the world of Edward Bellamy now. They are living 113 years ahead of themselves, so to speak, and must constantly be justifying that fact.

Barzun: I have the feeling that the only kind of criticism suitable for a reformer is negative criticism. He must state his principles; he must say this is wrong, this is intolerable; we can't go on this way. But to tell people what they must do then is both an impossibility and an impertinence. It is like what people call constructive criticism, which merely means telling a man how he ought to do his job.

Van Doren: Perhaps, Mr. Barzun, you mean that the reformer should be concerned with the present rather than the future.

Barzun: Yes.

Van Doren: On the other hand, when he says something is wrong with the present, what must he appeal to in order to convince us, what is the nature of his reference when he uses the word "wrong"?

Barzun: I should think it would be an inconsistency between what we profess to admire or to want and the way in which we do things. But he should not extend what we profess to admire to feasible but possibly one-sided modes of life.

Van Doren: Especially when we can assume that they have become feasible through processes that we don't particularly inquire into. You see, the process by which his world became feasible is not described by Bellamy. He asks us to assume that the thing happened almost by itself overnight.

Barzun: Like Karl Marx and others of his day, he trusted in an evolution and, like theirs also, his evolution ends in utopia. It stops there—it's the Grand Central Terminal.

Van Doren: Mr. Eastman, I am interested in your use of the word "pathetic." You have used it twice with reference to this book. Could you elucidate it?

Eastman: Looking Backward has a particular pathos for me and I'll tell you why. I just read it for the first time, and I read it while I was occupied in editing Alexander Barmine's memoirs of his life lived under the Soviet regime in Russia. Barmine was the head of the Soviet Legation at Athens who refused to go back and be shot during the purge and who is now in this country. And as he has been not only a general in the Red Army but the head of factories and the head of commercial trusts as well as a diplomat, he has a knowledge of the Soviet experience that is very relevant to this utopian prophecy. He knows how it operated, and how it operates, as a business institution. And it is exactly opposite to what Bellamy thought would come through exactly the same process—the nationalization of industry. They have really nationalized industry, and instead of getting freedom and virtue and general happiness, they've got a totally enslaved working class and bureaucratic inefficiency in business.

Van Doren: You wouldn't say that the failure of that picture to equate with Bellamy's picture is a failure that can be explained by the difference in industrial advancement between Russia and the United States?

Eastman: No, I don't think so, and Barmine himself is very explicit about that. He thinks that the experiment in Russia has general significance.

Barzun: I believe, at any rate, that this can be said, quite apart from the practical conditions, and that is that the greatest and most justified complaint against individualism is that it permits irresponsibility. But how does Bellamy take care of this? By preventing anyone in the state from being responsible for anything. There is irresponsibility at the other end.

Van Doren: Yes, I think that is why the book fails somehow or other to satisfy us. The book is interesting to me; it is often very touching, often admirable. The spirit of the author, even if it is slight, seems to me pure and disinterested.

Barzun: And eloquent.

Eastman: He is ingenious too. I am sometimes more impressed by his little gadgets than I am by his general plan. I like these umbrellas that move out over the whole sidewalk when it rains. Having one umbrella over all of Boston instead of a lot of umbrellas. It appeals to me particularly because I don't like to get wet, and yet I feel a little ashamed to carry an umbrella.

Barzun: But this uniformitarian idea he also extends to art, which bothers me a good deal. There isn't a single Philistine, or anybody interested in horse-racing or chess, in this book. Everybody listens to good music, and though I don't think that good music should necessarily be made a luxury, it shouldn't be forced on people.

Eastman: I felt sure it wasn't very good, either, when he was talking about it.

Barzun: But that of course is a trivial detail.

Van Doren: Yet details like that are important. Plato realized his commonwealth in detail, and of course Samuel Butler did. While we are speaking of details I must say I felt a great relief when I came to the description of the dinner which the doctor and his guest, Julian West, had, under perfect circumstances.

Having heard that the dinner was to be eaten at some community dining center, I was afraid there would be long tables with hundreds of people sitting together who didn't like one another. But there was enough sense in that day to provide small dining rooms in which one's family could eat a perfectly prepared dinner ordered the night before.

Barzun: This book has been called "a new embodiment of the American dream." Maybe eating at a community center is part of the American dream.

Van Doren: Well, the phrase suggests a question that we ought to ask ourselves. We have been assuming for the past twenty minutes that this book somehow fails. I think we all agree that it fails to be much more than pathetic at this moment. When the transformation which Bellamy saw as inevitable and painless has turned out to be one of the most painful things in human experience, what shall we say about the effort of any man to foresee the human future? Is there no sense in anyone's writing a utopia? Young people are likely to come under the influence of this book and to think that it is important, that it does a great deal of good. Is it actually misleading? Are you sorry that such books exist?

Barzun: Oh, not at all, because it seems to me that the simplicity and the perfection of the book have something of the quality of the stories of Jules Verne, or perhaps *Robinson Crusoe,* and start the mind thinking about problems which otherwise would not be seen at all by young people.

Van Doren: The reference of utopian literature is to the present after all, isn't it? Something is wrong with the world in which the author lives. He describes a world which is different from that world with respect to those details which he finds most unhappy.

Barzun: And he's always right. In this book Bellamy is always right about what is wrong with the present-day world; he isn't fantastic in that regard, it seems to me.

Van Doren: You did find realism there.

Eastman: He's right, and he's also eloquent. The only passionate place in the book is where he comes back or dreams he has come back home and gets kicked out of his sweetheart's house for denouncing civilization in Boston in the nineteenth century. That is really eloquent. Something comes through there that is lacking in all of the rest of the pages, which I find a bit bland.

Van Doren: Once in a while, however, the other note is struck. I think I shall always remember the doctor's remarking about our system of production. "The daydream of the nineteenth-century producer," he says, "was to gain control of the supply of some necessity of life, so that he might keep the public at the verge of starvation and always command famine prices for what he supplied. This is what was called in the nineteenth century a system of production. I will leave it to you if it does not seem in some of its aspects a great deal more like a system for preventing production." There the man is speaking with some sharpness—

Eastman: Very good.

Van Doren: —speaking with sharpness, speaking with passion, because he sees a world which is throttling itself and thwarting its own life.

Barzun: Yes, and Bellamy has a knack for hitting out aphorisms about what he sees; and it probably contradicts his notion of evolution that he can see what is there. But he cannot possibly tell what is going to grow out of it. And perhaps what we are suffering from today is an excessive desire to make a blueprint with a gap separating it from what we do see.

Eastman: I think so. I don't agree with you that a reformer should concentrate on the present. I think he should concentrate on the pretty immediate future. And he should concentrate on specific changes, instead of going into the struggle—the labor struggle, for instance, which is my particular interest—with some general ideal blueprint which makes his action religious rather than scientific.

Barzun: Of course a religious element is needed if you're going to get people to band together for any one common object.

Van Doren: The word "religious" reminds me that I was forced by the book to reflect on the theme of original sin. Bellamy

assumes that the thing once called by theologians "original sin"
was something accidental to life, something conditioned by life,
and that once these conditions were removed nothing ignoble in
human nature would survive. He failed to convince me there. The
very reason I suppose that his future is so much like a bathroom
lined with white tile is that sin is lacking in that life.

Barzun: Or at least a sense of contradiction. We could put it
that way.

Van Doren: Which is what original sin actually means. The
term "original sin" refers to insoluble contradictions in human
nature.

Eastman: It really means our biological inheritance. We are
at bottom animals and we have drives and impulses which haven't
got anything to do with our rational dreams.

Barzun: He also seemed to think—a curious assumption which
I think we've lost—that talent was very plentiful, that people
could stop working after the age of forty-five, and that the
elders after that age could, if they were willing, serve five years
as judges and not be re-eligible. The whole notion of learning
and performing a job in five years and having an endless supply
of people to do it struck me as quite extraordinary.

Eastman: They had the president elected by those who had
been through their course in the industrial army. That is, the
president of the republic was elected as in some colleges the
president is elected by the alumni. That struck me as a pretty
good idea.

Barzun: Perhaps we ought to get statistics first on how satisfactory that is.

Van Doren: How could you get them?

Eastman: We might ask Nicholas Murray Butler.

Van Doren: Can any theory of society ever be tested by statistics? That is to me one of the discouraging and one of the
fascinating things about social theory. No theory of society ever
seems to me to be possible to test.

Barzun: I meant statistics about the opinion of those most
nearly concerned in having a president so elected.

Eastman: I was just thinking that it is a little like Plato's idea that the guardians who rule the state should be people who don't want to. That is a wonderful thought.

Barzun: Yes. But how much energy would they have when they didn't want to rule?

Van Doren: This book reminded me of a conversation I had with a young man once after both of us had seen the moving picture made from H. G. Wells's *The Shape of Things to Come.* The imagination of Wells has spent a great deal of time in the future, as you know. The intolerable dullness of that movie was something my friend and I were discussing, and he finally said this: The future is not interesting if it is represented as anything essentially different from the present. You can imagine life going on only in the terms in which it is going on now. When there is a break, as you say, or a gap, when we are asked to consider a remote human future the connection between which and our own life has been broken, the imagination fails to operate, just as Bellamy's imagination fails here, and just as the imagination of any utopian must eventually fail.

Barzun: It would be fun to be cast away on Robinson Crusoe's island, but to go to Mars probably would be very dull.

Van Doren: That's right. Robinson Crusoe at least was within possible hailing distance of a vessel; Robinson Crusoe did take the clothes with him that he had worn in England.

Barzun: And he had the problems we all have.

Van Doren: When we cease to have those problems, somehow we cannot invent or imagine other problems.

Barzun: We've been pretty hard on this book. It seems to me that there are at least two perfectly sound ideas in it that we haven't perhaps done justice to. One is the notion of the industrial army by which young men for three years give of their best to the state and learn a trade for which they are fitted. The other, which is not a practical but a moral idea, deals with this question of rewards in society, of what people deserve. And here is a passage which seems to me to sum up a real insight that Bellamy had. The hero, Julian West, and Dr. Leete are discussing the question of what people deserve for the work they do. Dr. Leete, the man of 2000, says:

" 'We require of each that he shall make the same effort, that is, we demand of him the best service it is in his power to give.' 'And supposing all do the best they can,' I answer, 'the amount of the product resulting is twice greater from one man than from another.' 'Very true,' replied Dr. Leete, 'but the amount of the resulting product has nothing whatever to do with the question, which is one of desert. Desert is a moral question and the amount of the product a material quantity. It would be an extraordinary sort of logic which should try to determine a moral question by a material standard. The amount of the effort alone is pertinent to the question of desert. All men who do their best do the same. A man's endowments, however godlike, merely fix the measure of his duty. The man of great endowments who does not do all he might, though he may do more than a man of small endowments who does his best, is deemed a less deserving worker than the latter and dies a debtor to his fellows. The Creator sets men's tasks for them by the faculties he gives them. We simply exact their fulfillment.' "

A SELECTED BIBLIOGRAPHY

AESCHYLUS, *The Oresteia*
   The Complete Greek Drama, Edited by Whitney J. Oates and Eugene O'Neill, Jr., Random House, New York. 2 vols., boxed, $6.00
HORACE, *Poems*
   The Complete Works of Horace, Edited by Casper J. Kraemer, Jr., Modern Library, New York. 95 cents
SHAKESPEARE, *Hamlet*
   The Complete Works of Shakespeare, in any of the standard editions
GOETHE, *Faust*
   Translated by Bayard Taylor, Modern Library, New York. 95 cents. Translated by A. G. Latham, Everyman's Library, New York. 95 cents
IBSEN, *The Wild Duck*
   Eleven Plays of Henrik Ibsen, Modern Library, New York. $1.45
DESCARTES, *A Discourse on Method*
   Translated by A. D. Lindsay, Everyman's Library, New York. 95 cents
SPINOZA, *Ethics*
   The Philosophy of Spinoza, Edited by Joseph Ratner, Modern Library, New York. 95 cents. *Ethics and De Intellectus Emendatione,* Everyman's Library, New York. 95 cents
NIETZSCHE, *Beyond Good and Evil*
   The Philosophy of Nietzsche, Modern Library, New York. $1.45
AESOP, *Fables*
   Everyman's Library, New York. 95 cents. The Macmillan Company, New York. $1.00
LA FONTAINE, *Fables*
   The Macmillan Company, New York. $1.10
RABELAIS, *Gargantua and Pantagruel*
   Modern Library, New York. 95 cents. Everyman's Library, New York. 2 vols., 95 cents each. Oxford University Press, New York. $3.75

[429]

A Selected Bibliography

CERVANTES, *Don Quixote*
Ozell's Revision of the Translation by Peter Motteux, with 16 illustrations by Gustave Doré, Modern Library, New York. $1.45. Everyman's Library, 2 vols., 95 cents each. Oxford University Press, 2 vols., 80 cents each.

VOLTAIRE, *Candide*
Modern Library, New York. 95 cents. Everyman's Library, New York. 95 cents

FIELDING, *Tom Jones*
Modern Library, New York. $1.45. Everyman's Library, 2 vols., 95 cents each

CARROLL, *Alice in Wonderland*
The Complete Works of Lewis Carroll, Modern Library, New York. $1.45

JAMES, *The Turn of the Screw*
The Turn of the Screw and The Lesson of the Master, Modern Library, New York. 95 cents

DOYLE, *The Adventures of Sherlock Holmes*
Doubleday, Doran & Co., Garden City, N. Y. $1.98

HERODOTUS, *History*
The Greek Historians, Edited by Francis R. B. Godolphin, Random House, New York. 2 vols., boxed, $6.00

CHESTERFIELD, *Letters to His Son*
Everyman's Library, New York. 95 cents

BOSWELL, *Life of Samuel Johnson*
Modern Library, New York. $1.45. Everyman's Library, New York, 2 vols., 95 cents each. Oxford University Press, New York. 2 vols., $1.50 each

AUDUBON, *American Scenery and Character*
G. A. Baker and Co., New York. $6.00

PRESCOTT, *The Conquest of Mexico*
The Conquest of Mexico and The Conquest of Peru, Modern Library, $1.45

GRANT, *Memoirs*
Appleton-Century Company, New York. 2 vols. $10.00. O.P.

DEMOSTHENES, *Speeches*
On the Crown, The Philippics, and Ten Other Orations, Everyman's Library, New York. 95 cents

LINCOLN, *Speeches*
The Life and Writings of Abraham Lincoln, Edited by Philip Van Doren Stern, Modern Library, New York. $1.45

MONTESQUIEU, *The Spirit of Laws*
The Colonial Press, New York and London. 2 vols. N.P.

BURKE, *Reflections on the Revolution in France*
Everyman's Library, New York. 95 cents

PAINE, *The Rights of Man*
Everyman's Library, New York. 95 cents

MALTHUS, *Essay on Population*
Principles of Population, Everyman's Library, New York. 2 vols. 95 cents each

BELLAMY, *Looking Backward*
Houghton Mifflin Co., Boston. $1.50. Modern Library, New York. 95 cents

INDEX

[431]

Index

Index

Index

Index

Index